without a map

without a map

a memoir

Meredith Hall

Beacon Press, Boston

Beacon Press
25 Beacon Street
Boston, Massachusetts 02108-2892
www.beacon.org

Beacon Press books
are published under the auspices of
the Unitarian Universalist Association of Congregations.

10 09 08 07 8 7 6 5 4 3 2

This book is printed on acid-free paper that meets the uncoated paper
ANSI/NISO specifications for permanence as revised in 1992.

Text design by Bob Kosturko
Composition by Wilsted & Tyalor Publishing Services

Library of Congress Cataloging-in-Publication Data

Hall, Meredith
Without a map : a memoir / Meredith Hall.
p. cm.
ISBN-13: 978-0-8070-7273-8 (hardcover : alk. paper)
ISBN-10: 0-8070-7273-7 (hardcover : alk. paper) 1. Hall, Meredith—Childhood and
youth. 2. Authors, American—21st century—Biography. 3. Hall, Meredith—Homes
and haunts—Maine. 4. Maine—Social life and customs—21st century. I. Title.

PS3608.A5474Z46 2007
818'.609—dc22
[B]   2006027507

Credits: The following chapters first appeared in the following publications, in slightly
different form: "Shunned," "Killing Chickens," and "Without a Map" in *Creative
Nonfiction;* "Waiting" and "Outport Shadows" in *Prairie Schooner;* "Again," "A River
of Light," and "The River of Forgetting" as "A River of Light" in *Fourth Genre:
Explorations in Nonfiction,* vol. 8, no. 2, 2006, published by Michigan State University
Press; "Drawing the Line" in *Five Points;* and "Chimeras" in the *New York Times.*

Grateful acknowledgment is made for permission to include "Late Fragment"
from *A New Path to the Waterfall,* copyright © 1989 by the estate of
Raymond Carver. Used by permission of Grove/Atlantic, Inc.

To my children,
whose own stories start with these

Contents

Shunned

Even now, I talk too much and too loud, claiming ground, afraid that I will disappear from *this* life, too, from this time of being mother and teacher and friend. That It—everything I care about, that I believe in, that defines and reassures me—will be wrenched from me again.

Family. Church. School. Community. There are not many ways you can get kicked out of those memberships. As a child in Hampton, New Hampshire, I knew husbands who cheated on their wives. Openly. My father. I knew men and women who beat their children. We all knew them. We all knew men who were too lazy to bring in a paycheck or clean the leaves out of their yards, women who spent the day on the couch crying while the kids ran loose with the neighborhood. We knew who drank at the Meadowbrook after work each day and drove home to burn SpaghettiOs on the stove for the children. We even knew a witch. We called her Goody Welsh, as if her magic had kept her alive since the Salem days. But this was 1965. All these people were tolerated. More than tolerated. They were the Community. The teachers and ministers' wives and football players and drugstore owners. They lived next to me on Leavitt Road and Mill Road and High Street. They smiled hello when I rode my bike past their clean or dirty yards, their sunny or shuttered houses.

Then I got pregnant. I was sixteen. Family, church, school—each of those memberships that had embraced me as a child—turned their backs. Shunning is supposed to keep bad things from happening in a community. But it doesn't correct the life gone wrong. It can only expose the transgression to a very raw light, use it as a measure, a warning to others that says, *See? That didn't happen in our home. Because we are Good. We're better than that.* The price I paid seems still to be extreme. But I bet it was a while again before any girl in Hampton let herself be fucked in the gritty sand by a boy from away who said *love*.

A friend once told me that, when he was in seventh grade, he and his best friend, Nathan, fought. Nathan got everyone in school to ignore my friend the next day, incited them to the silent treatment. It only lasted until noon; one by one, my friend drew his friends back, outmaneuvering Nathan. But still my friend remembers the impotent shame he felt for those four hours. The injustice.

It didn't last because my friend was a boy, a boy who knew how to fight back, a boy who believed that he could interrupt the current and draw his world back into order. It didn't work because he felt powerful, after all, worthy of those friends and their loyalty.

And it didn't work because there was no moral to be exalted, no messy failure to be feasted upon. But pregnant in 1965? If this could happen to Bobbie's daughter, then, like contagion, it could infect anyone's girl. Unless we scared them so much they would never spread their legs again. Injustice. It had to be unjust. It had to be electrifying to work.

I have often wondered whether the grownups I went to church with, who made sandwiches for me and their children on dreamy summer days, who praised me year after year for my A's and my manners and my nice family, who paid me extra for watching their babies so well—I have wondered if they had to tell their children to shun me, or if the kids slid to it on their own. The motives of the grownups seem quite different from those of my peers. When Diane and Becky and Debbie and John and Tony stopped speaking to me, when they started to cross the street in tight hushed groups, when they left Tobey's Rexall, their cherry Cokes unfinished, because I walked in —were they told to steer clear of me? Did they understand that if shunning is to work, it must be absolute, no soft heart to undermine the effect? Or did they find their own reasons to cast me out:

"I never liked her anyway," or "She thinks she's so smart" or "Her father left, you know." Maybe I was simply too dangerous. If they did not abruptly turn away, they would be judged, by association, as being as dirty as I was.

This sort of shunning has the desired effect of erasing a life. Making it invisible, incapable of contaminating. I suddenly had no history with these kids. I had started school with them at Mrs. Winkler's kindergarten, in the basement of her husband's dental office. First grade, fifth, eighth, tenth—Mrs. Bean and Mrs. Marcotte and Mr. Cooper—twenty-four kids moving together year after year. We all knew each other's parents and brothers and sisters and whether they went to the Congregational or the Methodist or the tiny Episcopal church. We knew who practiced piano after supper and who lived with a grandmother and who secretly read in the field behind Pratt's barn.

No one in our class was bad. We believed we were good children, and were. The 1950s still breathed its insistent, costly calm through our childhoods. When we said, "I'm in sixth grade," we meant, *I belong with these boys and girls; we are bound in inevitable affection.* The grownups reinforced for each of us this sense of our lives being woven together, sticky strands of a resilient web. We liked each other as a matter of course; idiosyncrasies and conflicts, like broken rays of the whole, were quickly corrected, the flaw made invisible and forgotten.

I still can tell you that Larry had a funny, flat head. That fat Donny surprised us in eighth grade by whipping out a harmonica and playing country ballads. That he also surprised us that year by flopping on the floor in an epileptic fit. That Claudia, an only child, lived in a house as orderly and dead as a tomb. That I coveted her closet full of clothes. That Patty's father had to drag our muddy, sagging dog back every few weeks from hunting in the marshes; that he apologized politely every time to my mother, as if it were his fault. That Jay wanted to marry me in kindergarten, and that I whipped Jay a year or two later with thorny switches his father had trimmed from the hedge separating our yards. That his father called

me Meredy-my-love, and I called him Uncle Leo. That Heather's
grandmother Mrs. Coombs taught us music once a week, the fat that
hung from her arms swinging wildly just off beat as she led each song.
I still can tell you that Linea wouldn't eat the crusts. I thought
she was spoiled. That Sherrie smelled and was to be pitied, not os-
tracized. That Colleen wore my old skirts and dresses, found in the
Clothes Closet in the church vestry, and I must never mention anything to her, as though everyone had not seen those same clothes on
me all last year. That Janice was Mr. Fiedler's pet, that her mother
made cookies for the Brownies every Wednesday, when we sat like
grown women, gossiping while we sewed aprons and washcloth slippers for our mothers and grandmothers at Christmas. That Howie
was a flirt and liked to kiss girls, and he would come to no good, although he came to better than I did. That Sheila's mother sold us
eggs. That Brian was almost as smart as I was, but he was a boy and
never got all As. That I followed the rules and craved praise, that I
was cheerful and a pleaser, a leader who was headed somewhere.

These are myths, of course. We children touched ourselves in the
dark and stole money from our mothers' purses and listened at night
to our parents screaming obscenities. But the myths worked; none
of those secrets were visible. There was a silent hierarchy, based in
part on social class, but also on something less tangible—an un-
swerving sense of who came from a "good" family. They didn't need
to have money. But the good family must protect its secrets. No
grandparent could be a public drinker or an atheist. If Dad walked
out, Mother must become a saint.

Lucky for me, I came from just such a family. I was a good girl,
the darling of teachers and chosen as a friend by these twenty-four
kids I knew like cousins.

I have a very small box containing everything that survives that
childhood: a perfect-attendance pin from Sunday school; my

Brownie sash; a jet and rhinestone pin given to me by a crazy old woman up the street; my toe shoes, the pink satin worn through; one Ginny doll, her hair half gone, and a few clothes my mother and I sewed for her; a silver dollar my first boyfriend gave me for Christmas my sophomore year; my prayer book, signed in the front by my mother, *To my beloved daughter*; and a class picture, titled "My Class," from tenth grade.

I don't ever look at this photo, and I should throw it out. I loved My Class. I loved belonging. I loved the promise I thought I heard that they would become my past, my history. It is as if there was a terrible death and they were all lost to me, abruptly and all at once. But nobody died. The loss was only mine, a private and interior devastation.

Robin and I walked every day to school together, until the day I was kicked out. Ten years ago—twenty-four years after I walked home alone at eleven thirty in the morning with the green slip of expulsion in my book bag, my secret let loose and starting its zinging trip mouth to mouth—I heard from her when her mother, my mother's best friend, Margie, was dying of Alzheimer's. Now, when Robin and I get together, she tells me the stories of my own life that I have had to forget. Like an artist painting in the details of a soft charcoal sketch, she fills in the forgotten, the high school years that I cannot afford to carry. She says, "*You* remember, Meredy. Sharon lived on the corner of Mill Road. You used to spend the night at her house a lot." I don't remember. Maybe a certain flip of dark hair or a faint laugh. But I vanished in my own mind, along with all the comfortable small facts of my life, on that day of expulsion in 1965. Shunned, made invisible, I became invisible to myself. The photo of "My Class" is a record of the history I do not share.

I suppose they all get together every few years for a reunion. They would have been the class of 1967. I am certain that the space I occupied in the group for sixteen years closed in as fast as a shrub when one flower dies or is pinched out. I wonder what they would say if my name came up. I wonder if they ever think of me. I sometimes imagine that I will somehow find out where they will meet for the next reunion. I will arrive, looking clean and successful and proud. But what would I say to them? That this thing, this shunning, this shaming is an eraser, a weapon that should never be wielded?

Last year I had a student from Hampton in my writing class at the state university. I knew from her last name that she must be the daughter of Timmy Keaton. I told her that I had known her father all through my childhood. I didn't tell her that we weren't really friends, that I was important in class and he was one of those peripheral members no one ever really noticed. She came back the next Monday for a conference; to make conversation—or maybe, thirty years later, to reclaim some of my purged identity—I asked if she had mentioned my name to her father. She looked embarrassed, and I realized right away my misstep: I could not have a student knowing my dark and secret past. But she said, squirming in her chair, "He couldn't really remember your name. I tried to describe you, but he couldn't remember you."

Mrs. Taccetta played the small organ softly as I followed my mother and sister to seats up front. My shy brother was lighting candles on the altar with a long wand, his face shiny with embarrassment. This used to be Johnny Ford's house, a big colonial gone to seed between my house and uptown. The Episcopal church had originally met upstairs in the Grange Hall, my mother and Mrs. Pervier and Mr. Sargent setting up folding metal chairs and restacking them each Sunday morning for six years. Finally those pioneers, seeing some crucial and mysterious distinction between themselves and the Congregationalists and Methodists, raised the funds to buy Johnny's house and turn his living room and dining room into a chapel. The kitchen stayed, and my mother donated our old refrigerator; I could still smell our potatoes in the old-fashioned flip-out drawer at the bottom. The fridge gave me a sense of ownership in the church. So did my mother's role as president of the women's auxiliary. Exotic, deeply embroidered stoles and altar cloths hung in her closet, carefully washed, starched, and ironed, and laid over my absent father's wooden coat hangers. My mother walked up to the church each Saturday afternoon to set up, arranging flowers and replacing the grape juice and Communion wafers.

I felt important here, and loved. I heard every Sunday as we walked into church, "Oh, Bobbie, you have raised such wonderful children." My mother told us we were special, a family united by the trauma of my father's going, and made stronger for it. Church allowed us to parade our family's bravery and fortitude. Smiling, slim and tan and absolutely capable, my mother led us into the gaze of our congregation. I was proud. When Mrs. Palmer and Mrs. Riley and Mr. Kendall and Crazy LuLu and Reverend Andrews nodded and smiled their hellos, I felt the light of adoration shine on me. My mother held my hand in the pew, in the little chapel she had helped to build, and I was a child of grace.

I was kicked out of school on the day we returned from Christmas vacation. Four and a half months pregnant, a slim dancer, I had zipped my wool skirt over my hard round belly and prayed for one more day of hiding.

In gym class that morning, we had used the mats for tumbling. Over and over, Miss Marston had made us practice running somersaults, kips, and splits. When my turn came to do a move called the fish flop—a backward somersault, legs held high for a pause in the follow-through, and an arched-back slide down onto the chest and belly—I balked. I was starting to understand that what had ended my periods, what made my belly grow, was not just a terrifying threat, an ominous messenger telling me that I was doomed; it was becoming a life—a child curled inside me, perhaps in the same dread and fear of its future as I carried every minute. I felt, suddenly, watching the girls ahead of me slamming back down onto the mats, a confused and ferocious protectiveness, and a giving in, two of us too tired to hide anymore. The class watched as I ran out of the gym into the girls' lockers.

My best friends, Kathy and Susan, followed me. "What's wrong?" they asked earnestly. I hadn't showered after gym class for a month, but they had bought my excuses about not having time before biology class. This time, I turned and faced them in the clammy room. "I'm pregnant," I said. I remember now that they both visibly drew back, sucking in air, suspended. Maybe not. Maybe they just stared for a minute. Maybe they looked at me and considered how to react. But I was surprised, after all the months of rehearsing the scene in my mind, to see them turn silently to their lockers, fumble with their clothes, and leave together without saying a word to me. If I hadn't understood during those terrified months that everything I had ever been, everything I had ever believed in and dreamed of was gone, I understood it at that moment.

Miss Marston may have called Mrs. Duggin, the school nurse and my mother's helper on the women's auxiliary at church. Or maybe Mrs. Duggin watched me one day too many as I ran up the steps of the cafeteria into the bathroom to vomit lunch, my skirt stretched tight. Maybe she saw the change in my face, the darkness of fear and aloneness underlying the charade of walking and talking and sitting. She called me to her office. She was surprisingly tender as she handed me the expulsion slip.

"Do you want me to call your mother at work?" she asked.

"No, thank you," I answered. "How will I take my midterms?"

Mrs. Duggin sat back in her chair. "You understand that you may not return to this school?"

I left my books, left my notebooks with my childish penmanship looping phrases and doodles and who-loves-whom, on her desk. I walked down the silent, polished hallway to my locker, put on my jacket and mittens, and walked alone through the White wing, past the office staff staring at me through the big window, and out the door. The first phase of outcasting was done.

"Well," my mother said, sitting on the couch across the room in her trim wool dress and heels. "Well. You can't stay here."

The second phase.

I was supposed to move to my father's house the next morning. I asked my mother if I could wait until Sunday so I could go to church. She looked surprised. "Haven't you figured anything out?" she asked. "You can't go to church like that. They won't want us anymore." I don't believe my mother ever went to church again. When she died thirty years later, my brother and sister and I argued about whether she would want a minister at her grave. I believed that she would; I knew my own ambivalent heart. Finally, we asked a nice man from the Unitarian church to come, a neutral voice who was delicate in referring to a benevolent god.

No one from church ever called or wrote to me after I left Hampton. The silence made me feel as if I had never been part of their Christian body. The beloved smells of wax and leather prayer books and old women's perfume, the swish of Mr. Andrews's robes, the sweet wheeze of the organ, Mrs. Taccetta's tiny feet in stubby black heels pumping the pedals; the voices of the church rising together, proclaiming God's mercy and forgiveness; the refrigerator humming in the kitchen; my mother's hand wrapped around mine while we stood to sing and knelt to pray; Mr. Raymond or Miss Gleason smiling at me during the long sermon; the permanence and comfort of the affection of the grownups. The radiant, bored peace of church. All this evaporated when word got out.

Last Easter, I finally succeeded in getting my grown sons to accompany me to a service in the local Episcopal chapel. They had never been in a church, and I had not been in one except for funerals since I was sixteen. "Come," I said. "Easter is a joyous time in the church. Let's go sing about the rebirth of the Earth." They liked it. I sang by heart every word of "Christ the Lord Is Risen Today," and gave the responses to the Nicene Creed like a believer. I wasn't. But I was home—the sublime faces and the murmurings and the music and the candles and the lilies. The warmth felt deceptive, though, and seductive. Dangerous. My old defenses rose up again, instinctively, and I defied the beautiful place and the pious hearts and the father on the altar to catch me again.

I hadn't spent time with my father since he had remarried six years before. He and Catherine lived in a large old colonial in Epping, twenty miles from home. They were renovating the house themselves, and Catherine was a terrible housekeeper, so it was crowded with sheetrock panels and five-gallon buckets of plaster and boards and crushed boxes of nails and screws and tiles for the bathroom and old magazines and piles of mail and clothes strewn over chairs. The kitchen was greasy, and mounds of dirty dishes filled the sink. My father and Catherine both traveled for their jobs and were seldom home. Catherine told me to keep the thermostats at sixty-four; she bought cottage cheese and pineapple so I would stay thin and not "lose my shape." My sister, Sandy, agreed to stay with me while she completed her last year at the university. But her fiancé lived in Boston, and she, too, was seldom home. I had never slept alone in a house before.

I was not formed yet, not a decision-maker about my life. I was not yet born to consciousness. But here, suddenly, I was facing the results of *being* in the world. In those empty, slow, lonely days, I had to be born into my next life, as I lost my old self in a kind of death.

My stepsister, Molly, was still on her winter vacation from boarding school. The morning before I arrived she was moved from her home to her grandmother's house in western New Hampshire. We were told to stop writing letters to each other; my father explained that Molly was still only fifteen, and they didn't want her exposed to "things like this." I was forbidden to go outside because no one in town was told that I was there and pregnant. Once, after a deep, comforting snow, I shoveled the driveway and walks, thinking that my father and Catherine would be happily surprised when they came home the next day. They were angry, and reiterated that I must never go outside again.

I spent long silent days and nights in the house. When my father and Catherine were home, they sometimes had dinner parties. I was sent up to my room early with a plate of food and told not to make any noise. I didn't dare go to the bathroom down the hall, afraid that someone would come up the stairs. So I lay under the covers in my frosty, gloomy room, holding my pee, waiting. The laughter rose in bursts from the room below, voices from lives lived on another planet.

The winter was very long and very cold and very gray. The house, my room, were large and cold and gray. I waited for calls from Kathy and Susan, from friends at school who would be missing me, and then stopped waiting. Once I got a letter from a boy named Greg, a kind letter referring obscurely to my trouble and asking me to write back. It was a moment of tenderness that threatened to break my new tough heart. I could not afford to cry, and could not figure out what I—a dirty pregnant girl hiding upstairs in a cold, lonely house— could say to a handsome boy who still went to history class and shoveled driveways on Saturday morning. I never wrote back.

I know now that what happened that winter was a deep and scarring depression. Despair and a ferocious, watchful defiance saturated my young life. I was formed largely in those four months, those months that isolated me from any life, from any belief, from any sense that I belonged to anyone. I was alone. My fear and grief burned like wildfires on a silent and distant horizon. I watched the destruction day after day, standing by my bedroom window staring out over the snow-covered fields that belonged to my father.

My mother finally called in March. My birthday was coming, and she wanted to bring me home for dinner. I was pushed to excitement. I missed my mother badly, the mother of my childhood. I missed my bedroom and my cat. I missed that life, that girl, and wanted to reclaim her for a day.

I was exchanged between my parents' cars on the Route 101 overpass at noon. My mother stared at my large belly and didn't hug me. We drove in silence to Hampton; I wished I had not agreed to come. Being near her, being in our car, which belonged now to before, approaching my town on roads as familiar as my own body had once been, all agitated the deep, deep sense of loss which I had struggled so hard to kill. When we turned onto Lafayette Road near town, my mother told me to get down on the floor of the car. I didn't move. "We might see someone," she explained. I squeezed my baby and me onto her floor and watched my mother's faraway face staring straight ahead as we drove home.

My bedroom was a museum of another life. It was pink and soft and sunny and treacherous. I sat all afternoon on my bed, fingering the white chenille bedspread and stroking my purring black cat. I called up my numbness. A white lace cloth, ironed by me when I was a child in this house, covered the bureau. The blue plastic clock whirred quietly. Cars slid silently down High Street carrying people I knew: Mrs. Sargent and Teddy Lawrence and Sally and Mr. Palmer. They were in a movie, and I watched from beyond the screen.

I don't remember my birthday dinner, seventeen years old and seven months along. I am sure my mother gave me something nice. I hid on the floor of the car in the dark and was relieved to return to the empty obscurity of my father's house.

I had a keen sense of my baby and me being outcasts together. My father and mother had decided immediately that "we" would give the baby up for adoption. I didn't fight; I understood with absolute clarity that I would have no one helping me, that I had held one summer job in a candy store at the beach, that I could never return to high school. That we would be loved and protected nowhere. My sister and brother knew, but no one else in the family had been told. I still don't know where my grandparents thought I was that year. I do know that they were not there telling me that families don't give babies away.

The sense that I had a foreign and threatening force inside me had given way to an intense feeling of connection, of being lost together. We spent the dead-quiet hours alone, our heartbeats measuring together the passage of time, the damage, the unexpressed grief. We would be separated forever in two more months. We shared time in a strange and intense and encompassing sorrow.

My sister, six years older and longing since she was ten to have a baby of her own, said to me excitedly, "This is a baby, a miracle. A baby is growing inside you." I could not afford it with her.

"I hate this baby," I said to her, scaring her away.

I could feel his small heel or an elbow pressing hard against the inside of my belly as he rolled. I spent the days doing nothing but thinking, learning to live in my head, my arms wrapped under my belly, my baby absorbing my stunned sadness. He had hiccups in the night. I lay in the deep, cold emptiness of the house, the night shared with another living being. My blood flowed through him. Tenacious threads joined us, outside the world. I could not feel loved by him, ever. But we were one life, small and scared and alone.

"You have got to let this baby go," the doctor roared at me. He smelled of cigarettes. We had been here a very, very long time. "You cannot hold this baby inside you," he said angrily. "Push!" My baby was born on Memorial Day 1966.

Five days after the birth, my mother drove me to High Mowing, a small boarding school on a mountaintop in western New Hampshire, for an interview to enter in the fall. That morning she had found me crying as I squeezed milk from my impacted breasts into the bathroom sink.

"Oh, sweetheart," she had said. "My poor sweetheart."

I whipped around and hissed at her, "Get out." They were the first and only tears I had shed throughout the pregnancy and birth and the terrible, terrible drive away from the hospital. We had moved beyond mother and daughter forever. Whatever she felt watching me cry could not help me now.

She was cheerful and talkative on the way to the school. "This is a time to regroup," she told me, "to get back on track." She didn't look at me as she drove. "You need to forget these difficult months and make a new start," she said.

My belly was empty and soft; I had stuffed handkerchiefs in my bra to soak up the milk that spilled and spilled from my breasts. I felt old. The fierce sense of aloneness intensified. My other being, my baby who shared life with me, who was alive in me when everything else had died, was left alone someplace on the third floor of the hospital, the absolute outcast, a castaway.

"I'm relieved," my mother said, "that this whole ordeal is over." She reminded me again that some of her friends had dropped her when they heard about me; she had paid a big price, she said. I was lucky she had found this school, the only one that had agreed to consider me. She talked on and on while we drove toward my next life.

Mrs. Emmet met us in the old farmhouse living room. She was eighty-three, a wealthy eccentric and educator who carried her ideas from Germany and Austria. I felt at home; this was a world away from Hampton and Epping and my school friends who had become cardboard cutouts from someone else's past. If I did not get in here, I would have to go to work, without a diploma. I had always imagined I would go to Smith or Wellesley, the first generation. Now I hoped this old woman would let me finish out high school in her strange little school for fuck-ups.

She said I could come, even though I had "run amok." I had to promise I would never talk to any of the girls about what I had done; I would have the only single room, to isolate me from the possibility that the need to talk would compromise my promise. In September, ancient and so diminished I barely felt alive, I joined eighty children for a final year of school. I graduated in 1967, the same year my old class finished up in Hampton.

I occasionally went home for several years after that. I slowly grew bold and defiant, and would walk uptown and into the familiar stores. I always saw someone I knew. Inevitably, they stared and then turned away abruptly. If two were together, they bent in whispers and walked away from me. Barbara, who had been for six years the only other member, with me, of an experimental accelerated class, refused to sell stamps to me at the post office. Mrs. Clayton stayed busy in the back of the five-and-ten, folding and refolding clothes, until I left. Once, as I got out of the car in my mother's driveway, Cheryl drove by with three girls from my class. They whipped around in the next driveway and stopped in front of my house. Cheryl leaped out of the car, smiling at me. "Is it true," she asked loudly, grinning back at my old friends, "is it true you got knocked up?"

There are other truths, of course, behind this history, glimmers and flickers of understanding that underlie these memories. I was not the do-good child I thought myself to be. For example, I know now that I hated school. I was bored and arrogant, clamoring for more from better teachers. I once told the principal to go to hell; I offered to replace Mr. Belanger as French teacher when he couldn't answer my questions. My brother was a day student at Phillips Exeter, and I was jealous.

I think I was a skeptic—actually, a cynic—by the time I was in high school. I was outspoken, with strong opinions—even defiant. I was intolerant of ignorance or injustice. I read the daily paper and *The Atlantic Monthly*, and knew that people suffered terrible inequities. I laid blame passionately around me—the battle was between the haves and have-nots. I believed in the Truth, in what was Right, and must have been self-righteous. I tended to be a loner; I had lots of friends, but they knew, I think, that I always reserved some elemental piece of myself. I imagined myself always on the outside, by choice on the days I felt loved and by some inherent flaw on those other days. I was very serious, which was belied by my cheerfulness.

I did love my church. But I attended confirmation class when I was fourteen and grew increasingly frustrated with the lack of answers to my questions. I perceived this as a failure on the part of the minister and the church to own up to its limitations and hypocrisies. I challenged Mr. Andrews; he appeared to tolerate my confrontations, but I left each Wednesday evening confused and agitated. Two years before my expulsion, I realize now, my beliefs in God and my church had already started to fray.

It is true that my mother did not stay in the church after I left. But she had met Peter the year before; he was a jazz musician, a writer, a thinker. I remember going to church alone for a while, probably during that time of tumultuous changes in my mother's own life. She became a radical, started keeping a journal, sketched faces on the phone pad. She worked for Peter at a new job with a small, artsy magazine. After work, they joined friends at the house Peter rented at the beach for long nights of drinking and talk and cigarettes and music. That was the summer I got pregnant. Leaving the church may actually have happened for my mother months before my outcasting. Of course, I believed completely that she was a nearly perfect mother and any trouble I found was born in my own reckless, selfish heart.

It is true that my shunning was a message from our community to my mother, also: *Bobbie Hall thought she was so high and mighty, but she couldn't keep her husband, and now she hangs out with beatniks at the beach. And don't even mention her youngest. You get what you deserve.* Her rejection of me was a measure of the humiliation she felt. She believed until her death that I caused her to lose her friends and her stature in our town.

I struggle to reckon with my own silence, my lack of fight. I allowed my family and community to abandon me when I was drowning. Worst of all, I allowed my baby to be abandoned. I abandoned my baby. I never said a word. Sometimes my own failure of courage feels like the most hideous kind of cowardice, a flaw in me that confirms my unworthiness for love. Sometimes, rarely, I get a flicker of understanding about other realities, and feel a powerful protectiveness of that stunned and desperate girl.

These various truths sometimes collide with memories I have used to reconstruct the puzzle, but they cannot alter the perfect truth I carry of having been turned out.

It is a function of shunning that it must eliminate the shunned completely. It feels like a murder, and is baffling because there is no grave; no hymns were sung to ease my going or to beg for God's blessing on my soul. Shunning is as precise as a scalpel, an absolute excision, leaving, miraculously, not a trace of a scar on the community body. The scarring is left for the girl, an intense, debilitating wound that weeps for the rest of her life. It's quite a price to pay for having scared sex on a beach on a foggy Labor Day night.

Chapter One

The Lonely Hunter

The day is warm, gray and damp. Early July, but the horizon between the sky and ocean bleeds. It is 1965; I am sixteen. Hampton
Beach is almost deserted, with the crowds across the boulevard in the
shops.

"Hrrr," a young man says, dropping down beside me on the old
blanket. It sounds like a growl, or a low dark purr. "What are you
reading?" He takes the paperback from me. I don't say anything.
"Carson McCullers. *The Heart Is a Lonely Hunter.* Mine is," he says,
laughing.

He has black curly hair, dark skin, and a crooked nose. He wears
shorts and no shirt or shoes. His legs and chest are covered in thick,
black curly hair. The boys in my class have smooth skin still, and
most don't shave yet. I am scared, feeling myself caught already in
something dangerous.

"You don't say much, do you? You look really good, though."

I take the book back and open it again, pretending to find my
place and read.

"What are you doing here all by yourself? I think you need some
company." He makes that strange growl deep in his throat again, and
smiles. "Talk to me." He takes my book and slides it under his belly
on the blanket. "There. Now you're either going to have to talk to
me or go after your book. I'm happy either way."

He is self-confident. I feel silly and young, unable to talk, to keep
up with his flirtation. But I also feel a sudden rising power, a new
sense of my body and my skin—a recklessness, as if I am slipping
over a wall into something dangerous and intoxicating. I want this

boy, this young man, to love me. I have been embarrassed to be alone on the beach. What sixteen-year-old spends the summer at the beach alone—day after day, whether it is sunny or not—reading books and watching the tide move in and out? But suddenly my aloneness is a commodity, a mystery, payback.

"Cat got your tongue?" he asks.

I don't like the cliché. I haven't smiled yet. It makes me feel more grown-up, sophisticated. I am on my side, my head resting on my cocked arm. I like the way my hip rises from my waist. I roll onto my stomach, then feel his hand on the small of my back. It is shocking—skin to skin. I can't speak.

"Hrrr, Skeet, look what I found," he says to another boy walking up to us.

"Nice one!" Skeet says. They laugh.

"What's a nice girl like you doing down here at the beach?" my boy asks.

I try to sound aloof, careless. "I work here."

"She speaks!" he says. "This is good. Where do you work?"

"Nowhere," I say, turning my head away.

He suddenly jumps up. "Let's go," he says to Skeet.

A bubble of panic rises up in me. I want to hold on to this time, on to him and his admiring eyes and confidence and black hair. I feel as if I have missed something important for a long time and here it is, walking away. I feel hungry, desperate for him to stay, to lie back down next to me and pull my book away and touch my skin again.

"In the casino," I say. "It's my day off." I feel the heat rise in my face and neck. I am breaking every rule. "At the candy store and miniature golf."

He purrs again. "The casino. I love miniature golf, don't you, Skeet?"

I watch him walk up to the boardwalk and across the street. He turns just as he crosses the boardwalk and yells, "My name is Anthony! Don't forget!" I spend the afternoon looking up from my book every few minutes, trying to find his black curly head and dark skin in the crowds jostling in and out of the shops and arcade. Seagulls scream and call, floating overhead, pure white crosses against the dark sky. The afternoon wind comes up. Two months from now I will be pregnant. I put my jeans and shirt on over my swimsuit and wait for my mother to pick me up.

Hampton Beach, New Hampshire, is a honky-tonk place in 1965. Maybe it has always been. For years my mother forbade us children from going there except once a summer when my grandmother drove my brother and sister and me down to "the beach" in her '55 Ford. We'd park in the sandy lot behind the casino and spend the evening walking with the crowd, stopping at our favorite stores. My grandmother spoke familiarly to Mrs. Junkins at the candy store. We watched the big old taffy machine pull and twist and braid the shiny candy and left with a big box for my mother, who refused to "do" the beach. My grandmother gave us dimes in the arcade to play skee-ball and have our fortunes told by the creaking and faded and beautiful gypsy doll in the big glass box. We ate hamburgers at Wimpy's, sitting on the heavy green bench on the sidewalk and watching all the other tourists wander by. They were mostly French Canadians, with very short shorts and white socks in their leather sandals. They were a big part of why my mother refused to let us go down to the beach. She told us that we were too good to be around these people, that we shouldn't even want to be there. That there was something cheap and ordinary going on there, and we were not cheap or ordinary. The beach meant day-tripping workers from Massachusetts, from the mill towns of Haverhill—my mother's hometown —and Amesbury and Lowell. It meant old ladies and men dragging their beach chairs down the boardwalk and onto the sand. It meant families eating sandwiches on striped blankets and playing shoulder to shoulder with strangers in the cold rolling waves. And it meant young people, kids, boys and girls with different rules from mine, prowling the beach for beer and kisses and secret dates somewhere on the mile-long sands. The beach was a playground of the old world: 1950s America, a relic of both innocence and hidden transgressions.

But this summer, 1965, is a threshold time. My mother comes to Hampton Beach, too, every day, with Peter. The editor of *New Hampshire Profiles* magazine and my mother's boss, Peter has asked her to work with him for the summer on a federally funded project. My father left our family just a few years ago, a devastating loss for my mother. Now she is in love with Peter, or at least with Peter's life—the music, the art, the artist friends, the late nights with their underlying beat of love and heat. Before she met Peter, my mother was president of the PTA and chair of the church social events committee. She polished our silver-plated forks and knives and carefully hemmed my skirts below the knee. But she has entered a new life and is intoxicated with it. She starts to write short stories, to read Sartre and Camus and Hesse and Rilke. She lets her hair grow out from her short and practical wave, and the handsome dark wool and gabardine dresses she sewed with such skill are pushed to the back of her closet. She wears slacks and turtlenecks and Mexican sandals. Finishing her duties as mother to her last child at home seems unmanageable, a commitment she resents and resists. Suddenly, I find myself accompanying her each day to the forbidden beach and spending long lonely hours before and after work waiting for her.

Peter and my mother do important work, work that justifies her drive each morning to the mildewed, sandy office of the Hampton Beach Riot Committee. I don't know how Peter's editorship of a small New Hampshire magazine, how his jazz and writing qualify him to head the riot study commission. I don't know what my mother, with her cool judgments of others' misbehavior, wants to bring to a study of youth gone wild. But for the summer of 1965, Peter and my mother work in the glass-wrapped office of the Hampton Beach Chamber of Commerce, right on the boardwalk along the white sand beach, building a report on the causes of the riots the summer before.

On Labor Day eve 1964, the huge crowd of kids gathered at

the beach for the holiday coalesced into a rioting mob. The police and firefighters responded with force, driving the rioters across the beach and into the water. Each time, the crowd swept back into the streets, attacking the cops with rocks and Molotov cocktails. Finally, in the middle of the night, the governor called out the National Guard and declared martial law. The guard closed down all the roads into the beach and set up machine gun stations along the main road. It took them until dawn on Labor Day to contain the riot, with dozens of police and kids left wounded.

The Hampton Beach riots stunned the nation, which still clung to the passive, determined calm of the 1950s. The rioters were average kids from area towns, not troublemakers with a history. A year later, no one has figured out what they were all so angry about. Peter and my mother are charged with interviewing hundreds of rioters, finding answers and coming up with recommendations so this cannot happen again. They do a good job. The police receive extensive sensitivity training. Bongo drums and radios playing rock 'n' roll are finally allowed on the beach with no police action. Bikinis no longer earn a citation for indecency. My mother feels sympathy for these kids. At a moment of great transformation in her own life, she understands the surge of change that is gathering force in this seedy little summer town and is soon to engulf the country.

I feel the swelling energy, the inexplicable, restless hunger, rising in my own innocent life. I don't care at all about the music or the drinking or the gathering together of teenagers for fun and the thrill of belonging. But my father is gone. He has a new life, a new wife and daughter, and never calls or visits. I miss him badly. My mother is inaccessible. My older brother and sister have moved on to their own lives, leaving me very alone at home and on the beach while my mother works and plays with Peter. I feel lost, caught between my old life at home—a safe, small, family life—and the new life on which my mother has opened the door. A growing sense of dread, of confusion, of abandonment and desperation is starting to erase my childhood. I am hungry to be loved, and understand the rioters' anger, the eruptive release, the need to defy. I understand the pulsing impatience. I feel a powerful dark longing that throws me back into myself. Most of this I cannot name or explain. But as the summer slides along, I know one thing very clearly: I am drifting in over my head and want my mother to grab me out of the tide.

My mother was a guardian of the old rules until she met Peter and stepped into his world. Now, I teeter on a frightened edge between our two lives, understanding that I am to follow the old system, that I must be contained. I grew up with certain indisputable expectations for my behavior: I would dress modestly. I would never call a boy. I would never be alone with a boy. I would not lie or sneak. I would not talk back. But this summer, as my mother moves farther and farther into her new life, I spend more and more time alone. After her work on the committee ends late in the day and my work at the casino is over, my mother drives me home and then heads to Peter's house, up the coast five miles to eat, drink, make music and conversation with friends. She is happy and alive. Our house is very quiet.

The biggest change is that she suddenly allows me to date. My mother stops asking where I am going and with whom. She tells me to be home at ten, but she is not there to hear me come in. Suddenly, I am on my own to make up the new rules. Once, I told her how much I liked a boy putting his hand on my leg at the movie. She disapproved: "Meredy, never let a boy do that."

"Why?"

She was disgusted. "Because one thing leads to another." But she wouldn't tell me how to reconcile her expectations for my proper behavior with the new universe we both found ourselves in.

I spend the first weeks of the summer holding myself to the old rules. Then one day, I shop in the cheap little stores along the beach while I wait for her to get out of work. I find a bikini—white dotted swiss with big black polka dots and ruffles over the seat. I try it on in the cramped dressing room. I love what I see. I am thin, brown, mature. It confuses me, the good girl.

The next day, I strut all morning up and down the beach outside my mother's wall of windows at the chamber. Up and down, up and down. Only a few girls wear bikinis still, and I am the center of attention. Men whistle. Boys fall into step beside me and ask for my name, my phone number. I love their interest. I want them to love me, to hold me, to fill the vast empty space in my life that is starting to scare me so much.

I can see my mother bent over her desk on the second floor, answering the phone, walking out of sight and returning. Several times I wave but get no response. By the end of the day, I decide that this is going to be my new skin. I leap into a new life that afternoon, blind and alone, reckless. When I climb into my mother's car at the curb at five thirty, I don't cover up with a shirt. I wait, wanting her to draw me, to draw us, back to the safety of our other life, the life in which a father and mother hold ground. She looks sideways at me but doesn't say a word.

When I am back in the shelter of my small, sunny room at home, I fold my old one-piece swimsuit into the back of a drawer for good. I hear my mother's car pull back out. I close my door and stand in front of the mirror, studying my body. A trained dancer, I am strong and thin. The polka-dotted ruffles on my bottom look innocent, playful. I stroke the soft roundness of my breasts, the dark hollow between them, and the smooth curve at the small of my back. I have areas of baby-fine white skin on my chest and belly and back that need exposure, need to brown up in the open air. Except for that, I am ready. When Anthony puts his hand on my back that cloudy July afternoon, I am ready.

It is Labor Day 1965. There are no stars tonight. No moon. The beach is divided in two: the upper part by the boardwalk is a sad greenish-pink from the mercury lights overhead; the lower part is dark, with a silvery light from the wave crests rising and then seeping over the sand, rising and seeping. That's where Anthony takes me, over the line of light into the dark. The beach monument—a seated woman looking out to sea for her lost love—marks the spot where Skeet waits in Anthony's car. It has been exactly a year since the riots erupted and two months since we met. Everything at the beach is quiet, but inside I can feel rising something dangerous, a chaotic push and pull.

As we walk along the water's edge, Anthony laughs and teases me, as he does each time we are together, about how protected I have been, how naïve, how girlish I am. "Are you sure you're not afraid of the dark?" he asks. "Your mother must have told you never to let a guy like me take you to the beach on a night like this." Later, he says, "Don't worry. I'm here to protect you from the sharks." He doesn't hold my hand or put his arm around me. In fact, we have barely kissed all summer.

I have seen Anthony six or seven times since I met him. I have never been alone with him; he and Skeet are a team. They made their way to the second floor of the casino on a hot evening a few days after that first inflaming afternoon and found me at the miniature golf desk handing out clubs and balls to a steady flow of people. I was bored. When I noticed Anthony standing in line, I felt no surprise. I knew he would come.

The upstairs of the old casino is dark and musty and cold even on a hot, sunny day. The floorboards creak as people move around the cavernous room. Anthony and Skeet played three rounds of golf. Anthony has an athletic body and a confident, easy walk. He joked with me about the silliness of my job and the fact that I was all bundled up against the cold wind that blasted up the wide concrete steps of the casino. "Why aren't you in that cute little thing you had on the other day?" he asked. "The thing with the ruffles." I was busy and didn't have to do anything more than smile back. By the time he and Skeet left, Anthony knew my name and how to call me.

Carl, a friend who worked with me every day, asked, "Who was that?"

"Just a guy I met," I said. I felt guilty.

"He's got to be twenty years old, Meredy. Why are you talking to a guy like that?"

"He's nice," I said. "Don't worry. We're not going out or anything."

"Does your mother know about him?"

"Yeah," I said. "She just said no cars." He knew I was lying. I had never mentioned Anthony to my mother, and she had stopped worrying about cars.

In fact, I rode in Anthony's green MG several times. The first time, he took me to Salisbury, across the border in Massachusetts. Skeet was crammed into the space behind my seat, breathing over my shoulder. We were headed to a party. I was forbidden to go to Seabrook or Salisbury—tough towns of low-life people, my mother said. And I had never been to a real party anywhere before. On the way, Anthony hummed and beat out the time on the little steering wheel to a song I could not recognize. I felt a hard stab of fear, a flashing grip of warning. But the car was fast, Anthony knew what he was doing, and I gave myself over to his recklessness.

"Do you ever do drugs?" he yelled over the song. But he gave me no time to answer. "Stupid question. I bet you don't even drink." He growled, that low call, deep in his chest, which I knew was an enticement to trouble. "Okay. We're going to this place. I know some people there, but there are going to be some people I don't know. Open the glove box."

Inside was a small black gun. He took it out and turned it over in his hand a couple of times. "Here, take it," he said, laughing at me as I shrank away from it. He put it back in the glove box. "Okay. This is what you're going to do. Stick close to me. If things heat up, just follow me. Fast. Got it?"

I watched the road fly at us and under our wheels. The wind whipped my hair in my eyes. I was on my way to trouble, and I knew it. "Great," I said. "I know what to do."

The party was in a cottage on a crowded street that dead-ended on the beach in Salisbury. Everyone was years older than I was; they were doing drugs, selling and buying drugs, and passing out high. There was no trouble. I lost Anthony for a few hours and went out to sit on the beach alone. When I came back in to find him, neither of us asked where the other had been. We left with Skeet, and I snuck into the house at two A.M. without waking up my mother.

I decided that night not to be around Anthony anymore. I had learned that he was a senior at Boston College, that he was twenty-one and came from Andover, Massachusetts. His father was hard on him, but he was spoiled, with a car and a motorcycle and college and no job all summer. I lay in bed that night remembering the humiliating teasing, the lack of conversation, Skeet, the older people passed out in a dirty house in Salisbury, the gun. The fact that Anthony had never asked me any questions about myself. If he had, he would have learned that I was going to be a junior in high school, that I was a good girl, that the empty place inside me was not shaped like him.

But a week later, and another after that, I was back in his car, with Skeet sitting in the back. We went to a party in Rye one night. We drove up the coast once. One hot night we drove around and around the fifteen blocks that make up Hampton Beach, with Skeet yelling at girls and Anthony laughing and purring.

One rainy afternoon, they came to my house. I was alone. They walked right into the tidy kitchen without knocking. I was panicked that my mother would come home from work and find them there. She would know from one look that these were not the kind of boys I was allowed to date. Anthony found my cat's litter of kittens in a box by the phone and picked up three of them. Their eyes were still closed.

"Hey, Skeet!" he called. "Let's bake the kittens!"

I dragged at his arm as he put them in the oven and turned it on. I hated him suddenly, hated the way he made me feel both dirty and childish. "Get out!" I yelled. "Leave me alone!"

They did leave, laughing, with the kittens still in the warm oven.

I took my childhood cat and her babies into my room and sat crying on my bed, holding each tiny kitten to my face, feeling that I had failed at something and it was going to hurt me all my life.

This starless Labor Day night on the beach is the last time I will see Anthony until after Christmas. There are only a few people on the beach. My mother has done her work well—no pulsing anger churns at the beach, waiting to erupt into a riot. Instead, a scared and lonely girl who wants to be loved makes her way on a deserted beach toward the few minutes that will shape the rest of her life.

We walk side by side, without touching, deeper and deeper into the dark night. When Anthony and Skeet drop me off at home an hour later, the zipper on my white corduroy pants is broken. My mother's car is in the driveway. I shake as I stand next to her bed, answering her questions about where I have been and with whom. I hold my sweater across my belly to hide what has been broken, certain that the shift in my life is written over my body, in my eyes. It is very late, but she doesn't question me. She says good night and goes back to her book. I take a shower and bury my pants in the bottom of the trash barrel in the garage.

In late October, I track down a number for Anthony at Boston College. He says that he had fun with me but that he is committed to a girl named Christine, a girl his family chose for him when they were just children. I quietly, desperately, ask him not to hang up. He is embarrassed and says he has to run to class. "Wait!" I cry. "I'm pregnant." There is a pause, and then the phone connection clicks off. I crumple to the floor in the corner of the kitchen and sob. I don't care anything for Anthony, but I feel suddenly severed from the world. A violent undertow of dread and fear pulls me from shore.

The drawbridge over Hampton River is raised; I wait, the only car trying to cross. It is a heavy, gray morning in late January. The river, the ocean, the sky, the flat snow-filled marsh blend into a field of weight, of grief. Of shame. Anthony has agreed to meet me on the

Seabrook side, in the public parking lot, to sign his name to the adoption papers. A lobster boat chugs under the bridge on the dark current; the bridge slowly lowers, clanking into place like a cell door locking shut.

His little green car is there, in the far corner by a path through the dune grass to the beach. There is not another car or person in sight, as if this is a vast stage for the playing out of this act. As I drive up, I realize that Skeet is sitting in the passenger seat. Anthony gets out and stands facing me over the roof of his car, resting his weight on his elbows. I put my father's car into park and get out, holding the sheaf of papers. The wind catches at them, and I have to clutch them so they won't blow away. Sand and trash—candy and cigarette wrappers, paper cups, sheets of damp, yellowed newspapers—blow across the parking lot and wrap against my legs and the tires of the cars.

I am five months pregnant. I have numbed myself for this meeting. I wear a bright blue wool coat my mother made for me in eighth grade, just three years ago; it was designed for a girl, although it is full and covers my swollen belly. The lining is shiny white satin. I loved the coat once. Now I feel embarrassed, a pregnant sixteen-year-old in a child's clothes.

Anthony growls, "Hrrrr. You really are."

"Yes. I really am. You need to sign this." I want to cover myself, remove myself from his, and Skeet's, eyes. I put the papers on the trunk of his car.

"So what will happen?" he asks, taking the pen from me. He seems to have a little smile on his face. I am distressed by it, and struggle to read him.

"The baby will be given up for adoption." My voice is flat, hard. In the lonely despair of hiding from the world, I have slowly awoken to the life of my child growing inside me and feel a ferocious and protective love for my baby.

"What about you?" he asks.

"What about me?" I say. "Sign there." He puts his signature on the line above my mother's and my father's. There is one line left empty, waiting for me.

I drive away, leaving him beside his car. This time the bridge is down and I drive right across, back to my father's house, back to that quiet and desperate wait.

Nearly forty years later, I still have the same copy of *The Heart Is a Lonely Hunter*—a Bantam Giant edition costing thirty-five cents. The pages are yellow and brittle. I underlined and asterisked certain passages, small dark tunnels back through time to that lonely and catastrophic summer. I marked, "It was as though in some way she was waiting—but what she waited for she did not know. Sometimes she would look all around her quick and this panic would come in her." The last pages are underlined again and again: "He felt the old terror that always came as he awakened . . . The emptiness in him hurt. He wanted to look neither backward nor forward"; and, finally, "For in him he felt a warning, a shaft of terror. Between the two worlds he was suspended . . . The left eye delved narrowly into the past while the right gazed wide and affrighted into a future of blackness, error, and ruin."

In the margins I have written, *I know this* and *I am scared, too*. The handwriting is large and unformed, that of a child. I cannot remember exactly what I was thinking at the time these ominous and alienated ideas spoke so loudly to me. I only know that I was a lonely hunter.

Chapter Two

Waiting

"Meredy!" My mother is home from work, calling from the kitchen. Her voice is sharp, imperious. I have been waiting for this moment, waiting for more than four months. Still, I haven't expected this voice, and it stops me cold. I telephoned her when I got home from school, midmorning, wishing I had let the school nurse call her. When my mother asked why I wasn't at school, I said, "I'll tell you when you get home tonight." I spent the day trying to imagine this conversation, but I could not draw up my mother's concerned face, could not feel her arms around me. Now, I stand silent, watching myself in the mirror over my bureau. Everything in the house feels muffled, distant, as if suddenly none of it has anything to do with me anymore—not the hum of the furnace below my feet, not my diary under my slips in the second drawer, not the skittering shadows of winter branches shimmering on my wall—each piece receding into a past that belonged to the girl I had been up until this moment.

I am Meredith Hall, I think, looking back at the girl in my mirror. I am Meredy, a junior at Winnacunnet High School in Hampton, New Hampshire. I will graduate, class of '67, and go to Smith College. I am a sixteen-year-old girl who gets all As and is secretary of student council. The ocean flows in and out, in and out in perfect rhythm, every day and every night, across my beach, a mile beyond Mrs. Paley's and Old Billie's and Uncle Leo's, who is not really my uncle but who has always called me "my little sweetheart," beyond their bunched-together and friendly little houses with peeling paint. This has been my bedroom since I was born. I sleep under this soft worn bedspread. I ironed the white lace cloth on my bureau, whose drawers stick, and inside are my clothes. I come home after school and put apple blossoms in a vase or make brownies to surprise and please my mother. I am Meredy, with a brother named Michael, a sister named Sandy, and a mother who loves me.

I look back at myself in the mirror, my hands holding the edge of my bureau softly. Some things are right. My shiny blond hair and crisp white blouse. My girl's skin. But the awful fear, the aloneness, the waiting for four and a half months for this moment and whatever will follow, have settled into my eyes, my face. School and pleasing my mother and the soft shelter of my room are gone, I know, forever.

"Meredy!" The call is a summons. I suddenly feel too tired to imagine what is going to come next. My mother's voice announces that whatever I have hoped would be is not going to happen. The hush in the house is slow and deep, a warning I hear but cannot react to as I face her.

"You're pregnant, aren't you?" The words are hard, fierce. I cannot find my mother; she is gone, a million miles away, back in a place where there were no terrible surprises, where good girls didn't draw shame on good mothers. I am surprised that she has taken so long to come to this realization, surprised that after my round belly and morning sickness and fear and retreat slipped past her all these months, all it took was a small break in the routine, me coming home early from school, for her to pay attention finally to her daughter's despair.

"Yes." I struggle to react, to fight this new current, the unexpected coldness, the judgment, before it is too late. But my voice is tiny in the hollow room. Her cigarette smoke floats in the still air. I want cover. I want someone to hold me.

"How far along are you?"

"Almost five months."

"Michael!" my mother calls, looking at me steadily. "Michael!"

My brother, home for winter break from college in Montreal where he is in pre-med, appears in the kitchen doorway.

"Your sister is pregnant."

My loved brother's head slowly turns toward me. He looks surprised and then disapproving. Slowly he turns back to our mother; they look at each other silently, then he walks past me into the hall. I hear his bedroom door click shut.

I don't want to look at my mother; I don't want to look at the floor, don't want to allow my mother to see me, my belly round with this shame, me helpless and too scared to speak. I imagine myself erased. The cold gray light tumbles in through the window and absorbs me.

"Well," my mother says. It is a loud word, not ambivalent. There is no struggle in it, no doubt. "Go call your father and tell him what you have done."

My father sits stiffly in the faded brown chair we still call, six years after his leaving, Daddy's chair. The last time we all sat together in this room was when my father returned after having disappeared for a year and announced that he had married a woman named Catherine. Now, he has on one of his old Viyella shirts, worn out at the elbows, and canvas boat shoes with a hole in one toe. Once, I told him it embarrassed me that he dressed like that; my father laughed and said, "I've worked goddamned hard to be able to dress like this." He is tall and large-chested, and fills his old chair. His strong features are handsome. He grounds the room, the house, my mother, me in ways I have forgotten.

My mother, still in her green wool dress and black heels from her job at *New Hampshire Profiles*, sits straight-backed on the edge of the couch. The muscles of her face have drawn in, setting her eyes and mouth in a smooth, hard mask. I sit by the picture window, tugging at the pleats of my skirt to hide the small bulge of my stomach. I watch my father and mother silently, trying to remember at what point so much had careened off track. I have a vague sense that what is about to happen is somehow inevitable, a scene written in my hazy past and only now being acted out. I can't think what the scripted outcome is, though, and wait to hear my parents speak their lines. They do not say any of the things I thought they would.

"Do you know who the father is?" my own father asks. His voice is not cold. It is slow, uncertain, as if he also can't remember his part.

I am surprised by the question. I look quickly at my mother, hoping there might be a protest, some protection, but my mother returns my look without flinching and waits.

I think my voice will be a roar, will scorch the room, but it is small. I hear myself answer in a wavering voice, "Yes." I say the name.

"What?" my father says. "What? What is it?"

I say the name again.

My father looks at my mother. "What is that, Bobbie?" He repeats the name. "Is that Italian?" My mother doesn't answer. "Do you want to get married?" he asks me. He doesn't wait for an answer and asks, "Does he know about this? Jesus Christ. Jesus Christ. Goddamn that little son of a bitch. Jesus, Meredy."

I want to say something, to explain that I am stunned, too, frightened and wanting to climb back against these events to my life. But we are lurching blind through our scenes, and I cannot find my voice to say, *Help me.*

"Will he sign the papers?" my father asks.

It is so quiet. I can't tell if we are all hearing the same waiting silence. I understand that my father means I will have to see Anthony again. But papers? I have imagined this scene a thousand times, and it has never been anything like this. Papers. I try to think that he means papers having to do with my homework. Or maybe he means something to do with the police. Papers. A slow terrible dawning washes through me. I hold my hands tight against my small hard belly. I haven't answered my father's question.

He looks at my mother again. "Now what?"

My mother looks at me coldly. "Well, she can't stay here."

In the car on the way to Epping, my father tries to hold my hand. I pull it back into my lap when he has to shift. I am afraid I will cry. I hope that he will tell me what is going to happen to me, that he will say things will be all right. We cross the marsh, golden in the low afternoon light, and take Route 101 through the soft, overgrown, snow-covered farmland. The heater fan hums. We don't talk during the half-hour drive to his house.

I have never seen the upstairs of my father and Catherine's house. I put my bag on the bed. Catherine closes the door and goes downstairs. When I hear their voices from the kitchen, I open the door quietly and look down the hall. The house is an old colonial my father and Catherine are renovating. The ceilings are high, the rooms cubes of stripped gray plaster. What has been finished— the hallway, the bathroom, and the front stairway—are grand and striped and carpeted. There is a heavy strength in the house, some- thing authoritative that makes me feel small and vulnerable. A man's terry bathrobe hangs on the back of the bathroom door. There are only two towels on the rod by the sink. I wipe my hands on my slacks and quietly walk back down the hall. All the bedroom doors are closed. I want to find my father, but I don't dare go downstairs.

My room is in the back corner, with two big windows looking out over the old barn and fields and woods. There are no curtains. Boxes are stacked along the walls and in the small closet. The air in the room is cold, and old. I climb under the flowered bedspread, my arms at my sides, shivering, and watch the last gray light of the af- ternoon settle over the fields.

Catherine and my father leave on separate business trips the next morning. I sit at the breakfast table while Catherine uses the phone to confirm their flights and check in with their secretaries about pickup and hotel arrangements. Her face has a formal beauty that my mother's lacks; I can see the difference, see her sophistication, and understand my father's leaving for this new life. Catherine has an old, heavy brown cardigan over her black suit. The kitchen is cold like the rest of the house; Catherine tells me to keep the thermostat at sixty-four while they are away. The kitchen hasn't been redone yet. It is large and dirty; newspapers and old mail and stacks of dishes clutter the old linoleum counters. The ceiling and faded flowered wallpaper are clouded yellow from old cigarette smoke. Small cardboard boxes full of Italian tiles line the wall beside the refrigerator. The windows by the table face east, and thin, cold winter sun outlines the greasy gas stove.

Catherine's voice is commanding, with her secretary and then with me. She shows me where the light switches are, how to relight the gas pilot on the stove, and what food is in the refrigerator and pantry. She posts telephone numbers for my father in Houston. She will be home first, in four days. I nod at the directions but don't ask any questions. I have never spent a night alone. The coming days feel like part of a penance, punishment. I am suddenly scared of everything, of the back country road with no streetlights and the sagging unlit shed beyond the kitchen, of my mother's voice and being alone and the stove pilot. I am afraid of having a baby. I am afraid of giving a baby away. I nod yes to everything Catherine says.

When they leave, my father hugs me. I can feel the small tight knot of my stomach against his heavy coat. He pulls away from me and says, "I...I don't want you to go outside while we're away. Don't go outside. I don't think you need to, anyway." No one in town knows I am here, the hidden, shamed girl. I pull my sweater around my chest and belly and say okay.

I wash two days' dishes and scrub the sink, as if somehow I mirror the dirt and disarray of my father's house, as if by cleaning and organizing the rooms, I can somehow clean away my disgrace, bring sense and order back to my own life. I spend the morning walking through each room of the house, examining pictures and the books on the shelves, opening the drawers and closets. Everything is a mess, dirty and cluttered, plaster dust and piles of magazines and boxes marked *Keene: Study* and *Kitchen*. It is snowing softly, and the gray sky and gray plaster make the interior landscape as dreary as the country outside. I put on all the ceiling lights on the first floor, but the bulbs are low-watt and don't cheer up the cold rooms. I climb the stairs to their room.

The blankets are tossed aside. There is a television at the foot of the bed. This room has been finished. It is big, and big turquoise flowers bloom on the walls; the carpet is a heavy red. Their closet is full of shirts and blouses and skirts and suits in dry cleaner bags. Clothes spill out of drawers and over the chairs. I open each drawer and carefully close it just the way it was. My father's cuff links and tie tacks are in an open leather box. I remember it on his bureau at home. I dump them out on the bed, examining each one, remembering them, remembering something that lingers softly, sadly, at the edge of my memory, and put them back in pairs. My mother's bedroom slides like a film in front of this one, her worn chenille spread pulled neatly across her bed, the bed she used to share with my father, and her old sewing machine and the sun sweeping across the clean maple floor.

I take out one of my father's old work sweaters and pull it over my head. It smells of him, of linseed oil and sawdust. I go back downstairs to the front room, to a patch of pale sun on the couch. The clock on the mantel says nine thirty. I undo the top button of my skirt and sit down with one of Catherine's paperbacks, a mystery by someone I have never heard of. I wish I had brought *Demian* and the Austen my mother gave me for Christmas. When I packed to leave, everything in my room seemed to belong to someone who had died —things sweet and too painful to hold. I have come to Epping with a small bag of clothes almost too tight to wear. The clock ticks in the big gray room. I look up each time a car drives by, its tires *shoosh*ing through the slush.

It snows a lot in southern New Hampshire this winter. My father and Catherine are away most of the time. Sometimes Catherine is home without him. She takes over my diet: plain toast for breakfast, cottage cheese and pineapple for lunch, hamburger patty and a slice of tomato for dinner. Catherine speaks to me every day, at every meal, about the importance of not gaining weight, of using cream to prevent stretch marks, of wearing a tight bra to keep my young breasts high and firm. We do not talk about the child inside me, his future, my future, love, fear, betrayal, loneliness. I am always hungry, and fine, zigzagging lines are already webbing my belly. They feel like a mark on me, a mark to announce me forever as the girl who made a baby and gave it away. They feel like a warning to anyone who might think of loving me someday.

Catherine catches me one day in one of my father's shirts. She makes me take it off and gives me a blue one with the collar frayed off instead. I am careful to hide the belt I have taken from my father's closet to hold up my skirt, with the button and zipper wide open. My mother sends a maternity outfit finally, short-sleeved plaid with big buttons, cheap stiff cotton that collapses when I wash it. The pants embarrass me, synthetic, dark blue, enormous, with a panel of elastic that shows every time I move.

I sit on the edge of my bed each morning and rub in the cream Catherine gave me, goose bumps rising in the cold. My hands recognize the smooth long muscles of my arms and legs. But my breasts, barely formed before I got pregnant, are large and heavy; the small nipples are hard red nubs, tight and sore. I don't like to touch them. My belly hardens, a tight round world stretching inside my skin. I try once, holding on to the bureau in my cold dim room, to move through my old ballet exercises. But I can see my reflection in the window, a stranger, and do not do it again.

I write long letters to my mother, angry and frightened and pleading letters, but afterward I feel helpless and embarrassed, and I rip them up. My mother does not call or write. The house is heavy; the light is heavy; it is only six weeks since I left school.

Sometimes I try to pray at night in my bed, but my prayers always end up being to my mother. "Hold me," I pray. "Please help me."

"Do you know what this town is saying about me?" my mother answers from above. "They say that my daughter is common, that she is a slut."

The big empty house ticks along, slow and cold and quiet. I stay in my room, waiting, watching the light come and go over the pasture and woods. One morning, Catherine knocks on my door. I stiffen. I am lying on the bed under the quilt, dressed in the maternity clothes I wear every day, shoes on as if I might go somewhere, reading a book from the carousel bookstand by the bed. My back is to the door, my leg bent to make a hollow for my belly. Catherine enters, speaking.

"Meredy. You cannot stay in this room all the time. You have got to get involved in a project. Get some exercise." Her voice is critical, impatient.

I get off the bed and stand on the other side. I don't answer.

"I'll get you a rug. You can do exercises here on the floor." She shoves the boxes one after another into the corner.

I sit back down on the bed. It is going to snow; the room is still and gray. The boxes grate across the pine floor. Catherine walks back to the side of the bed, reaches around me, and turns on the lamp.

"There," she says.

I call my mother. She is silent after I say hello. I can hear the stereo in the background; my mother inhales on her cigarette.

"Mum, I just wanted to talk."

"About what?"

I hesitate. "I don't know. Everything."

"What do you want me to say, Meredy?"

"I don't want you to say anything, Mum." There is a long silence. "Mum, I don't know if I can do this."

"Well. You have no choice. You'll be fine," my mother says.

The first time my father asks me to eat upstairs when company comes for dinner, I have to ask why.

His response is more abrupt than I have ever heard him. "Why do you think?" he answers. After that, I know that when Catherine cleans the kitchen and living rooms and my father makes fires in the fireplaces, I should go upstairs. The house smells of roast lamb and garlic. I listen to their friends talk all at once about vacations and the snow and their children. Bursts of laughter flare and ebb. I can sometimes hear my brother's or sister's name rise above the murmur, and I stand with my ear to the door trying to hear my own.

Catherine buys a clock for my room. I listen to it flapping the time, minute after minute, for three days. When I am alone again in the house, I unplug it and push it under the sheets in the linen closet. I stand by the bathroom window, my fingertips touching under my belly. I lean my head against the frosted glass; snow floats in gentle eddies on the wind. I wish someone would come, but I can't think who. The weight settles hard. I roll my head slowly back and forth, eyes closed, fingers touching. The silence in the house leaves me marooned, unattached.

I have come only with sneakers. In the musty shed, I find Catherine's boots. I put on mittens and my father's old red hunting jacket and a hat. I walk out the shed door into the winter storm. A car rounds the corner slowly on the snowy road. I step quickly back into the shed and pull the door closed. I wait, listening for cars. When it is quiet, I move quickly around behind the shed, and, cupping my belly in my arms, I start to run before another car drives by. I have not been outside the house since I came; the cold wind burns my lungs and throat. As I move straight across the field toward the woods, snow comes over Catherine's boots, packing behind the loose tongue and soaking my socks. Everything is still. Small gusts of wind make snow eddies; stiff weed stems curve down to the ground and etch semicircles back and forth in the snow. The rotting plank door to the old cold cellar stands open. I have heard my father talk about this relic from the old farm, but I have never seen it. Dug into the hillside, the domed black pit smells of damp earth and mold. I stand just inside, out of the snow. I breath deeply, tasting the sweet decay, emptying my lungs of air I have breathed in and out, in and out for weeks in the closed-up house. Turning around, I face the woods; the falling snow softens the line of trees, and the air is sharp and clean.

I cross the pasture, plowing my boots through the snow, and crawl clumsily under the old wire fence. Two cars pass the house, but I feel small and inconsequential in the back fields. I don't run. Instead, I lie down at the edge of the woods, looking up through the bare oak and beech branches. The snow floats here out of the wind, drifting softly onto me like goose down. I am cold. I press my back into the snow and turn my head to the side, flicking little piles of snow with my tongue. I remember the coppery taste of the snow, its quick melt on my tongue. There is nothing moving anywhere. The woods and fields calm me, ease the groundswell of dread. Spreading my arms and legs wide, I slowly sweep a snow angel, remembering for just a moment my childhood life, gone forever. I lie still, my belly rising into the soft light, snow collecting around my eyes, my feet cold and everything perfectly silent.

I am seven months pregnant. Catherine hands me a bag holding three yards of nearly white pinwale corduroy and a pattern for a maternity dress. I know how to sew. My mother has been a good teacher. I lay out the cloth, pinning the tissue pieces carefully along the straight of the weave. I cut it out with pinking shears and sew it together on Catherine's portable sewing machine set on my bedroom floor. The dress is full, with a round neck and several big buttons down the front. I hem it carefully, evenly, at the knee. I iron it and hang it in my closet. It is much too nice to wear.

One morning Catherine tells me to put on my dress. We are going in the car. She is always serious and cool and does not tell me where we are going. She drives to Hampton and gets on the highway south. I sit in the new dress with my arms around my large belly. It feels good to be out in the world, but I feel great foreboding, things always out of my control. We drive to the airport in Boston and take a plane to New York City. Catherine is wearing her mink coat and high heels. We do not talk during the drive or the flight. We take a cab into the city. "Wait here for me," she says in the lobby of a large office building. "I have a meeting."

When she returns, we take another cab to a large theater with a gilded dome and velvet seats. The lights go down and the curtain rises. *Othello*. Sir Laurence Olivier. It takes a few minutes to begin to understand the archaic language. But I am ready to be carried away: Othello's love, Desdemona's commitment, Iago's treachery. I give myself to the story. In the dark theater, I lose for a few hours the life I have come to.

The lights come on and my future returns in the glare. We fly back to Boston and drive home in silence. I hang my new dress in the closet and lie in the cold dark room, the eternal language of love and betrayal in my ears.

Midmorning. The early March light is thin, silvery in the dark house. I have been alone for four days. I am almost always alone. Each day is the same. I am awake often in the night, sleepless, frightened, disconnected. Finally, I drift into welcome sleep before dawn, then wake with a jolt as the cold gray light comes to my room. Instantly, I remember: *I am pregnant. I am having a baby. I am at my father's, alone. I will give away my baby.* The nightmare of each new day.

I lie in my bed, unable to get comfortable, stroking my belly. There is not a sound anywhere inside or outside the house, a vacuum, emptiness. Time suspends, dropping me deeply into an aching, inescapable fear. I hunch into the covers for warmth, trying to will myself back into sleep. When I open my eyes, I look at Catherine's boxes against the wall with my limp, faded maternity clothes folded carefully on top. The table and small lamp beside my bed and the closed door to the closet. The two windows with nothing but gray sky beyond. My baby stretches, poking me from inside. I trace what I believe is an arm, and a knee. There is no time. Nothing changes day to day, week to week, in this gray lonely house, in my fear, except that my baby grows, moving closer and closer to being gone forever.

I finally rise into the cold air, lingering in the warm and hypnotic shower. Sometimes I think I hear the phone ringing, or the heavy knocker on the kitchen door. I turn off the water quickly and freeze, naked, round-bellied, listening. Maybe someone is calling for me. Coming to be with me. Hope, and shame. But there is no sound.

I eat standing at the messy counter, and then move to my place in my father's chair by the living room window. In one of the books on the dusty shelves, I have found a beautiful red crayon drawing I like to look at. By Leonardo da Vinci, it is of a baby in the womb, *The Foetus in Utero*. It looks like a chestnut cut away to reveal the kernel of life at its center. There is no suggestion of the mother's body, just a detached capsule of seawater with a baby floating inside. I study the way the artist sliced away the shell of the womb to reveal the child inside: as a large, wide wedge was erased, the womb became a heart with the baby curled tight within. He is beautiful, robust and ready to leave his cocoon and enter the world. He is big, taking up most of this heart-shaped vessel. His umbilical cord snakes from his belly into loops around his feet. A web of veins encapsulates the outer shell of the womb, his mother's sustenance encircling him. His feet are large, as if he will need them to move away from his site of birth, a child already gone. His head is tucked tight to his knees, his face hidden, a stranger to me forever.

I put the book away and sit in the silent room. A car passes every five minutes or so. I rouse to attention each time, straining to catch a glimpse of the man or woman driving, a face, a human being, some small connection that will pull me for a moment from the terror that has become part of me now. The cars speed by, a red collar, a glance in the rearview mirror, a silent laugh shared with the woman in the passenger seat. No connection. Life being lived beyond me, out of my reach. My baby nestles heavily into my lap. The old clock on the mantel slips silently through the slow, empty minutes, hours. The winter's snow recedes, inch by inch, from the foundation of the barn, the dark tree trunks, the roadside bankings, revealing the muddied earth beneath. I wrap my arms under my belly, holding my baby to me. Sometimes I feel his body tic, hiccups maybe, or his heart measuring the minutes with me.

Late in the afternoon, as the light falls again, I rise and wander through the house, my nighttime agitation rising. There is nothing to do. Wait. Each quiet step, each glance out to the road, each press of an arm or leg inside me. I have no idea how to prepare, or even what to prepare for. There is no one to tell me what is coming. Walking, sitting, lying through the night in the cold room upstairs. My baby, me, just waiting.

"I could take care of it," I say. I have been trying to convince my father about the maple sap all morning.

"Jesus, Meredy."

"Help me move the evaporator behind the barn. No one would see me. All the sap is just overflowing the buckets. It's such a waste. I can—"

"Meredy! If you want to do some work, sand the walls in the back hall. You haven't done a thing to fix up the house since you got here."

We are all embarrassed by my request. My father and Catherine don't want me outside in the yard. Catherine sips her coffee and turns the pages of the newspaper. My father gets up, pushing his chair back hard against the wall, and moves to his chair in the living room. I go up to my room and lie under the blankets, my face absorbing the closed-up cold of the room.

Two days later, my father and Catherine spend the morning packing, arguing, and confirming flights.

"We'll both be back at three thirty on Friday," Catherine calls up the stairs to me. "We're meeting in Baltimore and flying up together."

"Don't go out, Meredy," my father calls up. Each word is spoken distinctly, slowly.

"I know," I answer. "I won't."

Their car pulls out of the gravel driveway onto the tarred road. I stand by my bed, running my hands over my hard, mounding belly. I think of calling my mother. The late March sun floods the overgrown paddock by the barn; snow drips off the roof and pelts the terrace below. I sit on the bed, then stand again. I walk to the window and lean my forehead against the glass. Someone rolls inside me. I turn back to my room: a bed, boxes, the new rug, a lamp.

The sap is running hard. At first, as spring comes, I feel the old excitement, the child's release as the sky clears; the buds swell, the air carries the rich sweet smell of earth, the birds return and remember their mating songs. I want to be outside, where the world feels orderly, where there is life, the reassuring cycle. But as the days warm, the sap rises from deep below the snow-covered soil and overflows the buckets my father set on the taps. He is too busy, away too much, and I watch the sap fill and drip over the buckets day after day. Some days, my father walks tree to tree and pours the sap out over the melting snow, replacing the empty buckets one by one. It frightens me to see the sap rising to nothing, the days roaring on, the fullness of the earth wasted, discarded. My own blood courses through my enlarged veins, the fullness of a new life coming. I want to slow and contain the flow, bring the swift current of time, of growth, under control. I can't bear to watch the sap released onto the ground, my baby now weeks from slipping into the world, leaving both of us alone.

I struggle to drag the old evaporator out behind the barn, but it is big and heavy; its metal legs catch in the mud, and I leave it beside the shed. I go back inside, find Catherine's lobster kettle on a shelf in the shed, and wash it carefully at the old sink. I put it on the stove and head back outside, careful to listen for cars as I leave the cover of the house for the open yard. The sap buckets hanging from the old sugar maples along the driveway drip into the muddy snow beneath each tree. I put my mouth over the tap and suck the cold, sweet water down my throat. Bracing against the rough bark, I lift the gallon buckets off the hooks and carry them, one at a time, into the kitchen.

I empty them into the kettle and hang them back out on the trees. Each time a car approaches, I walk heavily for the shed, setting the sloshing bucket in the snow. Five buckets fill the pot. I light the stove. A loud *shhh*, and the pop and crackle of expanding metal cracks the silence of the kitchen. I stir the clear liquid with a long wooden spoon, watching the swirl and eddies of the simmering sap.

I stay in the kitchen all day, stirring the kettle and cleaning up the counters and sink, feeling calmer than I have for many months. Late in the afternoon, I put my sweater back on and light a fire in the fireplace, something my father has told me not to do when he isn't here. I look for a book, pick up one of Catherine's romances, and settle into my father's chair by the window. I sit with my legs crossed under me, my large tight belly braced on them, the sweater stretched tight and thin. Maple steam fills the house.

I stay downstairs by the fire. Sap flows through the trees outside, dripping into the emptied buckets. It boils on the stove. I tend the kettle every half hour until midnight and then, turning the flame low, climb upstairs to bed. I leave a light on in the hall, a luxury.

The sun wakes me as it edges the east window. I can smell maple even up here. I stay under the warm covers, the quiet of the house thick in the early light. I lie on my side, watching the wedge of light widen. My hand slides down over my belly, a foot or elbow answering in a tight quick arc. Closing my eyes, I cup the tiny point in my hand. My baby rolls and flutters. A crow calls from the woods across the road.

From my father's closet, I take down a thick sweater I haven't worn before. I button it around myself, standing back from the mirror on their closet door. My hands spread wide over my hard belly. The girl I was a year ago is gone. Now, I am old, tired with fear and shame. One of Catherine's sheepskin slippers is on the unmade bed, a newspaper beside it on the floor. I have a sense of conversation, even laughter, happening in this room when I am not here.

I hear the mailman stop at the end of the driveway. Downstairs, I watch him on the slant from the edge of the living room window, keeping myself hidden by the drapes. I lean on the casing after he leaves, staring down the road. The kettle *shush*es quietly in the kitchen, a reassuring sound, a hushing sound like a mother's love. I look at Catherine's couch, the glass my father left by his chair, at the quickening woods. It was cold last night, but the sun has warmth finally, and the buckets will be overflowing again. Three months here.

I walk into the kitchen to stir the sap. Over the stove, the old wallpaper has pulled away from the wall in large sagging sheets. Yellow steam, stained with old nicotine, beads on the ceiling and drips yellow onto the counter and floor and stove and boxes, onto me. I turn. The paper, the greasy brown wallpaper, hangs in limp sheets four feet down from the ceiling all the way around the room. The stained and pocked plaster underneath glistens gray with steam.

I turn back to the stove and slowly stir the thickening syrup. I put down the spoon. The filthy steam drips from the ceiling onto my hair, my arms, my belly, the floor. My fingertips hold the edge of the stove lightly. The crying comes, silent, the kettle *shush*ing on the stove.

Chapter Three

Stronghold

Girls who run amok in 1966 get kicked out of public school and can't return. This is a second chance, my only chance to find my way back to anything resembling the life my parents and I have imagined for me. Mrs. Emmet, the old, eccentric head of this strange little school, has agreed to let me in to finish high school, and has given me a full scholarship. I had a baby ninety days ago. I left the baby in the hospital for someone else to claim and walked out into the day. I am no longer a girl, and feel too old for the world. I will be here for nine months, a gestation time for my next life.

My new classmates at High Mowing School, all seventeen of them, greet me on the back lawn that first day with warm smiles, and teasingly introduce each other. This is my first glimpse of the kids at this school; when my mother drove me here to beg Mrs. Emmet to let me in, everyone had left for the summer. I'm shocked by what I see. Their clothes are strange. There is a carelessness, a complete disregard for the tight fashion fads that pervaded my old school: girls' hair curled into flips, Peter Pan collars with circle pins at the neck, nylon stockings, and knee-length kilts with large gold safety pins holding the front together. Here, the girls and boys both wear faded Levi's and loose shirts, untucked. They are barefoot in the warm September sun, although class will start soon. In fact, some of the teachers sit in the sun with us, wearing the same faded jeans and loose shirts and talking with the students easily. I have never seen anyone like these people.

I am an observer. Jake smiles and sings bits of arias to no one in a perfect soprano, his voice rising over the old farm fields and moving toward the soft peak of Mt. Monadnock to the west. I have never heard a male soprano. It sounds like a prayer. John is taking pictures with a professional-looking camera. His classmates are used to him and don't stop laughing and talking with one another. Someone plays strands of guitar, and the rich woody resonance of what I will come to know is a recorder drifts from somewhere inside. Everyone lies on the grassy back terrace or sprawls on the wide stone steps that lead down to the garden below. I have a photo still of that day: I am lying on my side in my prim clothes, my head propped in my palm, smiling into the sun and John's camera. My hair shines gold. Under the smile is a terrible, dark, exhausted sadness.

"How come you're just here for one year?" a blond, smooth-faced boy asks.

"I just wanted to change schools," I say.

"What didn't you like about your old school?" someone asks.

"Oh, you know, it was just so stupid. I was really bored."

That works. Almost everyone here came out of other schools which were a bad fit. "Yeah," a girl with long dark hair says, "I came here because I wanted to be able to paint and draw what I wanted. I hated my old school."

"So how come High Mowing?" someone asks.

"I just really liked what I heard about it. I liked how different it is from my school."

This is the beginning of the lies. Last night when I arrived, Mrs. Kroehne, a kind German woman who is our dorm mother, showed me to my room. After my conversation in Mrs. Emmet's living room, I expected a single. But I had a roommate, a junior named Janet. By the time it was lights-out, Mrs. Kroehne had returned. "You come with me," she said very tenderly. With no explanation to Janet, we picked up all my things and carried them to a small single room. Its inhabitant, Ellie, had earned the single as a senior. Now she was moved in with Janet, and my separation from the other girls began. "We must protect the girls," Mrs. Kroehne said. "You understand." I do understand. I am a contaminant and must be kept silent. It has been three months since my baby was born, three months since I walked away from my baby with milk dripping from my breasts. I will not say this to any of these young people during my time among them. I will construct careful lies and memorize them to explain myself, my dark inward life, my hunger for love, my tough resistance to trust.

On this first morning, the fields and woods glow in the autumn sun. I am alert, watchful. "We call it the Hill," Jen tells me. "There is the world out there, off the Hill, and the world here. No one wants to have to leave the Hill. When we go downtown, people always look at us as if we come from a different planet. We just want to come back to the Hill and be ourselves. You're going to like it here." I sense that I have joined a small troop of misfits, the first I have met in my life. I like them. I feel easy with them. The gnawing grief and shame don't calm down. But for a moment I feel the sun's light on this beautiful old farm on the Hill, and the innocence of friendship my classmates share.

Someone is ringing a large hand bell. Everyone jumps up and makes their way through the tall narrow door into the Big Room. Jake is playing short bits on the old grand piano that takes up the bay window. The whole school—seventy-six students and all the teachers—sits on three long low steps that cross what was once the farm's barn. Mrs. Emmet stands beside the piano, waiting for us to quiet. She is eighty-three years old, a small woman in a soft dress and slippers. Her white hair is twisted into a loose bun; she pushes back a wisp again and again as she speaks to us. Her middle finger—fine-boned, and almost translucent—has an odd crook to it at the end. I watch it as she tucks her hair into her bun. She is not grandmotherly, yet she seems very kind. I want her to notice me, to like me. Her voice is strong as she welcomes us to the new school year. The students are very attentive. She jokes with a few of us, reads the day's announcements, and then says, "Let's greet the day."

Voices rise together all around me. "I gaze into the world, in which the sun is shining, in which the stars are sparkling. . . ." This is some sort of prayer, with no god. The voices are so earnest. My chest aches. Mrs. Emmet smiles to all of us. "Time for classes, children," she says, and we make our way to block class. I think of that one word for the rest of the day: children. It confuses me. I certainly am no longer a child. I go to sleep feeling like an impostor hiding among good and unsuspecting people, a girl who has given away a child secreting herself among children.

Mrs. Kroehne says I can paint my little bedroom. The girls live on the top two floors of the old barn, among the huge beams and ancient wide boards of the floors and walls. The cupola rises from the middle of our living room, a square tower with windows letting angular blocks of sunlight lie across the old rug. My room is tiny, a dormer pushing out onto the slate roof. The windows are diamond-paned leaded glass with an old brass catch that doesn't pull them tight. When it snows, I find a small drift of snow neatly edging the top of my dresser. My room feels separate from the cluster of double rooms, a different kind of space, a place where I am kept outside the daily flow of relationships. But it is the only home I have now, and I attach myself to it. I paint the plaster walls white, except for the little nook under the sloping roof where my bed fits just perfectly. There, I paint the walls and sloping ceiling black.

Mrs. Kroehne is shocked. She holds me to her bosom, stroking my hair and whispering, "My poor girl. My poor, poor girl." Her reaction surprises and embarrasses me. But this dark corner becomes my refuge. I say to myself, "I am in my Black," or, "I want to go to my Black." At High Mowing School, this numbing non-place is physical, but it introduces me to a psychological space I will call up for many years to come. "I love my Black," I will say to myself. I cannot see how troubling this must be for the adults watching me at High Mowing. I feel I am coping pretty well. I am alive, even, some of the time. But as that black retreat eases my pain, it also erases me. I am a girl who has left the world. Luckily, High Mowing gives me a very long tether.

Sabina moves freely across the Big Room floor in her flowing blue robe. Her bare feet are strong and root themselves as she dances. She speaks lines of poetry as she circles her arms, stepping toe-first in a powerful choreography of feet, legs, body, arms, head. There is no music. No rhythm except the pacing of the poetry. I am in love with beautiful and strong Sabina and this strange dance form called eurythmy. It is only taught at Waldorf schools. High Mowing is a Waldorf school, although at seventeen I don't know what that means. We hear frequent references to the three aspects of the human being— the mind, the creative spirit, and the will—but I don't think about these abstractions. I only know that eurythmy is compelling and mysterious to watch, and that I want to learn its movements.

Eurythmy manifests the sound of human language in movement. The dancer is a sculptor in space, carving the emotional life of words into the air. The short vowels are embracing sounds, and the arms draw the world into the body to make these sounds visible. Hard sounds like *k* and *t* and *p* are expressed with short, abrupt movements—movements that suggest finality, closure, barriers: *contagious* and *dirty* and *pain*. *S* is, of course, a hissing sound, slithering, the hands painting quick curves on the air. *Loss*. *Silence*. *L* and *b* are the soft round sounds of *love* and *breast* and *baby*.

Sabina's powerful middle-aged body sculpts the world as she fills the room with her calm rich voice. I watch her, trying to imagine her strong movements in my own body, my arms and legs. I studied ballet for many years. When Sabina calls to me, "Meredy. This isn't ballet. You are a sculptor. You carve the world," I know that she is telling me I am potent. I imagine my feet grounded, rooted on the earth, and I move on my own path across the floor, carving my grief silently into the air.

It is three o'clock in the morning. It is my first block night—the last night to work on my copy book. I am just completing my first block of the semester, an intensive three-week study of light and optics. I had not cared what the classes would be here; I had felt no engagement in the first days. Mr. Swanson, the physics teacher, is an older man the other students like. In fact, they seem to like every teacher here, and like to spend time with them outside of class. I don't. If I

am not in class or doing required afternoon activities, I am in my
room or wandering alone in the fields and woods.

I am lost in this classroom at first, waiting impatiently for the
teacher to teach. But Mr. Swanson has been patient with me. The
classroom doesn't have desks and chairs. There are long science tables and stools, old and beaten-up like everything at High Mowing.
We don't sit and listen here. We make things that play with light. We
make things of our own design that often don't work. We play with
cameras and binoculars and telescopes, prisms. We observe light and
shadow, color. We ask questions. Mr. Swanson asks us question after
question, giving us time to figure a problem out. He smiles a wide
pleased smile when we make a discovery.

Tonight, I am racing the clock to finish the final project of the
block. I have not seen exactly what a copy book looks like, but I have
a lot to say about light and how we perceive it. The whole school
is up—the traditional end-of-block all-nighter. I have been given a
large blank booklet, a box of soft, fat colored pencils, a ruler and
compass, and a lined master to lay behind the blank white paper so
my handwriting will be straight and neat on the page. I sit on my
floor under the lamp drawing careful diagrams of the sun, of the eye,
of light as particle and light as wave. I think my drawings are clear,
and beautiful.

There has been no textbook, no memorization, no tests. Whatever I write is mine—my thoughts, my ideas and wonderings, my
questions and solutions. I am wildly excited. I suddenly realize that
at this minute I am happy. I have escaped my grief through my mind.
I want to rush out into the world and confront every mystery, to
think my way into the world. A deep gratitude rises. I have needed
this. I have needed this place, in its quiet beauty, its people who
are offering me the world in its vast complexity, feeding the terrible, gnawing, unnamed hunger. Somehow, they have made their
way to the child I was a year ago and drawn her back to life, at least
for this small moment. She sits on the floor next to the broken
girl and greedily creates her book. At the end, she writes a shy note

to Mr. Swanson: *Thank you*, the child says. *You have taught me to think.*

I take a shower at dawn, before the other girls come out of their rooms, and lie on my carefully made bed reading my beautiful book. I think of my mother, wondering if she would like it as much as I do. Mr. Swanson hands it back to me at breakfast three days later. He has written, *This is magnificent work*. There is no grade. *Magnificent work*. For the first time in my life, I am proud of my work.

The new block has started; I am studying early Renaissance art with Mrs. Emmet. We sit in the large old living room. Mrs. Emmet perches on the cobbler's bench, her love for these old paintings like a light shining out to me. She gives us postcard-sized prints of the art she has seen herself all over Europe; everything is a rendition of the Madonna and child. Everything is about me, about suddenly being pregnant, about a baby, a mother's immense and already resigned love, about loss and grief. I understand these paintings: Donatello's tender *Pazzi Madonna*, the young mother holding her baby face to face, their foreheads touching, an eternal connection which will outlast the trauma of loss coming. Fra Angelico's radiant *Presentation in the Temple*, the baby held out toward God as a luminous gift from the mother.

Most of all, I understand Botticelli's dark and confused *The Mystical Nativity*, the sharp lines like lances through the scene of the birth, the small devils of pain creeping toward the child and the mother, the arms of the baby reaching up through too much space to his mother, her face drawn with grief and love and foreboding. At night, alone in my dark room, in my Black, I think of my baby. I think of my mother and my father. A dim misty circle of moonlight hangs in the sky outside my little room. My baby is four months old.

"I don't know if I can do this anymore," I say. I am leaning against the wall in the tiny old phone booth in the classroom wing, my forehead pushed hard against the wood.

"Do what, Meredy?" my mother asks. Her voice is neutral. It is the middle of the night. Only the light by the outside door is on. I need to hear tenderness. I need to hear her cry for me.

"All of it."

"School?" she asks. "You have to do this, Meredy." Her voice toughens. "You have no choice. If it isn't High Mowing, it's nothing."

"It isn't school." Suddenly I am wailing. I can hear my cry rise from deep inside. I struggle to contain it. It terrifies me, as if I have loosed my devastated self. "It isn't school!" I cry.

My mother is quiet. "What is it you are scared of, Meredy? What are you afraid will happen?"

"I don't know! I'm so scared." My high, wild keening fills the hallway.

"Of what?" Her voice has not softened.

"I don't want to do any of this anymore, Mummy! I can't do any of this anymore. I just don't want to do this anymore." The wailing scares me, a girl who never cries. I am out of control. I feel ashamed, exposed. I suddenly realize what I am saying. "I feel like I'm going crazy! I'm going somewhere and I can't stop. I'm so scared." The crying squeezes up through my chest. "I'm so scared!" My head is rolling fast, side to side, against the wall. "I want all this to be over! I can't do this anymore!"

"Meredy!" my mother shouts at me. "Meredy! You need to pull yourself together." Her voice fills the phone booth. "You listen to me. You are going to make it through this because you are a survivor! Just like me! You are a survivor! Don't you ever forget that!"

I want her to tell me she will be here in two hours. That she will hold me and listen to me. That we will talk about my baby. "But I can't." I am whispering. "I don't want to anymore."

"Yes, you do. I want you to get off the phone and go to your room. Wash your face and get into bed. Tomorrow morning, you will get up and do what you are supposed to do. And the morning after that you will get up and do what you are supposed to do. Do you hear me? We are survivors, Meredy. You can do whatever you have to do."

In bed in my black corner, I say, "I am a survivor. I am a survivor. I can do whatever I have to do." I think of finding Sabina, or Mrs. Kroehne, but I don't know what either of them knows and I'm not supposed to tell anyone what I have done. I am ashamed of the crying.

"Let us go see something in the fields," Dr. von Baravalle says to me. He says *sompsing*. We are walking in the woods and fields behind the school. It is late afternoon in early October. I feel terribly shy with this old man. He is legendary, the brilliant mathematician who comes to High Mowing School every fall to teach a block in geometry. I already had geometry as a sophomore, but Mrs. Emmet insists that I study it again with Dr. von Baravalle. "I am certain that you missed the whole idea," she says. I don't know why this old, stooped man has asked me to come with him. I don't know if this is meant to be a tutorial, remedial math for the girl who missed Waldorf until her last year in school, or if I have been, for some reason, chosen. I barely speak.

"Now look at this, my dear girl," the old mathematician says, lifting a pale violet aster between his thick fingers. "What do you see?"

I freeze with uncertainty. I just want to return to my room. A cool breeze blows across the field from the southwest, rippling the stiff brown heads of timothy.

"It's all right," he says. "You can at least lean down to look. Tell me what you see."

"A little purple flower?" I say.

"Well, yes, it is that. What else do you see? Tell me exactly what you see."

I feel as if this is a test. "I see a little purple flower with frilly petals around a yellow center that's like a button."

"Exactly!" he says. "Now, what about those petals?"

I bend close to the aster. "Well, they're tiny. And short. There are three rows of them, actually." I'm surprised at this. It seems interesting.

"Yes. Three rows. One below the other. Now, what else do you see?"

I am lost. There doesn't seem to be anything more to observe. "Look at those rows," he says gently.

"Oh! Each one is offset from the one above it. Like dials."

"Exactly. Now what do we have here?" he asks himself as he wanders slowly into the field. "This is called what?"

"I think it's Queen Anne's lace?"

"Exactly. Queen Anne's lace going to seed before winter comes." He says *vinter*. "Now tell me what you see."

I know this flower and its musky scent from the field beside my childhood home. But I look more carefully this time before I speak. I describe the familiar flat white flower head with its little drop of blood in the center. Then I see that the big flower is actually made up of several dozen groups of little flowers. Every tiny flower has five petals shaped like mittens. And rising from each minuscule flower are golden stamens. As I hold the flower closer to my eyes, the sun illuminates it as if it is glowing from inside. "Oh!" I say. "Each little antenna ends in a tiny little ball!"

"Exactly!" he says. He is animated. "You see today that every creation of God is made in perfect symmetry. He designed this flower. Its symmetry is what makes it beautiful to our eyes."

"And the light coming through it."

"Yes, and the light coming through it. We will draw these flowers tomorrow. I will show you how. We will use your compass and trace out the universal perfection of form."

I don't really understand, but I don't want to go inside yet. We walk slowly in the fields and woods that are filled with leaves, fall seed heads, dark branches reaching toward the light, vines, fungi, the old mathematician patiently asking me to see.

The days and seasons at High Mowing are in perfect rhythm. We feel safe in these rhythms. First breakfast and our simple prayer to greet the day. Then our academic classes—the intellect. After lunch, our creative work—weaving, pottery, drama, music, dance, art. In the late afternoon, our physical work. I have missed the building of the new gymnasium, but Bob Pittman, who graduated with the first class in 1946, is stocking in lumber for an addition to the boys' dorm. I am helping to cut the trees, drag them behind the tractor to the sawmill, and saw them into boards.

It is snowing lightly. A thin sun lies pink across the snow. Six of us tromp behind the tractor down the hill into the woods. We are on an old tote road, cutting through the woods toward the Frye farm that supplies our milk. The woods and fields and mountains and big sky are exciting and mysterious to me. I know the tamed beach, and my mother's small garden, but I have never been in places where people are only visitors. It feels wild and full of promise. I fill with a sense of love for the calling crows, the lacy white birches at the field edge, the grass drawing a perfect semicircle on the snow in the northeasterly wind. I notice sounds now. I notice the light. I am finding a home here.

Bob stops the tractor and hops off into the soft snow. He is wearing olive green overalls and a 1950s plaid wool hat with the earflaps tied on top. He whistles as he gets out his chain saw and gas can. I don't really know anything about Bob, except that he is the one who drives us to concerts and soccer games in the school's only bus, an old army truck with canvas sides. Today, he smiles and says, "Let's go," to his crew. No one complains. There is a strong sense of pride in our work projects, in the poorly designed, poorly built buildings laid up by students and inexperienced faculty. I'm excited. I am going to saw down a tree and make it into boards. This is boy's work, and feels significant. The day is clean and energized. We walk into the hardwood grove. A chickadee calls his warning, *Fee-bee. Fee-bee.*

Bob sizes up each tree, leaning his head back and running his eyes all the way up the trunk. I don't know what he is looking for. "This one?" he asks us. It is bigger than the others nearby, its old bark grooved and splotched with lichen. "This is an old maple," he says as he puts down the gas can. "It will make a nice floor in the front hall." The boys stand close to him. "You're going to have to stand back now. I want you to stand over there."

We cluster fifteen feet away. I wish I could do the cutting, feel the power and weight of the old power saw as it cuts through the wood. I want to hitch the log with the chains to the tractor and drag it myself to the sawmill. Bob yanks on the cord and starts the saw. It's louder than I imagined. I have heard Bob and his crews working in the distant woods, but this is a sputtering mechanical whine that startles me. Bob checks to be sure we are standing clear and bends beside the tree. He looks so small next to it. The saw slides right through the wood. First, a large notch on the downhill side. Bob flicks out the wedge he's cut with his foot. Then he slices through the base of the tree toward the *V* of the notch. It only takes a minute. The excitement is gone. I am starting to feel a deep dread. I want to call out to stop this, but I don't understand what it is that needs to stop.

"She's going!" Bob yells, stepping back. The tree leans gently at first, as if a breeze is pushing against it. Suddenly a loud crack booms through the woods and the tree topples through the air, crashing in thunder onto the cushion of snow. I start to cry. I don't know what I am doing. I run toward the tree crying, then turn back away from it, trying to run toward the school. Bob catches me and holds me to his cold chest. "It's okay, Meredy. It's okay," he says softly. The other students watch me, circling awkwardly.

Silently, Bob holds me close to him. The branches have snapped off and lie crushed in the snow all around us. The tree is enormous and lies stretched, broken and helpless, in the snow on the floor of the woods. The windows of the school buildings glint across the fields behind us. The woods have hushed. I hear my own hard breath rising and falling in the quiet afternoon. My baby is seven months old.

I lie in Frye's Field in the soft spring grass. The ground rumbles beneath me as thunder explodes over the hill. I am spread-eagled on my back. It is midday, but the sky is purple-black and it weights me down into the soil. Heavy rain pounds into my body, my legs, my arms, my breasts, my belly. My empty belly. Lightning cracks in the field, blinding me for seconds. Thunder booms and rolls over me and on across the hills. Lightning flares, white-hot, through the sky above me. Again. The storm is here. Thunder follows each bolt of light, the crack and roar and rumble. I am pushed hard into the earth, laid out under the pummeling rain and searing light and godly roar. I am not terrified. Palms up, I stare back at the sky. My voice is lost. The earth fights back. I am this storm.

Mrs. Emmet's voice, soft and sure, fills the tiny chapel. The candles in the wall sconces and on the mantel give the only light, a pure light refracted by the leaded glass windows. It is Sunday night. We sit on the narrow raised platform on long wooden benches, students and teachers. Mr. Tallerico plays the ebony baby grand piano. I love his gentle face, the beauty of the music he gives us. I love the shining, receptive faces of my schoolmates. I love Mrs. Emmet's hand as she strokes the ancient Etruscan lamb that lies on the small table by her chair. The darkened fireplace and mantel came from Renaissance Italy. On cold winter nights, the fire is our only heat.

This is a transcendent place. Perfect beauty. I am at peace in this tiny room, one of the old farm sheds made into a sanctuary. Mrs. Emmet teaches us about Michaelmas and the rhythms of the ancient Christian calendar. I don't believe any of it. But Mrs. Emmet tells a good story. She believes it. The names and places are mysterious, so I listen. Mostly, I watch the light, watch her hand stroke the lamb, watch Mr. Tallerico patiently waiting, his feet silently stroking the pedals of the piano as if he is playing a tender accompaniment. The students listen. The candles waver.

"Let us now sing the vesper hymn," Mrs. Emmet says. This is what I have waited for. We stand, holding the old red Waldorf hymnbooks. Page fifty-five. Minor key. *Now, our wants and burdens leaving to his care who cares for all, cease we fearing, cease we grieving. Hope and faith and love rise glorious, shining in the wondrous skies.* Mr. Tallerico plays softly beneath our voices. Old Mrs. Emmet sits calmly watching us, her eyes moving face to face, her hand gently stroking her lamb. I am expectant. I rest here. When we sit down, the old benches scuff against the worn floor. There is dark beyond the windows. Mrs. Emmet starts to speak again, and the candlelight continues to waver gently in the refuge.

Chapter Four

The Uprising

"I'm *not* staying here," I say to my mother. We have just walked in the door from a silent ride home after my graduation from High Mowing School, marking for me the final closing on my life at home. Something had shifted violently as I packed to leave school and faced returning to my mother's house. The stunned grief of the past twenty months had suddenly flared into anger. I felt myself snap away from silence into defiance, an understanding that I would not survive if I didn't, finally, start fighting back. I carry fury in me as we stand in the living room, the room where I was turned away by my mother a year and a half ago. The boxes and suitcase I have just brought home from school still stand by the door.

"Where do you think you're going?" She looks uncertain, shaken by the confrontation.

I am emboldened. "I know some girls who graduated from High Mowing a couple of years ago. They're renting an apartment in Cambridge for the summer. They said I could live there until I leave for Bennington in the fall." This isn't true. I have not yet dared call them to introduce myself and try to barge into their summer. But I am taking a bus to Boston that afternoon. I have an address and two names. It is enough for me. I sense a power rising inside, finally—reckless and tangled dangerously with a feeling that I am beyond hurt, that whatever comes from now on cannot harm me.

"You just turned eighteen!" she says, her voice familiar in its implication that I am again doing something bad, dirty. "You are going to work at the beach again. You are living at home until you go to school in the fall. You are not moving to Boston."

I stand eye to eye with my mother. I know and she knows that she will never again tell me what to do. "Stop me," I say, staring hard, my voice fierce. "Try to stop me." I pick up the suitcase and walk out the door, heading uptown to catch the Greyhound bus. I am scared, but with each step I throw fuel on the fire that is starting to burn inside. That anger is becoming a blaze, my only protection against the past. It is late May 1967. I am on a collision course. The country is erupting in a cataclysm of change. I will meet that eruption with my own fierce and compressed rage.

Walter Cronkite and Chet Huntley and David Brinkley tell us every night on our televisions that the conflict in Vietnam is not going well. They report the war, the body counts, the anti-war demonstrations each night on the evening news.

There are 486,000 American boys in Vietnam.

We drop napalm, a bomb filled with incendiary gel designed to burn human bodies, on the villages of Vietnam. A photograph of Kim Phuc, a nine-year-old girl with third-degree burns over half her tiny, naked body, is broadcast around the world. Protestors rally against Dow Chemical. Photographs of boy soldiers sewn into body bags flash across our television screens.

11,058 American soldiers die in Vietnam this year. 56,013 are wounded.

The Summer of Love. Hippies gather by the thousands to smoke pot, listen to music, and spread a message of peace. Flower Power.

I have no practice living in the world. I have been to Boston only a few times in my life. I know nothing about taking a bus, finding a job, holding ground in the blare and rush. But I do know about making my way through my days and nights alone, about facing the next day with no one to rely on but myself. I move in with five girls I do not know, sleeping on the couch in a sunny apartment on Garden Street near Radcliffe. They don't want me there. I am lost, engulfed in sorrow and anger; anyone near me must feel frightened away. I find a job making pâté sandwiches with foreign students at a patio restaurant in Harvard Square. I never speak to anyone there, and watch the play and banter as if it is a movie. Each day confirms my feeling that I am an outsider, that I will be forever a stranger watching from a dark and detached world. But I feel safer in the impersonality of the city, in the swelling noise of the early mornings and the broody nights. I walk Cambridge and Boston, anonymous, with no connection anywhere on earth, me with no history, a girl catapulted by loss into a grown woman's life. I learned while I was pregnant to live in my brain. Here, strangers live energetically in the world, and I watch from a fortress.

I am an intruder at the apartment. It lasts just three weeks. When I walk in the door after work one beautiful, breezy day in June, all five girls are waiting for me. "You need to leave," they say. "It's too crowded."

I smile. "No problem. Give me two days."

But it is a huge problem. I will never return home. I have not been able to save any money yet. I don't know how to find an apartment. I do not know anyone in the city, and have no connection with anyone from my old life. I am on my own. I do nothing the next day to create a plan. I am scared, but the fear is an odd, disconnected, drifty feeling. On the second day, on my walk home from work, a handsome boy with a long red beard and ponytail pulls up beside me on an old beat-up motorcycle.

"Want a ride?" he asks. His teeth flash white when he speaks. Erik tells me later that I never even smile. I just climb onto his bike behind him and wrap my arms around his waist. Silently, I drive into the next new life.

A black cabbie is beaten by the police in Newark. Riots flare and burn for five days. Riot police riot. 23 demonstrators are killed, 1,000 people are injured, 1,400 are arrested.

Four days later, Detroit explodes in fury. Federal troops are called out with loaded rifles and tanks. 43 demonstrators are killed, no police; 1,189 are injured, 7,000 people are arrested. For one week the streets burn. It is the worst riot of the century.

While Detroit blazes, uprisings break out in Toledo; Rochester; East Harlem; Pontiac, Michigan. Within a week, riots flare in more than 100 cities. President Johnson calls out the National Guard. Films of police and National Guard brutality fill our television screens every night. Films of raging blacks flash across our televisions. Films of boys halfway around the world with limbs missing, screaming, artillery fire bursting around them. Of Vietnamese lying dead in their burned-out villages. A Buddhist monk immolating himself in the streets of Saigon in protest of this American war, his face the last to disappear in the flames.

"I need to tell you something," I say to Erik in the dreary evening light coming through the old sheet over the window. I met him three weeks ago and am camping out in the dirty, bare apartment he and his Harvard friends are renting for the summer. We are on his bed, a mattress on the floor in a small dark room. The walls are dingy yellow. The smudged ceiling looms miles above us. Erik is silent, and my serious tone hangs tense and heavy in the dreary room.

"What's up?" he asks, lighting a cigarette.

I have thought about this conversation a thousand times. Each time, I imagine something terrible happens as soon as the words are out of my mouth.

"I'm not who you think I am," I say.

He laughs a little. "Who are you?"

"A girl who got pregnant and had a baby."

He sits up and stares at the shrouded window. "Where's the baby?" he asks.

"I don't know."

He is quiet. I wait for one of the terrible things I have imagined to happen.

"When?"

"Last year."

We lie back down together, side by side, in the thick summer heat.

"Jesus," he says, his hands clasped behind his head. "Some secret."

We never speak about my baby again. For the next four years, I never again mention anything about my life before Erik.

Boys are scared. They strategize to avoid the draft: Volunteer—you get a better deal. Go to school full-time until you're 24. 2-S. This works for the rich and middle-class boys. For the others, flunk the induction physical: a bar of soap under the arm raises your blood pressure. Show up tripping. Say you're gay. Say you love killing people. Flunk the eye test. Flunk the hearing test. Shout, "Fuck you! Fuck you!" at the top of your lungs at the doctors. 1-Y leaves you vulnerable; 4-F gets you out, the prize. Or this: Join the National Guard.

More than 20,000 boys flee to Canada just this year to avoid the draft, expecting they might never be allowed to return. Families support them, or not. Draft card burnings and turn-ins and sit-ins take place across the country. Civil disobedience activists break into draft offices and throw the files onto the streets for public burning.

The Flower Child movement ends with a call for a militant response to the war.

I stand at the door to the dining hall at Bennington College, the familiar dread rising. "Twenty feet," I say to myself. "You just need to walk twenty feet." Inside, in the small living room, six or seven Bennington girls lounge, their long legs and elegant arms draped over small upholstered chairs by the fireplace. They are older than I, juniors and seniors, and are comfortable here, belong here.

After living with Erik for the summer, I have come to Bennington to start college. It is a pretty place; even I, in my shell-shocked trance, can see that. Twelve white colonial houses face off across the large mown lawn in two rows, like guardians of privilege looking out over the soft Vermont hills in the hazy distance. Dance and art and music studios nestle under the trees at the edges of the tiny campus. At the head of the lawn, Commons looms, a mansion, the gathering place for food, friendship, mail.

I have been here for two months and still skip most meals, coming to Commons only when hunger drives me to it. I pull the door open and, head up, walk toward the dining room. I miss Cambridge. This innocent little island of girls still being girls is claustrophobic. Here, I feel as if the gutted-out detachment that has helped me get through the past eighteen months marks me as a failure, a misfit, a shamed girl with a very big secret.

I quit Bennington College at the end of the first semester.

"I didn't raise you to be a quitter," my father yells over the phone.

I try to tell him that the dance program is a sham. That my roommate, Sasha, is a heroin addict, that sometimes I have to loosen the rubber tubing from her arm after she escapes the world, that I live in daily fear that I will be implicated when she is caught. That the girls are rich, and spoiled. That college has no relevance to my life. I want to say to him, "I have a baby floating somewhere in this world. I am an old woman. These girls are children. Here, I know every single day that I have left that world forever. Here, I feel broken and very scared." I want to say, "I feel helpless here, and I cannot afford to be helpless."

"You're just a goddamned quitter," he says. "I'm ashamed of you."

By Christmas, I am back in Cambridge, ashamed but invisible again.

1968. Rumors circulate: Lt. William Calley has overseen the massacre by American boys of 367 women, children, and old people at My Lai.

401,566 North and South Vietnamese soldiers are killed this year. No data are available for numbers wounded, or for civilian casualties.

10,000 anti-war demonstrators march in the streets of Chicago during the Democratic National Convention. Mayor Daly orders 11,000 riot police onto the streets, 6,000 National Guard armed with .30-caliber machine guns, grenade launchers and tanks, 6,500 army troops, 1,000 CIA and FBI agents with cameras. After 5 days of rioting and police brutality, 668 are arrested. 1,113 are injured. A federal investigation calls the event a "police riot."

Students strike on campuses across the country. San Francisco State closes for 8 days.

Lyndon Johnson announces the end of bombing in Vietnam. Richard Nixon beats Hubert Humphrey by 1 percent and becomes our new president.

Apollo 8 circles the moon 10 times. We watch on our televisions as the earth rises behind our moon.

After work, I make dinner in the closet-sized kitchen in my first apartment. I chop onions and parsley and mushrooms on a board laid over the stove, add bread crumbs, and spread it over pork chops, adding a can of mushroom soup. When it is done, I sit on the edge of my bed and eat, listening to Chopin. I have an eighteen-month-old baby somewhere. I am a college dropout. I have a job, a place to live, a boyfriend named Erik who lives his own separate life and asks for very little from me. I hold on fiercely to this flimsy structure. I like keeping house, like sweeping the worn linoleum and pulling the Indian bedspread tightly over the mattress on the floor. Big cheap pillows serve for chairs, and I sew curtains from a bolt of red cotton I buy in Filene's Basement. This first apartment is on Clinton Street, halfway between Harvard and Central Squares; semi-basement, it feels private to me, hidden away. I create order here, a tight containment of my grief and loneliness. I struggle to move through each day, to hold to routine. Wake early, tidy the apartment, shower, walk the mile to work. Work a long day. Walk home in the dark. Cook. Read. Listen to music. Sew or write or try to draw with pastels. The conversation with my old life never ends.

Some days the feeling of being a refugee, disconnected from my childhood life, eases. I work at a new Xerox shop near MIT, running hundreds of pages of doctoral theses and science research across the glowing green screen every day. I clean up the dingy, narrow shop, vacuuming the stained rug and painting the warped shelves, making signs to organize the work alphabetically. By March, I am made manager, which means filling in for the stoned-out workers when they fail to show for their shifts, staying into the night to finish jobs for desperate doctoral candidates, and making up an accounting system whereby whatever amount of money is in the till at closing jibes with the receipts on the spindle. I like the clear expectations of my job: make copies quickly and carefully.

Each morning when I make my way down Massachusetts Avenue, I become part of the orderly start of another workday. Men back trucks up to side doors, swearing or laughing; a woman in heels and a gray wool hat unlocks the heavy bronze door to the bank; paper swirls over the black and gritty snow banks; and the crazy man with no teeth smiles hello—"Hey there," he says to me as I walk past his bench. "Where'd you go?" I buy an Italian sandwich from the place next door for lunch each day, and eat standing up at the Xerox machine. I am a wary watcher in this new world, isolated and silent. The war, the draft, demonstrators being beaten. My baby. Wreckage. But work fills the days, the rhythmic click and flash and roll of the Xerox machine softening the hard edge of fear and loss. I can feel a strange pressure building, an inescapable compression that scares me. I like my neighborhood in Central Square, with its old brick factories and warehouses and scrappy yards of weeds between old tenements. But I feel most at home in Harvard Square, with its leafy, brick-and-ivy calm barely containing an incendiary mood of insurrection about to erupt.

Erik and I live together, but I am alone most of the time. He is a sophomore at Harvard, a restless and disinterested student. He moves a few things into my apartment—his guitar and amplifier; his motorcycle, an old BMW he squeezes into the furnace room; a few shirts and a jacket on the hook by the back door. He never sleeps at night, prowling, always stoned, on his bike along the grimy docks where stevedores bend under the weight of loads on their shoulders. Each morning when I leave for work, he is in bed, often in his clothes, the bike back in its place by the rumbling furnace.

I don't mind. We know very little about each other: He is Swedish, a failing Scandinavian Studies major at Harvard on a swimming scholarship, although he is too stoned to swim anymore and too radicalized in his politics to care. He is an only child. When Erik was seven, his mother and father moved from Sweden to New Britain, Connecticut, where his father was a machinist, so Erik could get an American education. He graduated from a small private school for boys and made good on his parents' dreams by getting into Harvard. Our visits to his parents' house are stiff—suffocating, in fact. Through the long afternoon in their hard little living room, we sit straight-backed on horsehair chairs, drinking aquavit. Erik's bronzed baby shoes sit on top of the television, perfectly dusted. Occasionally, Sven says into the silence, in his strong accent, "You are doing your studies, aren't you? That is why we are here, you know that."

Erik giggles. "Sure I'm studying, Dad. We're reading Strindberg right now."

His father looks at him for a minute, then turns away. "Well, I don't know who Strindberg is but you should. That is why we are here."

Erik giggles again, and his mother, Frida, leans forward in her chair. "Erik, you're not taking this seriously."

"Sure I am, Mom. I'm taking it plenty seriously." He grins and crosses his legs. The silence hangs in the little room.

"Did you win last week?" Sven asks.

"Win what?" Erik recrosses his legs, beaming kindly at his parents.

"Your swim meet. Don't you have swim meets anymore?"

"Oh, yeah, absolutely, Dad. I won!"

"That's your money for school. Don't you forget that. You need to be the top one or they'll take that money away from you."

They understand little about their son, with his long ponytail and dirty jeans and greasy, slouched engineer boots, his perpetual, compelling smile in the face of their questions and comments. Still, they believe he is a gift from God. I am quite sure they are not enthusiastic about me—a dropout in a miniskirt, with Xerox toner under my nails and a secret I am certain they can smell—but they are unfailingly polite with their son and with me. I am very jealous of the formal love they all share, the commitment and the permanence.

Martin Luther King Jr. is murdered in Memphis.

For a week, there are violent black uprisings in Chicago, D.C., Cincinnati, Boston, Detroit, Philadelphia, San Francisco, Oakland, Toledo. 125 cities explode in rage. Fires burn, police and National Guard attack.

Robert Kennedy is murdered.

The world catches fire: Paris, Madrid, Rome, Berlin explode in antigovernment violence. 10 million workers strike in France. Students peacefully topple the Soviet government in Czechoslovakia during Prague Spring. After several weeks, the Soviet Union retakes the country with tanks and 200,000 armed troops.

Erik starts a band, writing bluesy songs and playing lead guitar. The group finds gigs every weekend around town. They practice each night. Sometimes I go to their shows, getting high and dancing hard by myself. I don't like the music; it is loud and boyish. But I like the release of the dancing and the noise. I like the image I am working on: the strong and mysterious and hip girl, untouchable, arrogant.

Somehow, without any conversation, Erik and I settle quickly into an arrangement that allows him to have sex with other girls. Theoretically, I share the same freedom, although I am not interested. I don't feel much jealousy. I do not feel much of anything. Alone or in a group, with or without the boy I am supposed to be in love with—always, I move inside my own thoughts, years beyond the normal loves and fears and jealousies and doubts of a nineteen-year-old. The grief I carry every single day has burrowed deep by now, and its residue is recklessness. I am an isolated and pissed-off girl. I buy my own bike, an old BMW like Erik's. It is a huge, heavy, low-slung, black machine, a perfect vehicle for my crystallized sense of a world lost to me forever.

I run the Xerox shop, and get high, and cook, and move again and again, making apartments into momentary homes, and read and drive my bike fast and walk the city. Erik comes home in the still-dark morning. I hear his bike rumble closer and closer. When he slides into my bed, I ask him, "Say it."

"*Jag alskar dej*," he says, curling around me. *I love you.* It is enough. I lie in the darkness of this room, or that, or another, my transitory home, the fire inside burning.

Nixon orders secret bombings of Cambodia. 3,650 B-52 raids are carried out, dropping more than 4 times in tonnage what was dropped on Japan in all of World War II.

Massive protests are held at UC-Berkeley. Governor Ronald Reagan declares a state of "extreme emergency," calling in riot police and National Guard. Berkeley is closed down.

The demonstrations spread. Howard University, University of Massachusetts, Rice, Penn State. At the University of Wisconsin, thousands of students and area blacks go on a rampage over low black enrollment. The University of Chicago. City College of New York. After intense confrontation with riot troops, San Francisco State is closed for 134 days.

On a cool fall day, a girl my age walks into the Xerox shop. No one else is there. She is very small, with long, straight brown hair, bell-bottom corduroys, and a wrinkled blue shirt. She carries a big woven bag over her shoulder. She smiles. I am shocked to see a tooth missing. She is polite, but there is something noticeably withheld by her. She looks right at me, smiling all the time, but I see a veiling in her eyes. "Can you copy this?" she asks, digging around in the bag. She pulls out a card, creased and worn, and hands it to me. It is a print of *The Last Judgment* in the Sistine Chapel.

"Sure, but it will be in black and white. It won't look like this."

She laughs, a small and contained politeness, but she keeps her eyes on me. I feel an odd connection between us, a sense that we are each seeing our own sorrow written on someone else's face. I see in her an instinct to run, some dark, consuming ruin. I see my reflection in her face, in her tense body, her guarded eyes.

"Wait," I say, although she is not turning to leave. "Wait!"

The machine behind me whirs out copies while we stand looking at each other. I suddenly want to cry. I want to be held. I want to soften, to say my story, to say, *I am lonely.* To say I feel crazy with longing for my child, my family, my old beliefs. To say, *I am frightened of who I am.*

"Um," she says, still smiling that tight, careful smile with the hole on the side. "Um, we could get a cup of tea sometime."

"I could close up right now for a while," I say.

We walk silently to the lunch counter down the block and sit in the front by the open window. We order tea and sit awkwardly looking around the small restaurant. But each time she looks at me, I feel the punch of recognition. "Do you live here?" I ask.

"My name is Marni. I live in Harvard Square on Mt. Auburn with my boyfriend, Curt. He's a junior at Harvard." She never stops smiling. Now I can see that she tries to curl her upper lip down over the missing tooth. Her voice is reedy, and slides up and down between the notes.

"My name is Meredy," I say. "I live in Somerville with my boyfriend, Erik. He's a junior, too."

"Uh-oh," she says, smiling her empty smile. "What sign are you?"

I think this is silly. "Aries, I guess."

"Me, too." Marni is smiling, but I am not.

I watch her eyes. "So, how come you're here?"

She stares back at me for several seconds, and the smile suddenly disappears. Without it, she looks very tired, maybe even sick. "Oh, I don't know, a bunch of trouble at home. I quit school."

"I didn't exactly quit, but I barely finished."

"What happened?" she asks.

I sit silent for a minute and then speak the secret that seethes just under the surface of everything I say and think and do. "I got pregnant."

She takes her turn watching me. "Yeah, me, too. I was sixteen. That was two years ago. I never saw her."

The waitress comes toward us but walks away again. Someone shouts in the kitchen at the back. Cars line up in two rows at the light outside, then surge ahead. Silverware clatters.

"I was sixteen, too. Two years ago." We watch each other silently.

"I can't go home," she says. She turns the cup of tea around and around in her hands. "I don't really want to. But..." She smiles again for a second.

"Yeah. Well," I say. "There's nothing at home."

"No. That's for sure."

We stare at our cups. "Want to get together sometime?" I ask.

"Sure. I don't have any friends here. That would be good."

We do get together. Three or four times she and Curt and Erik and I go to hear music together. A few times Marni and I cook good food together. She teaches me how to toast the rice before I steam it. We never mention our babies again. We try to be friends, girls with lost babies, girls sharing a big secret, girls burning with guilt and grief and a deep sense of abandonment. It is comforting in a way to find a girl in as much trouble as I am. But it is also too much—this recognition, the mirroring in each other's devastated eyes, and after a few weeks, we never see each other again.

I think of her often, but I walk back inside the fort, my own mind. More than thirty-five years later, I will still carry a small piece of pink paper Marni gave me. She folded and colored it to look like a window. When I unfold it, there in the sky outside it says, *Tomorrow*.

In the last six months of 1969, there are 174 bombings on college campuses.

In one year, there are 64 airplane hijackings by terrorists.

By the end of 1969, almost 50,000 American boys have been killed in the Vietnam conflict.

The anniversary of the murder of Martin Luther King Jr. triggers 3 days of massive race and anti-war marches across the country. The Mobilization brings a half million marchers to Washington, calling for complete withdrawal from Vietnam, Cambodia, Laos.

I am somewhere in Nebraska, headed west. I am on a straight ribbon of tar that lifts and dips through vast fields of wheat and corn and on out of sight. It is early morning, and already the June heat rises in a wavering, steamy blur. My dress sticks to my waist and back. Goose, brown and white and black, a smart, crooked little mongrel, trots along beside me as I walk. I settle my satchel on my shoulder and put out my thumb. I haven't decided yet where I am headed. The last guy who picked me up said Montana is a good place to hitchhike because everyone takes you home and gives you food and a shower and a bed. I'd like a shower. I've been on the road for a week and feel grimy. I didn't make this plan. I just wake up sometimes and want to crawl out of my life.

I have plenty to eat—bread and peanut butter and an apple. There isn't a car in sight, just the half-grown crops, brilliant green in the moist morning light. Goose and I walk down the middle of the right-hand lane. It feels good to be in motion. Walking, turning and walking backward when I hear a car, sizing it up—an old pickup, a tractor-trailer, a VW van, a flashy Cadillac, a salesman's sedan. I prefer the tractor-trailers and the VWs. No matter what is coming, I stick out my thumb. The charge is in the anticipation. You never know who is going to pull over and smile a *Sure, get in, where you headed?* I almost never have trouble.

I hear a car coming up in the distance behind me. I turn and face the oncoming possibility. Goose keeps on trotting beside me. I can't tell yet what it is, not a tractor-trailer. I walk backward while the first ride of the day approaches. When he gets close enough, I put out my thumb. He'll ask a lot of questions. I have another minute or two to come up with some answers.

1970. We drop 125,000 tons of napalm on Vietnam.
We drop 8.4 million gallons of Agent Orange on Vietnam.
Nixon orders the invasion of Cambodia by American ground troops.
Anti-draft and anti-war and civil rights demonstrations flare. By spring,

the National Guard occupies 21 campuses in 16 states. Anti-war demonstrators rally at Kent State University in Ohio. The National Guard fires into the crowd, killing 4 students, wounding 8 more.

Two days later, strikes are called at 448 colleges. 4,000,000 students participate. Another 1,200 colleges hold support demonstrations against the shootings at Kent State, against the undeclared war in Cambodia. Students and police riot. Schools close. 75 campuses stay closed through to the end of the year.

The streets of Harvard Square are already filled with demonstrators milling around, looking for direction, a focus for the night's rally. Erik and I stand shoulder to shoulder in the crowd in front of the Holyoke Center, and are pushed and jostled as more people join the demonstration. Thousands of demonstrators fill the streets around Harvard Square, up Mass. Ave. to Brattle Street and Boylston Street, young people packed in from curb to curb.

It has turned cold, but the crush of bodies blocks the evening wind. We know we can pressure Harvard into changing its policies if enough of us raise our voices together. Someone has a bullhorn and the night begins. Swaying calmly, we chant in unison, "Out Now!" and "No ROTC!" "Black Studies When?" and "Dow Chemical Kills Children! Cut Ties Now!" Our voices echo off the walls surrounding Harvard Yard. Hope and a sense of power, of capacity to have effect, of belonging to something good and right rise in me.

Suddenly the deep, rhythmic drumming of police batons against their riot shields thunders behind our voices, the beat marking their military march toward us. We can't see it, but we know what is coming: a phalanx is marching down Mass. Ave., armed and committed to crushing the demonstrators. There is no place to run in the packed-in square. We know we are in trouble.

"Don't move! Don't fight back or the pigs will kill us! Stay where you are and don't fight back!" bellows a frightened voice over the bullhorn. The swaying changes its rhythm as people try to pull out of the crowd. "What's going on? What's happening?" people shout.

"The pigs are coming!" I grab Erik's arm and we try to move back toward Brattle Street. The low hard drumming comes steadily and unrelentingly toward us. Young men and women scream at the oncoming wall of riot police, "Pigs! You fucking pigs!" And then the police are inside the crowd, their baby blue helmets moving like jolting dots among the demonstrators. Some try to run, but others face off against the surging police, creating their own wall, defying the cops to use their batons and boots against an unarmed crowd. The police march into and through the line, swinging their batons against heads and shoulders and bellies, kicking people, the pretty blue helmets bobbing as they work.

Suddenly the crowd explodes in fury, grabbing newspapers and magazines from the news stand at the subway kiosk and lighting them on fire. Soon the stand and kiosk are on fire, the flames rising into the night. The crowd turns on the police, throwing bricks and bottles at the oncoming surge. In a rage, they break out store windows on both sides of Brattle and Boylston Streets. The streets fill with the crash of glass, shouting, smoke, sirens, gunshots. The cops fire tear gas at us, causing the crowd to split and flow through the back streets and converge again when the gas has subsided. Police sirens scream from the edges of the Square, their lights swinging in great red and blue arcs across the storefronts. People call frantically into the crowd as we are carried along down Boylston Street: "Tim! Susan! Where are you? Don't run! Kill the pigs! They're going to kill us all! Down to the river! Run! Don't run! They'll kill you! Russ! Russ!"

I lose Erik and back my way up Brattle Street. I am not afraid. As glass shatters and fires ignite, I feel an answering of my own private sorrows. Here, finally, is a momentary release. I stand backed against a store wall, the thunder of feet rising through my legs and into my belly. At last, the eruption. I start to run the streets, taunting the police, the fury flowing. For a few hours the fire burning inside flares with the street fires. "Fuck you!" I scream at the rioting police and soldiers. "Fuck you!" Someone grabs my long hair and jerks my head down, dragging me backward. He lets me go to raise his baton at someone coming up on his back. "Fuck you!" I scream, fixing his eyes with mine.

The ambulance sirens wail as they make their way slowly into and back out of the surging crowd. And then it is quiet. The National Guard holds the Square, the fires still smoldering. They announce a curfew, and clear the streets. We have been beaten into fractured and stunned groups. We wander slowly out of the Square with our eyes burning still from tear gas, many with blood on their hands and faces, calling across the streets to each other, "It's over, man. Let's go. Are you hurt? Fucking pigs. They won't get away with this."

I make my way along the quiet back streets down toward the river to Leverett House, Erik's old dorm, to see if he is there with his friends. He greets me without his customary grin, and says, "Jesus. The fucking cops went nuts out there. I was worried about you." I sit on the old couch in the dark. All the grief and loss and hurt of the past several years has risen to meet the chaos on the streets. In my mind I can still hear the thundering collapse of windows onto the sidewalk, can smell the fires burning, feel the tear at my hair as my head is jerked backward. I want to be purged, cleansed of all the dark and hidden and weighty sorrow. But here I am, nothing changed, still a girl living a lonely and fractured and makeshift life in Cambridge.

Later, in the dark night, I hear a noise from the street three floors below, the familiar beat of heavy boots marching on patrol. I rise and lift the window quickly, a loud smooth growl of wood against wood, and bend out to see what is happening below. Five soldiers stop abruptly, jerking their heads at the sound, and raise their rifles in unison, pointing them at me without a sound. We stare, a girl beyond fear and five young men with guns. "Do it," I call out to them, as if I am flirting with them. "Do it." They look embarrassed and walk on, their boots measuring their even steps.

I lie back down beside Erik, waiting for the long night to pass. "Say it," I ask.

Chapter Five

Again

It isn't even my father who does it. I call him on the telephone. Catherine answers. What do you want? she says. Your father doesn't want you calling for him.

That's a lie, I yell in a sudden and tearful rage. My father loves me! He wants me to call him! You're the one who always hates it when I call. Go to hell, Catherine!

She waits for a minute, then says coolly, You may never come to our house again. You are not welcome.

I love my father. But my father is a weak man, and he does not object.

I am nineteen years old. I never return to my father's house again.

When I am small, my father whistles. He is tall and handsome, with shining blue eyes and a ready smile. He has big hands and can build a boat or a house. He sings *Aida* and *Carmen* in his bathrobe and white cowboy hat, pacing the living room, his smooth tenor voice filling the small room, looking to us for encouragement and praise. "Do you like this song?" he wants to know. "I think I sound like Caruso, don't you? Huh? What do you think? Do you think I sound like Caruso?"

Although he enjoys it when people tell him he looks just like Hemingway, he never reads. "Just don't give me any books for Christmas," he tells us. He often speaks in baby talk. "I'm the best driver I know," he says in the car, pulling me into his lap and letting me feel the wheel slide through my fingers. "Right? Huh, Merky? Don't you think I'm the best driver you've ever seen?"

"I'm going to bring you a baby crow," he promises, "and we'll teach it to talk." And "I'm going to bring you a baby bear," he promises. "There's a little monkey who lives under the hood of the car," he tells me. "Don't you hear him sometimes? I'm going to train him for you and give him to you." My father lifts a pinch of garden soil—the garden he tilled and planted, the seeds flicked out of his palm one by one with his thumb down each furrow, the garden he loves but always leaves to my mother to tend—squeezes it and breaks it open again. Then he tastes it, putting a bit on his tongue, looking off while he makes his judgment. "It's acid," he says matter-of-factly. "We need more lime."

My mother and father both graduated from high school at sixteen, and moved directly into their work lives. But they wanted up and the 1950s were waiting for them. They studied the mannerisms and accoutrements of upper-middle-class life and replicated it in the tiny box house they designed and built themselves on a small lot in an apple orchard in Hampton. The little tract house we live in is a low-budget expression of my father's creativity and very high aspirations. Linoleum and paint and wallpaper have to do the trick. The kitchen has black, chrome-edged linoleum countertops, a black and red floor. The bathroom counter is curved, and the white brick fireplace is set into a modern expanse of dark green wall. The furniture is sleek with clean curvy edges. The curtains my mother sews have splashed-on scenes, pink and black, from a Paris bistro. My parents' desire for sophistication, for a life that will let them pass as educated and successful, is so powerful it becomes its own fuel. I grow up the envy of my friends who live in the same little houses but with beige walls and dull straight lines.

My father comes home from his business trips, selling on the road for Gates Rubber Company, and leaves his battered leather suitcase on the kitchen floor for my mother to take care of. "Daddy's home! Daddy's home!" we all shriek with joy. He usually turns right around, packing up his hunting gear or his fishing gear or his cameras or his watercolors, and walks back out the door. Sometimes he comes home from these trips to the woods with a string of fish, or three pheasants my mother plucks and cleans. Or a watercolor of ice glazing a rocky woodland stream, the water slipping under the shelf of ice in his other world. He comes back from these weekends unshaved, smelling of spruce and snow and bug dope and oil paints and Hoppe's rifle cleaner. Years later, my mother tells me he also came back with lipstick on his clothes, little oversights reminding her of what she already knew. By Sunday night each week, she has his white shirts ironed and folded and back in the suitcase. My father wanders the house, singing and talking baby talk and teasing us, an enormous person with a waiting family hungry for his magnificent and elusive love.

But sometimes on Friday afternoon, he changes into his old pants and the worn Viyella shirts which smell of him, of strong, sweet Cuprinol preservative and sawdust. He works all weekend on the boat he is building in the garage. He has lofted full-sized plans onto enormous sheets of white Masonite nailed up on the long wall. When he is away, those crisscrossed lines, in their lovely confluence of curves, feel like a map reassuring me that everything leads home in the end. For years after he leaves for good, those beautiful sweeping lines, with his penciled measurements and notes, haunt me, reminding me of his large and compelling presence. The tools of his work—an old table saw, the massive vise on his beat-up workbench under the windows, dried-out scrubby paintbrushes green with Cuprinol—stay where he has left them, as if he is coming home one of these days to get back to work.

My father steams his own planks for the boat over a fire behind the garage. He uses a section of black sewer pipe, stopped up at the ends, laid over a bed of coals. Listening to the escaping steam, he draws out the hot board and tests the plank for spring against his

thigh. "Think it's done, Merky?" he asks. "We're going to get this
board just right." He takes on the Yankee accent of his country
friends. Or the Texas accent of his business clients. Or the Midwest
accent of his secretary, or the soft Georgian drawl of his boss. "Yup,
Merk, you watch me now. We're going to lay this board up just as
tight as a mouse. Mouse tight." He isn't talking to me. I am his au-
dience as he seals the pipe back up for another few minutes. Suddenly
he knows he has what he wants from his jerry-rigged steam box. He
pulls out the plank and rushes into the garage, steam rising around
his intent face as he races time, easing the plank and securing it with
a dozen heavy clamps before it cools. He whistles as the plank wraps
without cracking over the graceful curved frames. "I'm good at this,
you know," he says. "You know that, Meredy. I'm a damned good
boat builder." His sweet home talk and chameleon salesman's talk
blend as the steam rises and drifts into the cool fall air.

   He has moved out for good by the time I am ten, and hadn't been
around much before that. But he shines in me like a light. I believe I
am the center of his brilliant, hungry world.

My father was an only child, growing up through the Depression in
an old first-floor apartment in Lawrence, Massachusetts. His father
and grandfather shared this small world, but were, my father believes, weak and invisible men. He was raised by adoring women.
When I am a child, his mother and grandmother still live in his
childhood apartment. Lawrence is a brick and water city, with shoe
and textile mills packed along the filthy Merrimack River. The water that comes from the tap smells and tastes of the hard, noisy,
crushing work lives of generations of men and women, including my
family. By the time I can remember, Grammy Hall has left the stitching floor and works as a clerk and fitter, selling foundations—girdles
and bras—at Cherry & Webb's department store downtown. Great-
Grammy Melling sits all day in the bay window talking to her blue
parakeet, Petey, waiting for her daughter to come home.

   I never see my father speak tenderly to either his mother or grandmother, although I am sure he loves them. His speech is always impatient and critical. He is still, two decades after leaving home, lord of the place. His mother and grandmother prepare his favorite meals for him—meat gravy over potatoes, chicken pie, pot roast—although he never seems grateful. "Mother! Are you still using that old pot? I thought I told you to throw that thing out. Christ! You'll save anything." This is accompanied by a small snort, a sort of snicker of disbelieving contempt at the end of the scolding.

After my parents divorce and my father remarries, he does not want to upset his mother and grandmother. For two years, for each holiday and birthday, my mother, sister, brother, and I meet him on the highway and drive together as a family to Lawrence. No one needs to tell us the rules of this game: we are a happy family, a special and wonderful family. My father jokes and teases us. My mother, astonishingly, plays her role of contented wife perfectly.

We gather up the food from the car and the mending my mother has done for Grammy and file behind my father up the walkway, through the little gate, and along the unpainted wall of the tenement house, waving with big smiles to Grammy Melling in the window. We don't knock. Grammy Hall is cooking already at the huge old range. The kitchen is big and empty except for an old wooden day bed along the back wall and a round table by the big window. It is dark—dark wood, dark floors, a gas light converted to electric hanging from the high gray ceiling. My father says hello and immediately seems restless, bored, pacing around, jabbing at Grammy. "Mother, that's going to take hours to cook. I told you I can't stay all day." His mother placates him: "Leslie, dear, it won't take long. I can hurry it up." She has blue hair and wears a lot of perfume. She takes great pride in dressing up the dining room table with Depression glass and china. Grammy Melling bobs her head from her chair at all of the hubbub, and my mother helps cook and set the table. She stands next to my father, sits next to him, shares our news from the past few weeks. She smiles. My father sits at the head of the table with his children and ex-wife and mother and grandmother all attend-

ing him. My mother pretends she is still the wife. We children pretend that we are still the only children, that my father, their beloved
Leslie, still comes home to us, that his new wife and stepchild do
not exist. It is an audacious act for my father. I don't know why
my mother goes along with it; she is in love with my father, and
may find a strange comfort in being allowed to play wife again for an
afternoon.

During these charades, I feel deep confusion. Whatever griefs
and fears I am experiencing about my father's leaving do not seem to
occur to him. He asks me, at ten or eleven years old, to put on an act
for him, to pretend that I am still the happy girl from our earlier life.
He tells us that he just wants his mother and grandmother to be
happy. I know, though, even as a child, that my father will ask the un-
thinkable of me in order to smooth the way for himself. I learn in
those tenuous afternoons, with the old mantel clock ticking, that my
father is a weak man, and he will not protect me.

My father marries Catherine when I am ten years old. He has disappeared for a year. Disappearing isn't unusual, but his wanderings
around the backcountry of New England have never lasted more
than a week or two. One day, after a year of silence, my father comes
home. He sits forward in his old chair, tanned and animated. His
eyes are crystal blue, flashing with new dreams. "I have some good
news!" he tells us. "I got married!" There is a stunned silence. "Her
name is Catherine and you're going to think she's terrific." My
brother, sister, and I turn to my mother for a softening of the news,
some signal that this is not what our father has meant to say. But she
is crying, and the three of us start to cry with her. "Jesus Christ!"
my father says loudly. "Jesus Christ! I didn't expect you to jump up
and down with joy, but I thought you'd be happy for me. Jesus! This
isn't what I need today!"

He stands up, walks to the door, and makes his way to his car.
Small enough: a divorce. But my father's inability to imagine our
loss and grief is what will pull me back to this little scene years from

now. His expectation is what holds me, that we will share in his own great relief, his happiness that his new love promises him a wonderful future.

Catherine is not good news. Intelligent and cold, she claims my father from us unapologetically. He still whistles and sings opera and teases, but I become an infrequent visitor in his new life. He and Catherine are passionate together, arguing and laughing and yelling, claiming all of each other. A fire burns there I have never known before—eruptive, consuming, fed by needs I sense in my father but cannot understand. I am suddenly a stepdaughter, and I know I have to be careful.

I think Catherine—"Kitty," my father calls her in baby talk—is beautiful, partly, maybe, because my father tells us that she is, and because, even at ten, I can see that she possesses a powerful, handsome face. She is sophisticated, a business executive who lives in New Hampshire and works in New York City. Her fine brown hair is short and feathery, her nose straight and strong, her lips wide and sensuous. Her father was Greek, and I see her face and strong, full body in the classic marble statues in the Greek Hall at the museum. My father admires her large breasts and often comments on them, in baby talk, as he cups them in his hands.

In contrast to my father's childish playfulness, Catherine is still, contained, and forbidding. Her severity, the intimation of calm, cool judgment, surround her like a cold light, a large and powerful caution to anyone in her presence. Often, she and my father erupt in fury, hurling magazines and coffee cups and insults at each other. I am scared of her, and of the passionate, tumultuous connection between her and my father. Their complex and potent personalities mesh in strange and volatile ways: childlike, immature, supremely egotistical and narcissistic, my father seems to find in Catherine's remote silence an anchor, or maybe a challenge. They are in love. They are two enormous characters, creating the beginnings of an exclusive and destructive interdependence that will cost me my father.

He tells us happily about the house he and Catherine are building themselves at "the lake" in western New Hampshire. One snowy Friday night after work, they pick us up in his new convertible sports car, a shining red Triumph. Michael and I squeeze behind their seats with Molly, Catherine's ten-year-old daughter. Our winter gear and food for several days is stashed in the trunk and around our shoulders. On these rare trips to the lake, my father is the center of the show, good-natured, teasing and happily baby-talking all of us. Catherine is not playful; she sits hunched into her heavy coat, distant and self-contained. We make the three-hour trip in the flapping cold, the engine humming a loud throaty growl every time my father shifts. We unload our gear and make our way into the icy, pitch-black kitchen.

My father is a dreamer. The house is big, framed up but not yet insulated, a hulk of modern angles crouched on a steep rocky slope to the water. It looms with a high slanted ceiling, long glass walls, and almost no furniture. Piles of lumber and building supplies and my father's and Catherine's usual mess of boxes, old mail, clothing, and bags of building debris take the place of furniture. Late at night, I am tired and lonely for something I can't name; our entrance to my father's new project feels like a threshold I want to resist. Catherine moves abruptly, giving us orders to unpack the groceries, roll up newspaper for the woodstove, gather kindling from the piles of sweepings around the house.

The bedrooms are in the daylight basement. They have windows looking down the wooded slope to the lake, but no stairs to the living space above. Overtired, uncertain, feeling a deep dread, I follow my brother and Molly out the door into the night, down the steep hill along the side of the house, the flashlight beam swallowed by the immensity of the snowy woods. It is the middle of the night. I feel that we are being asked by Catherine to do more than children should be asked to do. But Michael, at twelve, dutifully faces those expectations, and Molly and I silently follow after him. I sleep in Molly's room on the upper bunk. Everything is frozen and gray and hard in this strange space. We undress in the deep dark, feet aching from wet socks and cold, and climb into the unwelcoming beds.

Molly and I each lie curled tightly under the heavy blankets, my father and her mother thumping around upstairs in this ice-cold house
with no stairway connecting us to them.

My father tweaks Catherine's breasts and talks baby talk. He
needs her to keep track of his things and remind him what he is
thinking. "Do I like chutney?" he asks his wife. "Do I, Kitty?"
"Where the hell is my pencil, Kitty? I can't do anything without my
pencil. Help me find my pencil, Kitty." "Kitty, where did I get this
shirt? I like this shirt. Where did I get it?" I have had nothing of my
father for several years. Now here he is, but the terms for sharing are
very steep. I know I am on the losing end of a silent struggle that
is already in full motion. My father and Catherine are building a
future together, and I understand it has very little to do with me.
When I sit in my father's lap in his new, modern black leather chair,
Catherine immediately chases me away: "Meredy, you and Molly go
sweep the bedrooms. Now." Or: "Your father doesn't want you always hanging on him. You don't see Molly doing that. Get up." My
father, ominously, never says a word. I get up and do as I am told.

Once, doing errands in the nearby town of Keene, my father
holds my hand as we walk down the sidewalk. Catherine watches us
for a few minutes, and then says sternly, "Meredy. You are too old for
that. Your father doesn't want you holding on to him like that." I
drop my father's hand, burning with a confusion of shame, anger,
and a sense that something vital to me is slipping away forever. My
father, typically, does not react, and we walk from then on side by
side, not touching. After a few minutes, my father says quietly, "You
know I love you, Merky." Catherine is fighting a war, and with my
father's refusal to protect me, she wins each of these quiet battles. I
feel that Catherine is a catastrophe in my life, that something crushing is coming my way because of her. It will take another seven years
for the explosion.

Charles Simic, the great poet, writes, "I am in dialogue with certain
elements in my life . . . Meaning is the matter of my existence. My effort to understand is a perpetual circling around a few obsessive im-

ages." Simic, who as a child lived in Serbia under the terror of both German and Allied bombs, writes about stones, the pebbles in the ditch where he flattened himself one sunny day while the world exploded around him. Death and suffering surrounded him. He might have died. The stones linger, haunting images that try to tell the whole story. The meaning is there, in the weight and smooth grain of rocks. If Simic remembers them well enough, truthfully enough, surely he will understand why the entire world went mad, why his father left his mother alone to protect their young children, why his poems arise from that ditch.

I circle my own obsessive images, examining each small fragment in the light, laying one against the next until the image becomes memory. They are the permanent record, aren't they? Burned into the chemistry of brain cells, they do not play tricks, do they? What happened has become part of me, etched and immutable. I want to rely on these truths.

Obsessive images, a life becoming story, story becoming meaning. These are my memories, filed and cross-filed in my mind. Is this really how it was? I know, and then the flash of doubt. I want to get it right. These are shifting sands. Say it, then turn your back for a moment, just long enough to see the light move through the high branches of an oak, hear a few notes from a song you heard long ago, catch a flick of a smile or a trembling hand, then return, and you will tell a different story. Every detail counts: Was it snowing? Was my sister there? Did he speak to me in *anger* or in *fear*? Of course, as the sands shift, so does meaning: there is a gulf between anger and fear.

I say, "This is what happened." I examine each small piece of the puzzle and come up with an idea: "And this is why." It feels important, necessary.

Slowly, over years, my father's guilt over my outcasting becomes anger, and I become the cause of all our trouble. Twice in thirty years I call him, desperately seeking some understanding of his rejection of me, some righting of the terrible injustice.

"Look," he says fiercely to me. "I don't need to explain anything to you. If you don't love me enough to even come see me, I don't want to talk to you."

"I'll come!" I say. "I'll come tomorrow!"

"Don't push me like this, Meredy. You're just like your mother. And remember—I divorced her for a lot less than this."

I go to sleep, wake, and the images slice across my vision. I circle them, making meaning. It matters. I need to get it right.

I have a strange artifact in my small box of keepsakes, a three-inch green plastic disk, translucent and etched with tight rings spiraling to the center. My father used these disks on his Dictaphone machine, recording business letters for his secretary to type up later. No one has the old machines anymore. But I can play the little disk on an old turntable. Warbling along at 78 rpm, there I am, my child voice from 1957.

My message is clear. "I love you, Daddy," I say. My voice wavers. "I love you, Daddy. I love you, Daddy. I love you, Daddy." There is a question in my sentence, a beseeching. I don't know what strange flaw in the disk causes my appeal to play over and over. I listen to me calling out to my father for three or four minutes. It is as if I know what is coming, as if I can hold him to me against the current. I am a child, resisting exile.

Chapter Six
Drawing the Line

I have never been seasick before, but the heavy smell of rancid fat in the galley and the fish guts that oil every inch of beaten-up wood saturate the air. Even below deck, the wind roars like a freight train; the ancient Cummins diesel whines and vibrates the chipped mugs hanging over the sink. The bare bulb overhead flickers as the *Jenny D* pitches and heaves and rolls in the August southwester. The shovels in the empty fish hold thud hard, back and forth, on the other side of the bulkhead. I can't predict each sickening rise and bottom-out drop; I bend my knees and lean into the counter hard with my hips, and still I am slammed again and again against the stove and icebox and bolted-down table. I move three greasy milk crates of tools and used engine parts onto the bunks in the forepeak, their bare mattresses strewn with old army blankets, and wedge myself into the cramped corner bench behind the table. I close my eyes; the surge of the sea is met with an answering surge in my stomach. Pots and dishes clatter in the filthy bins beneath the stove; sweaters and vests and jackets, stiff with salt and sweat and fish juice, grate back and forth on their hooks above my head.

A sense of dread, the seeping uneasiness which has nagged me lately, rises again. Erik and I have owned the *Jenny D* for over a year, fishing out of Gloucester, Massachusetts, our latest escapade. But lately I have started to wish that things were different. I don't want to be here. I feel a deep panic rise as the boat heaves. So much seems to be at stake between us, and none of it is spoken.

I open my eyes, wishing for a long smooth horizon to define up and down, a clear and unmovable line to navigate by, to delineate me from this grimy and thundering boat.

I can hear Erik and Billy laughing in the wheelhouse above. The sweet, heavy smoke of Bugle tobacco from Billy's pipe floats down the companionway and mixes with the smell of grease as I cook eggs and hash for breakfast. Gooey black fat tars the edge of the grill. I lift the eggs onto buns, squirt ketchup on them, and lay them with the hash on two paper plates for the men. I let my legs roll with the boat as I reach for the chips stashed behind the sink. Balancing the plates, I hitch myself up the stairs to the wheelhouse.

It is a relief to be above deck, in the presence of these confident men and eye to eye with the storm. Outside the cramped, dingy wheelhouse, the sky is a dark gray dome clamped down close over us. There is no horizon; the chaotic sea and roiling sky meet and fuse, becoming each other. Green water breaks over the bow of the *Jenny D* every few minutes, thundering through her old wooden hull. Erik stands rooted to the floor, his compact, athletic body negotiating with the wheel as he maneuvers the tired old fishing dragger into weather she shouldn't be asked to endure. I stand behind him and wrap my strong, thin arms around his waist. He looks over his shoulder at me, surprised. We are buddies, *gumbas* like Gloucester's Italian fishermen—loyal and dependent, saving each other's faces at every turn. We never hug.

Erik eats as I wedge myself between the port side door and counter. He glances at me and laughs. "You all right? Told you you shouldn't come this trip." He holds the wheel steady, legs straddled, his black rubber fishing boots tight around his strong calves. The fishermen tell stories of men who can't swim filling their boots with stones if they get in trouble; the loaded boots take them down fast. Erik likes to say he keeps a bucket of stones on deck, but I know he was ninth in the nation on Harvard's swim team.

Erik likes to say a lot of things I know aren't true. That he is a

Viking, destined to live and die heroically on the sea. That he is a simple man, a workingman, uneducated, with animal smarts. That he isn't afraid.

The truth is that he barely graduated from Harvard with a 1.8 in Scandinavian Studies, almost a year into fishing the *Jenny D*. That he reads the *Eddas* in Old Norse for pleasure. That every half-truth —the long, rough red beard and wild, tangled hair, the fishing boots worn even to slop along the streets of Cambridge, the perpetual grin, the *Jenny D*—all of these are gestures to ward off his fear, images to create a character that will not, cannot, be ignored or diminished by anyone. The truth is that the *Jenny D*, a hard-used, thirty-eight-foot stern dragger we bought together for two thousand dollars, is just the kind of surprise Erik likes to drop on his friends. The truth is, Erik loves me and needs me, but after three years of living together, we don't know anything about each other. We are mythmakers. Vikings need fellow warriors, and I am the perfect fellow. But lately I am getting tired of our big stories. I am starting to understand that my own mythmaking is running dry, is keeping me tied to something not mine. I am getting lost in our stories, and feel as if I am missing something, something ordinary and very important.

"You okay?" he asks again, smirking at me.

"Yeah. Of course. Of course I'm all right," I say cheerfully. I do feel better. I look from Erik to Billy, trying to absorb their eagerness to be heading out for a day of fishing in twenty-five-knot winds and eight-foot seas. The truth is, I love Erik. But the storm seems to be churning things up. I want to be at home, sitting in the gray light by the kitchen window, sorting me out from my stories, getting ready for what might be coming next.

Billy digs around in his pipe with his pocketknife, his small body resting against the starboard door; he is grinning. His jeans and long brown ponytail and fingernails are all dirty. He is clean shaven, though, so his lean and tired face looks open and receptive, as if he is always ready for the next surprise. He relights the pipe with his Zippo, flicking the top of the lighter open and shut, open and shut before his hand finally obeys the command to be still. He wipes his knife on his oily Levi's and drops the lighter and knife into his pocket. I know that in several minutes his pipe, forgotten, will be out again, and he will repeat this lurching, spastic ritual.

Billy isn't one of Erik's Harvard buddies. Twitching and jerking from years of too much cocaine, he drifted into Gloucester with a small wave of hippies whose lives had run out of control. He arrived burned out, jittering, and earnest. His wife, Sonya, is twenty, large and soft-spoken, with dreamy eyes. They sleep with their two-year-old daughter, Beth, between them on a mattress on the floor in their drafty apartment on Portuguee Hill. The hill is home to generations of Portuguese immigrants. It is a tumble of very old houses painted the bright colors of the boats in the harbors of their old Portugal and right here in Gloucester's harbor—white with red trim, yellow with blue trim, blue with red trim—the houses squeezed together down the narrow, twisting streets. The old men and women on the hill have grudgingly accepted this tenuous and mystifying family. Sonya seldom leaves the apartment. Sometimes, on hot summer days, she and Beth walk down the hill to the new state pier to sit on the boat while Billy works on the nets and gear. Sometimes, they walk up Main Street, past the old closed-up storefronts, to Goodwill, or to Sterling's Drugstore for milk shakes at the counter.

I like to sit with Sonya and Beth on blankets spread over the clean, bare floor, drinking tea and eating enormous fluffy muffins Sonya bakes. One May day, with the sun floating through the big, dusty window, Sonya says, "Erik was over yesterday. I think it's great you don't mind us fucking." She smiles, her wide mouth soft and easy.

I don't speak. I imagine Erik here, Sonya's full white body, red hair, and breathy laugh, and Beth nearby murmuring quietly to her dolls. I return to the apartment just once after that, when I have silent, retaliatory sex with Billy in Sonya's bed among her quilts and soft pillows. I wonder if Erik imagines my small, strong body, my long blond hair, my eyes open in the bright, sunlit room. Now, Sonya and I always keep a careful distance, although Erik and Billy don't seem to notice.

What I like most about Erik is his ability to hold his show together. He is solid, in an irreverent and careless way. What I like is his ability to stay right on the edge, threatening to slip off at any minute but never losing his footing in the end. So far, I haven't fallen off the edge, either, but I feel that it is going to happen some day. I never tell Erik I am scared. I like hanging on that edge with him, anchored just enough by him to let me think I can do—and be—anything.

We do odd and exciting things together, creating new identities every few months, one story always leading to the next, with my dropping out of college and his disregard for his grades at Harvard adding to our sense that we can make up the rules as we go. We ride Erik's bike to New York and Montreal and Quebec, yelling, "Fuck you!" to men in Buicks and Lincolns when we stop next to them at red lights. We live for a summer in a decrepit, tick-infested hunting cabin among the Ojibwa Indians on Red Lake Indian Reservation in far northern Minnesota, getting lost each day in the woods and celebrating like children when we come back across our little camp and fire ring. We argue utopias with black student activists with guns in dark, sprawling apartments in the Columbia Heights projects. We drive across the border to sell Erik's steamer trunks full of homegrown marijuana in Montreal. We sit in with strangers in put-together rock bands in run-down, dirty apartments in Roxbury.

Erik and I are a good pair. We need each other, partners in myth-making. I have my own image to make—aloof, solitary, arrogant—an angry and isolated girl struggling to create a new self that can hold its place in the world. I construct myself, the strong and independent young woman who breaks all the rules.

I take on Erik's Harvard friends as my own, five men half in love with me. I like being the female at the center of all these young men,

and make each new apartment a home for them all. I construct myself: daring, flirtatious, laughing, and assured, a loner who likes to
feed hungry boys. I cook big meals for whoever is there, then close
my bedroom door and slip back into my stunned dissociation.

We move, and move, and move again, every new neighborhood,
every dirty old kitchen affirming that we are brave and brash and
ready for it all. I like to move, to make the decision that someplace
else looks better. I love disconnecting; I can set up a house in half a
day, any place we go. We travel light. I box and unbox the blue-and-
white dishes my grandmother earned with Green Stamps, and our
books, and cheap Indian bedspreads that cover windows and ratty
couches and holes in plaster walls. Erik says he doesn't care what a
place looks like, but it is always our place and my food his friends
gravitate to, and Erik likes to watch his friends wishing I were theirs.
"My old lady rides a bike like a man and cooks like a mama," he says
appreciatively. Erik expects a lot from me—to never ask questions,
to make him look good, to keep up with his roles as he dreams them
up, to prove I don't depend on him. Love is tricky with Erik. But I
expect a lot from him, too—to tolerate my absences, my solitary and
mysterious days, to confirm to the world that I am an independent
and irreverent girl, to substantiate my own imagemaking. Maybe
love is tricky with me, too. "Quicksilver girl," Erik says.

When Erik comes home one day and tells me he wants to move to
Gloucester and buy a boat, I am game. I love telling people what is
coming this time, this round the best yet: "We're buying a fishing
boat. We're moving to Gloucester, and we're going to be fishermen."
I love owning the *Jenny D*. Erik and I are seamen now, and we master the new vocabulary as if we had been born on the water, as if it is
the language we have always known and just recently recalled. We
move from the city to Rockport, a tiny fishing town beside Gloucester. The old cottage with the oilskins hanging in the kitchen excites
me, a little nest facing up against the moody sea. Erik has instinctive
skill as a fisherman—"I told you I'm a Viking," he says—and I know

my determination to be a good deckhand pleases him. This is a place
I think I will be happy to stay for a little while. I secretly want Erik
to change the name of our boat—the *Meredy Ann.*

I am surprised when Erik tells me after two months of fishing together that Billy is going to start making trips with us; I see that I
am extraneous, that Billy is strong and fearless in ways I am not. I
don't tell Erik how shaken I am. But I have a slip-sliding feeling, as
if I am untethered. If we aren't fishermen together on the sea, if I wait
onshore for the boat to come in loaded with fish, what am I? At first
I stay home, reading and putting in my first garden and driving my
bike for hours every day, a restless wandering that quiets my ceaseless loneliness and grief. I start waitressing at a cavernous tourist
place looking out on the breakwater and am fired for mocking the
customers when they give me small tips. For a while I deliver newspapers before dawn each morning, a solitary job I like but which pays
next to nothing. I wind transformers in a little room at the back of
an empty warehouse, working alone at night, covering my mistakes
with a few orderly turnings of pretty wire.

I always seem to end up back in the fish plants. I work shoulder to shoulder with about forty other women. The packing shed is
falling down, a long low structure on one of the rotting wharves that
line Gloucester's shore. I can see the harbor through the gaps in the
boards beneath my feet. It is so dark I cannot see the end of the line
in either direction; I work in a pool of thin light. It is always frigidly
cold, with water sloshing everywhere. We wear heavy black rubber
aprons over our winter coats, and layers of wool socks inside our
rubber boots. We cannot work in the cold water without gloves, but
we can't handle the fish with them on. We try the fisherman's traditional black rubber gloves, the newer orange gloves, boiled wool
gloves, or wristers—fingerless gloves—we knit ourselves. The wristers usually win. The cuffs of our coats are always soaked and slimy.

The foreman never has a name. We women never speak to him
and refer to him only as "the boss." He walks the catwalk under the
dim bare bulbs that hang from the roof every twenty feet. His black

rubber boots clomp along at our head level. I have never seen him smile. I dislike him, although he has never bothered me. As long as we do our job, he doesn't say a word. As soon as we screw up, he yells, "Hey! Two hands! Use both hands or we'll never go home tonight."

There is an art to packing herring. You have to pay attention. The fish are sluiced past you in a river of ice-cold Atlantic seawater. The right hand grabs a fish running tail-first along the chute. As you draw that one to you, keep watching the chute. With the left hand, grab a fish moving headfirst in the rush and roar of machinery and water. As the left hand draws the second fish toward you, the right hand lays its fish tightly, neatly, specifically into the box in front of you. As the left hand follows, placing its fish tightly, quickly, specifically alongside the first, your eye is watching the chute for the fish pointed just right, running tail-first down the cold river, right hand. There's a rhythm you have to keep: head to tail, head to tail, head to tail, right, left, right, left, right, left, twelve to a box. When your box is full, you lift it and turn, placing it on your cart behind you. You'll be paid in cash at the end of the day, ten cents a box.

I believe that this is a choice for me, that working here is temporary, that I will be moving back into adventure any day. For most of the women, it is what they will do all their lives, and their jobs are never certain as prices or fish stocks rise and fall. The tension among them runs very high. "You fucking bitch! I told you I'm not putting up with any more of your shit! You reach across me one more time and I'll slit your fucking throat." The rest of us keep our eyes on the river of fish, head tail head tail. The foreman walks back and slaps his hand against his leg. "Knock it off or neither one of you comes back tomorrow." The women step back into place, right hand, left. My feet ache. My hands ache. I am cold to the bone. I wipe my running nose on my filthy sleeve without losing my rhythm.

I wait for the months or the year I imagine it will take for this life, this adventure, to peter out and give way to something new, the next big idea, something that will give me a name for the self I am working so hard at creating. But it has been more than a year, and

the hovering, expectant sense that has bound us from the beginning
—that things are in the making, ours to imagine—is suddenly gone.
We have grown up together, have been good partners in imagemaking for four years, sticking to the scripts we improvise day by day.
But I have started to feel out of step, as if something is tugging at me
from the side.

I start to badger Erik. "This isn't what I banked on," I tell him.
"This is great for you, but I hate it. I didn't move to Gloucester to
serve lobsters to tourists and pack fish. What are we doing? Why
don't we sell the *Jenny D* this summer and head out? You're done
with school. We can do anything we want. Let's take the bikes south
somewhere. Let's buy a farm in Vermont. Let's go live in the caves
around Grenada."

"We will," he always says.

"When? You've been saying that since we got here."

His voice is playful, boyish, coercive: "I haven't caught that two-
hundred-pound halibut I promised you."

"Erik! I hate that fucking halibut. Let's go."

"We will," he says, again and again.

After months onshore, I am excited when Erik asks if I will make a
trip with him. "Tell Billy to take the trip off," I tell him. I am surprised when I wake up in the morning to a strong southwest wind.

"Still want to come?" Erik asks me.

I feel that a lot is at stake, that this trip is part of our story and I
have a chance to write myself back in. If the weather is a little rough,
all the better. We are Gloucester fishermen. "Absolutely," I say.

When we get down to the boat, there is another surprise: Billy
is coiling lines on the deck, with the engine already running. Erik
tells me to stow away the food.

I try to find the horizon as the *Jenny D* banks and rolls. My belly has
quieted down since I came up from the galley, but I dread the long
day ahead. We loaded ice and fuel at Tony Giuliano's dock at four

o'clock this morning; it was still dark, and raining. The American flag at the end of the pier snapped hard in the warm, wet wind. Tony's is on one of the old, decrepit wharves in the inner harbor. Long low windowless sheds, the sardine factories that mostly closed in the early 1960s, tilt on the rotting pilings. Businesses like Tony's—selling ice and fuel, buying the fish that men lump out by hand from the holds—occupy sections of the old factories that haven't rotted beyond use. Old fish crates and abandoned nets and rusted lumps of machinery litter the narrow wharves.

"Goin' out?" Tony asked. "Quite a blow. What're you doin'? Cornerin' the market?"

The men hanging around the wharf all laughed while the ice *shoosh*ed from the crusher into the hold. The docks were noisy with engines running and men's voices yelling over them. But no one joined us when we untied the spring line and shoved off. The harbor was lead gray, slapping at *Jenny D.* Our running lights fell dead in the air a few feet from the boat.

Billy hummed as he nosed the *Jenny D* east of Ten Pound Island and headed for the mouth of the harbor. Surf crashed over the breakwater ahead, sending plumes of white water ten feet into the air. The massive granite blocks seemed to float freely in the tumult. I resisted my fear, leaning against Erik's sturdy body, absorbing the boat's pounding through him. I wanted to question Erik's decision to go out; I wanted to say what common sense said: This is crazy. Why would you do this? But I said yes, wanting to be part of the big story again. There was no common sense. Billy would follow Erik anywhere, and Erik had a townful of men watching him leave the dock.

The Gloucester fishermen are not the first people to criticize Erik—or me. After every trip, Erik and Billy sit at the kitchen table drinking beer, telling the same story twenty times to the parade of Gloucester men coming over for a firsthand account. I sit with them, the only woman, serving thick, black coffee and cans of cheap beer and big pieces of pizza I make myself. "Mama Maria," they call me as I serve them food. The Italian and Portuguese fishermen listen, laughing and shaking their heads. They disapprove of these two, and I know it. They all have families to support, boats to preserve for their sons. They are cautious men. The whole town is filled with families missing someone to the sea. Fishing is a living, a tough one, something they are proud of in a defeated kind of way. It isn't anything to play with. Erik and Billy are suspect here. These two always fish where they have no business going, but that isn't the point. There are fifty other things Erik and Billy could do to make a living. They act as if this is a thrill, a charge, a story to tell later. The Gloucester men wait for the disaster they are sure is in the cards for these boys.

I look at the clock over the dripping windows: 7:25. A morning as dark as nightfall. I stay quiet as we head into the churning Atlantic Ocean. Here I am, scared and pretending I'm not, on a leaky old boat in a storm, the floorboards still smeared with oil and a sleeve from Erik's old blue shirt wrapped around the throttle where hydraulic fluid always leaks. I have never imagined Erik belonging like this. I know he needs me to play my own big role beside him, whatever we are calling ourselves at the minute. The problem is, I am starting to realize that there is a line, a horizon between the inside and the outside, between who I am and who I say I am. The problem is, I am starting to understand that there is no such line for Erik. The problem is, I am starting to understand that who I say I am doesn't matter. Erik seems happy with me as his *gumba*. But as the old boat rolls and pitches, our big heroic saga feels false and empty.

Billy stares out the side window, ducking just a little when a wave smashes against the wheelhouse. He turns for a second and catches my eye. The hull shudders. Billy snaps his lighter again and laughs. "I think old man Neptune's ruining your old lady's day," he says to Erik, who turns from the wheel and studies me a minute. I feel obliged to smile at him.

"This?" he asks, turning back to the wheel. "This is just kiddies' playtime in the bathtub." He drawls his words long and slow. Erik always has a new voice, something surprising, playful, not his own.

He is in profile to me, a self-conscious composition: his sharp, handsome face, the big red beard and wild hair, the seething ocean,
cockscombs whipping off the tops of the eight-foot swells, the salt-
sprayed cabin windows. The Viking at sea.

"I don't know what kind of kid you were," I say. "This is enough
for me."

"Too much?" Erik asks, turning again to face me square. There
is a quiet pause; for a minute, the sea and the engine and the tinny
radio and the constant roaring wind silence.

"Uh-uh," I say. My voice is tight, defiant. "It's never too much."

All of us, braced, legs apart, watch out the front windows as the
boat heaves and shudders her way out to sea.

"Wanna check out Jeffreys?" Billy asks. "If this thing's gonna
keep moving in from the southwest, there are gonna be a lot of pretty
cod moving into the shoals. That's our kind of business."

Erik whoops and laughs. "Jesus, Dawson. The last time we swept
the ledge we spent four days mending the net."

But I can see that they both already know that is where we are
going. Its shoal water means wild seas, barely submerged ledge, and
a shot at huge schools of cod. We'll be forty miles offshore, while the
rest of the men drink beer down below on their boats at the dock. I
know it is just the kind of game Erik will want to play. And Billy
knows it, too.

"Perfect." Billy smiles. "Let's go catch us some fish." He clacks
the lid of his lighter back and forth, dropping it and catching it
midair.

I feel fear rise, undeniable, tightening my throat. I look back over
the stern. The low coastline is long gone across miles of heaving
black sea.

"Want me to set the course?" I ask defiantly. I prop myself between the compass column and the chart counter and pull out the
chart for Jeffreys Ledge.

"You want to take the wheel or work with me on deck?" Erik asks me.
It is midmorning, and our work is just beginning. I don't want to do

either. Making it through a day of working on the deck in this storm will require a degree of defiance and skill I don't possess. And taking the wheel means being responsible for taking every single wave just right, not a single mistake, not a moment of forgetting or dreaming. I haven't eaten and have been up since three. I reach up and snap off the crackling AM radio.

"No, I'll—" I start to say, but Billy cuts me off.

"Are you serious, man?" he asks. "She'd be overboard in three minutes." He pulls on his hip boots.

Erik laughs as he zips up his oilskins. "She's my *gumba*. She can do it. Right?"

I suddenly flare. "Not being nuts about spending a day on this leaky piece of shit in a storm doesn't make me a coward. What the hell are you two doing? Do you think everyone's going to think you're heroes? They don't. They think you're just stupid. Stupid college boys who should have stayed in the city. They think you're crazy." I turn around to Erik, close to him, looking straight at him. He stops moving and stares back at me.

Billy pulls on his orange fish gloves, his back to us. *Jenny D* heaves. The surf out on the shoals roars around my words.

Erik strokes his beard slowly and looks out the side window. "What happened to my old lady?" he asks the storm, his voice tight. Then he turns calmly back to me and says, "Okay. Look. Billy will take the wheel and I'll work on deck. You keep Billy company." Erik lights a cigarette, pulls his woolen cap over his hair, and grins at Billy. "I'm gonna go catch us some feesh," he drawls, and he shoves open the door.

The storm whistles into the wheelhouse, then beats at the door again as it slams shut. I lean over to latch the door top and bottom. *Jenny D*'s deck glows against the froth on the shoals; the dark sky and blue-black sea merge, violent force meeting violent force, at the horizon. The diesel's pistons fire one by one in the dark heart of the boat.

Billy is silent as he maneuvers the boat through the surf. I pull on one of Erik's grimy jackets and draw the stiff wool closer to my chest. I turn sideways and look out the small stern window onto the deck. It is a bad design; I can't see the deck or Erik on it. Erik and Billy have always talked about opening up the back wall of the wheel-house with a larger window, but the engine has never been rebuilt, the sludge has not been cleaned out, and the window has never been installed. If there was ever trouble, the helmsman wouldn't know anything about it until no one came in after setting the net.

I can just see the tops of the gallows frame and the half-ton oak doors that hold open the throat of the net banging wildly from their cables. The net reel suddenly screams as the net is released, drowning out every other roaring, booming, rattling noise on the boat. I hear the cable race off the reel, the hundred-foot net running out and the huge doors thundering off the gunwales into the churning sea. I know that a dragger's deck is one of the most dangerous places a man can be, even on a calm summer day.

Gloucester is loaded with injured men—men missing fingers, arms, legs; men with furious red patches on their heads where hair used to grow; men who look fine but can no longer remember their wives' names or how to find their way home; men sitting on door stoops looking frightened still and embarrassed—men who have misstepped by a few inches, or have forgotten to focus every cell on that net reel, or who have done everything they should have but remember that sometimes cables part and take off men's heads, that doors crash to the deck and crush hard-working men. The stories get passed around and around, the teller never the one injured. The other men listen, knowing it might have been them; they cluck their tongues, suck air through their teeth, shake their heads, tell their wives to take some food up to the family. But slowly the stories accommodate the pervasive fear; jokes are inserted, men dare to laugh, and pretty soon it is all the fault of the careless, dumb son of a bitch who doesn't know how to fish.

I can't see Erik. I try to picture him scrambling for a hold every time a wave buries the deck. The worst stories—the haunting stories—are about the deck awash with no man in sight, about men being hauled in with the cod, their boots and orange gloves mixed in with the shimmering silver fish, their mouths filled with salt water like unborn babies. My body is rigid. I know that if no one comes in off that deck in twenty minutes, I will be the one to get the net in while Billy turns the boat around and gets us back to shore. I also know that if Billy lets *Jenny D* slide just once under the lip of one of the million waves rolling at us, we will swamp and go down too fast to call anyone; too fast, maybe, to fight over the two old survival suits stuffed behind Erik's bunk below.

I suddenly think of the sunlight in our small yellow bathroom at home. I want a shower, hot and steamy and silent in the soft golden glow of the light. I picture our bed, my rough, blue wool cape spread neatly over the pillows; books wait for me on the table. The pale blue morning glories I have trained on the rickety old fence by the kitchen door will be closed up tight in the storm.

The boat pitches. I listen for any sound of Erik working on deck.

I check the clock. We have been out for eight hours. Billy struggles to hold the boat along the edge of the ridge, fighting the sea moving in across the starboard beam. We listen to the depth sounder ping. Erik hauled in the net thirty minutes ago and reset it. I know he is awash on deck in glistening fish and seawater, sorting the catch into the fish pens and shoveling them into the hold. Straining on tiptoes, I look out the side window trying to see more of the deck, hoping to see Erik's bulky shape moving in his work. I can't see any movement.

Panic sweeps me, tightening my chest and throat. I think of stepping outside, peering around the edge of the wheelhouse through the driving rain to see if Erik is there, busy with the work I know by heart. I think of peering around the wheelhouse and finding no one, the deck sloshing seawater and fish. I stand frozen, uncertain.

Jenny D suddenly pitches forward and then heaves herself, bow skyward, out of the sea. Short, high barks erupt from my chest. The boat slams back down, her hull groaning and shuddering, and then the boat settles. The bilge pumps suck rhythmically below in a sudden eerie calm.

Erik's face appears in the window of the port door. I jump, then feel a rush of anger. When I unlatch the door, he fills the small wheel-house with water and wind and a ferocious, wild energy.

"Odin and I just did battle and I won!" Erik roars, his fists raised over his head.

Billy snickers. Grinning, he picks up his pipe and reaches inside his jacket for his lighter.

"What the hell were you doing, you snaky little bastard?" Erik asks him, grinning, pacing in the cramped space. "I turned around and was looking through green water!" His voice is tight with ex-citement, his eyes shining. He looks untamed, unconfined, too big and raw for this little boat.

"I couldn't see you," I say, trying to sound matter-of-fact. "I thought you were gone."

Erik peels off his drenched oilskins and throws them down the companionway stairs as we pitch and wallow in a trough. "Well, you know what to do if I don't come in from the next set, don't you?" He is laughing loudly. "You get the net on board and hustle your little ass back to Tony and tell him you want forty-three cents a pound! Tell him the mighty ghost of Erik said so!"

"Or jump overboard with rocks in my boots," I say. My voice is hard, and it erases Erik's grin.

"Let's tow for an hour," he says to Billy, flicking on the radio.

The sweet, suffocating smoke from Billy's pipe tightens the space around us all. I lean over, holding onto the compass column, and push a filthy towel around in the water on the floor. I want Erik to tell me what a good job I have done today, and I feel silly for want-ing it. I don't tell him, after all, that he has done a good job. But there is a thick silence in the midst of the storm, a waiting, a pause, that tells me he knows what I want and is not going to give it to me.

He turns to face me. "Guess what," he says. "I have a surprise you're gonna like."

He is serious, the perpetual bravado gone.

I am caught off guard. The panic starts to rise again. "What?" I say quietly. "I don't like surprises."

"You've been wanting to sell *Jenny D*, right? Do something new? Well, I sold her. We're going to Alaska."

"Alaska?" Relief starts to rush in over all the waiting. I feel a sudden gratitude and a lifting of the fear. Here is a next step, a move away from this story, a chance to find out who we each are beyond our big stories. "We are?"

"Yup. We found a boat for sale on Kodiak Island. Cheap. Billy and I are going in fifty-fifty."

I watch beads of water drop from Erik's beard to the floor. The depth sounder blips green points of light. Billy holds his lighter to his pipe, a faint hiss and bubbling of inrushing air.

"What about me?" I ask. "What am I going to do on Kodiak Island? You two are doing this? What about me?"

"You're coming."

"To do what?"

"I don't know. Whatever you want to do."

"What could I do on Kodiak Island, Erik? Why didn't you talk to me about this?"

"I don't know why you're pissed. We never tell each other what to do."

"I can't go there!"

A flicker of hurt or fear moves across Erik's face. He glances at Billy and back out the window. "Do whatever you have to do."

He adjusts his feet to take the pitch and roll of his boat, edging her along a hidden ridge of submerged granite, hunting. A wave breaks over the bow and she shakes. I stand beside Erik, my body tight, withheld. I see that my future is not rising up to meet me in ways I have ever imagined. A rush of the unceasing sadness and loneliness sweep over me. I follow his eyes out the window into the chaos of churning water.

On the third set of the day the net catches on the bottom and we lose the whole set. Luckily, we get both doors back on deck with the wrecked net. At sunset we head home, the hold half full. Erik is happy. The wind dies down as the gold light spreads like a river before us, the horizon slowly smoothing, marking the world of sky from the world of water. The boat is a mess. I clean up the wheelhouse around the men's feet, mopping salt water as best I can. I cook all the hamburger and beans and potatoes Erik bought, and we eat it all. I wash up the dishes and put them back in the cluttered cupboard, turning the latch to be sure nothing falls out the next time the boat rolls and heaves on a chaotic sea. Billy climbs into one of the grimy berths, his boots still on, and is asleep before I finish the dishes. I climb back up into the wheelhouse and lean on the counter. The sun feels good on my face, but I feel heavy, weighted. The storm is over and my fear has passed, but a different kind of dread is settling in. Erik smokes, the wheel slipping more easily now through his hands as he helps *Jenny D* lift and rise over the silver swells.

"I'm not going to Alaska," I say quietly.

"Yep. I could tell." He flicks his cigarette out the window and closes it again. Salt crusts his long beard and hair. In the sun, it looks like gray making its way into his thick, coppery hair. He adjusts the wheel, holding *Jenny D* with her load against the roll of the deflating storm. We don't speak for a long time.

"So you're going anyway?"

"Yep. We already put a deposit on the boat."

"You thought I'd just go with you."

"Yep. You're my Mama Maria. We do all this stuff together." He is very serious. His eyes are guarded. His voice is softer than I have ever heard it. We stand two feet apart, neither of us moving. He lights another cigarette.

"You're not really a Viking, you know. You're just a guy. You're scared to death and you make a lot of noise to hide it. But you can't just keep making up who you are." He turns suddenly and grins at me. "Why not? Watch me. What the hell do you think you're going to do that will be half as good as moving to Kodiak?"

"I don't know. But I don't think I can keep up anymore. I don't think I want to. This one is yours, not mine." I am afraid I am settling for something small, ordinary. But maybe ordinary is going to be a relief. Maybe inside ordinary there will be a horizon, a line between what I say I am and what I really am. And maybe on that horizon I will find some calm finally, a release from the losses that have held me to this made-up life.

"Yeah, well, you do what you need to do." Erik looks like a photograph, or an old etching in a children's book—the sun flashing through his wild beard, his strong body tired after wrestling with his Odin, his restless eyes looking out to the distance, ready for the next ordeal. I want to go home. I want to pack up my things again and move. The truth is, Erik and I love each other. The old boat slogs back to Gloucester. We'll get a great price on the fish. The stories will already be running. Later, Erik will sit at the table with the Gloucester men, cigarette held between his teeth, his eyes squinting against his own smoke, and laugh loudly as he tells his good story.

I imagine myself alone after Erik leaves for Kodiak, an ordinary young woman with a big history. The myths are done. They have helped me step from day to day for four years. I cannot picture what is coming next, how I will delineate the past from the future. The old boat makes her way steadily home in the shimmering evening sun. The land comes into view finally, a low, dark, uncertain line on the western horizon.

Chapter Seven

Without a Map

Don't be mad, I telegram James, care of the American Express office in Amsterdam. heading off alone. see you in india. The telegram takes a startling $4.50 out of the $70 I have left after paying for my hotel. James has the other $600. I feel some concern about this, but I stuff the $65.50 into my jeans pocket and walk out of the telegraph office into the streets of Luxembourg. It is a cold, drizzly, metallic winter day. I am scared, but I like the feeling.

The city is just waking up; delivery trucks park on the sidewalks, and men in wool jackets lower boxes and crates down steep stone steps to men waiting in basements below. Bare bulbs hang in the gloom; voices come in bursts of yelling and laughter. I can't understand a thing they are saying. I shoulder my new red backpack—fifty-six pounds, including the lumpy cotton sleeping bag I bought at the army/navy store—and shift it on my small shoulders until it feels less painful. The men on the street stop their work and turn to watch me walk by. One of them smiles and tips his cap. There is a murmur among them and then laughter. I feel shaky and powerful, recognizing a reckless potency as it takes over decision-making. Nothing can hurt me. I smile back at the workers, lean forward against the weight of the pack, and choose a direction. Luxembourg is silver in the morning mist. Men and women come, one by one, out onto the sidewalks to make their way to work. I walk among them, the human stream, but I have been outside that life for a long time, and make my way alone now.

James and I had been working at the difficult edges of love. I lived alone on Dartmouth Street in the Back Bay section of Boston, in a small shabby apartment with high ceilings and stained glass windows in the bathroom door. At night, I sat in the big bay window at the back of the house with the lights low, watching rats take over the nighttime alley. A man up a story across the alley stood each night at his window, watching me through binoculars. I stared back. Sometimes I filed my toenails for him, or read poetry out loud. I returned each night after work to the rats, my books, the man who watched me. I was very lonely. James and I had argued and had barely seen each other for several months. But when he came one snowy December night and asked me if I wanted to go to India with him, I immediately said yes. Maybe on the road to a faraway country I would find release from the griefs of my past.

The plan was that James would fly ahead to Amsterdam on his own. I would follow two weeks later, flying to Luxembourg on a cheap flight and taking a train to Amsterdam, where I would meet him. He would simply wait at the station on January 6 until I climbed off one of the trains, and we would start our four-month hitchhiking trip, joining the flow of American and European hippies, young people seeking adventure and maybe enlightenment in India. I was nervous as I flew to Reykjavik and on to Luxembourg, anxious about getting from the airport into the city alone, about finding a place on my own to spend the night. I decided I would just sleep in a chair at the train station, but when I got there it was locked up. It was a very cold and damp night. I didn't have the right clothes; I had packed for India, forgetting the continent in between. As I made my way to a nearby hotel, I felt inept and alone. I went to sleep worried about the train ride to Amsterdam the next day, and what would happen if James for some reason never showed up. He had almost all our money and our maps. Our only line of communication was through American Express, the hub for hitchhikers in Europe. Our plan seemed, in the damp, lonely room, flimsy and uncertain.

Before it was light, I was up, frightened. I washed in cold water at the stained sink behind the door, watching myself in the mirror. I was a girl in big trouble, and I knew this as I stared back at myself, at the guarded, haunted eyes, the tight and closed face, a record of loss. My baby, five years old now, was somewhere, maybe loved, maybe not. Mourning with no end, and a sense that I had lost every-thing—my child, my mother's love and protection, my father's love and protection, the life I had once imagined for myself—hollowed me out. I floated every day alone and disconnected, and could not find comfort or release. I understood clearly that my history had harmed me, had cut me off from the normal connections between people. Every day for five years I had been afraid of this disconnec-tion, feeling the possibility of perfect detachment within my reach, like a river running alongside, inviting me to step into its current.

Something shifted in the early morning's coming light as I looked back at the broken life reflected in the mirror. In that mo-ment, the river swept in close beside me, the current smooth and swift. I stepped in finally, reckless and grateful, a calm giving up. I had nothing more to lose. I walked toward the telegraph office. I did not care what happened to me anymore.

The winter air is heavy with sweet coal smoke as I walk and hitch-hike, following the Rhone River through eastern France. I am walk-ing blind, with no maps, and learn the names of the cities I am passing through from small brown signs: Nancy, Dijon, Lyons, Montelimar, Arles. Everything—buildings, fields, chugging facto-ries, workers' faces and clothes—is gray. Snow falls and turns to slush. I am cold and wet, but I am strangely excited. My money is go-ing fast on bread and cheese and hot soup. Each late afternoon, I have one purpose—to find a dry place to sleep where no one will find me. I am furtive as each day closes, slipping into farm sheds and fac-tory storerooms and derelict warehouses. Sometimes I am caught and an angry or indignant man or woman sends me back out into the night. I sleep lightly, listening for footsteps. If I am near a town in the morning, I like to find a public place—a café or market—and spend a few minutes warming up, my backpack resting against my legs near the sweaty windows. Often, the owner realizes I have no money to spend and shoos me out. Sometimes, a man or a young woman, a mother with a small, wide-eyed child perhaps, smiles and motions me to sit down. My French is poor: "Yes, I am walking to India," I say. "Thank you," I say again and again. I eat a pastry and drink a bowl of steaming coffee. Sometimes, a man who picks me up in his green Deux Chevaux or blue Fiat or black Mercedes pulls over at a market and buys me bread and tins of sardines and cheese. The world feels perfectly benign, generous even, and I go on my way, following the river.

I think of James, hoping he did not sit long in the train station waiting for me before he realized there was trouble, before he made his way to the American Express office and ripped open my telegram. I half-expect to see him waving at me across an intersection where roads meet and part again. I have no idea where I am.

One cold, windy day, as I walk through another little town with no name, I meet a man named Alex who is AWOL from the British army. He is tall and very, very thin, with hollowed-out cheeks and sunken eyes. His boots are rotting away; he has tied newspapers around the soles. In his dirty, wet canvas satchel, he carries a brown wool blanket, which is thin and filthy, and a miniature chess set. He has no passport. He has not contacted his family for over a year. He looks haunted, as if he no longer belongs to the world. He teaches me to play chess in the back stairwell of an apartment building. He is curt with me, and never smiles. He smells unwashed, but more than that: he seems to be fading from the world. I feel as if I am looking at myself a year from now.

Alex tells me the next morning, pointing down the empty road, Go that way until you reach the Mediterranean Sea. Turn left there. It will take you to a warmer place. I leave him sitting on a heap of stones at the edge of a field and head in the direction he pointed.

My backpack is lighter. In dirty Genoa, I sell two pairs of Levi's, my high red suede boots, a black lace shirt, and a bra to a girl from Chicago who is hitchhiking with her boyfriend. She gives me $20, and the rising worry about money that I have been trying to ignore eases. I have lost weight in just three weeks, and think about food as I walk.

I see lots of kids traveling together now that I have reached the warmer Mediterranean coast. Like me, they carry heavy backpacks and stick out their thumbs for a ride. They look happy, and well-fed, and sleep each night in a youth hostel they have chosen from their *Europe on Five Dollars a Day* guide. They congregate, little international communities, in cafés and clubs and parks in the centers of the quaint southern towns, finding a common language and sharing tales of their adventures. Sometimes I walk from town to town with someone I have met, but I feel detached from their youth and the ease with which they travel through the world.

The hole in me grows. I am becoming more and more isolated and recognize that I am walking my way into perfect disconnection. I think of my baby, a boy now, every single day. I make up stories: my baby is a boy named Thomas, with black, black hair. My baby is a boy lying on his back under a maple tree watching clouds—clouds just like these above me now—spin by on an easterly wind. He has blond curls and crooked fingers like me. He is shaped like this hole in me. I think of my mother. I think of my father. I walk under the weight of my backpack away from home.

The cobbled sidewalks in Florence have been worn down in the middle by centuries of people walking to the market and to work and back home, people who have carried burdens on their backs and in their string bags and in their hearts. The ancient stone steps of the Palazzo Medici and Pitti Palace are worn so deeply they seem to sag in the middle, as if the weight of all these lives has made its mark forever. I am at peace here, trudging down the center of the sidewalks.

I learn to steal oranges and bread and dates from indoor markets, leaving my backpack outside by the door so I can make a fast run with my day's food. At night, I comb my hair and present myself as an American college girl at the doors of *albergos*. Skeptical women in black dresses and stout shoes size me up, but each night someone agrees to take me in. In rapid-fire English, I refuse to leave my passport with them, arguing that I am going to meet friends later and will need my identification out on the city's streets. I cannot understand their answers, but if I get away with it, I find myself in a clean room with stiff white sheets on a high bed and windows looking out on a quiet side street.

I request that the hot water burner in my room be turned on, an extra cost. While the widow turns the gas valve and lights the match below the heater, I smile my gratitude. The woman doesn't smile back at me. Left alone, I put the lamp on and ease into the long tub. I soak clean in the deep steaming water, easing some of my aloneness in its embrace. I climb out, then wash my clothes in the tub and lay them for the night across the chugging radiator. In the morning, the woman brusquely brings me a tray of hard-crusted toast and sweet butter and strawberry jam in a little white pot. Later, of course, I lift my backpack onto my shoulders and quietly take the stairs past her rooms. I enter the day in Florence clean, my hunger appeased, and troubled with guilt. The beautiful old city wakes slowly while I watch, the red tiled roofs catching the coming sun as it rises over the Arno.

I make my way toward the rising sun. I no longer care about India. I have no destination. I speak briefly most days to one or two people, but I am worlds away. The road is leading in. The walking is a drug.

I cross mountains and find myself again on a sea. Rimini. Ravenna. Ferrara. Venice in the springtime, a liquid pink city. I am a reluctant but accomplished thief in these cities, stealing food and a bath and sleep. I sell a red dress I like very much and black tights and four T-shirts. I put the fifteen dollars in my pocket. I study a French girl's map and see that I am headed away from tourist cities, from food and beds, a roof. Worry nags at me. I linger in Venice, sitting in San Marco Square or on the boulevard looking across to the Lido.

Men in the freight boats on the canals call out to me with white smiles. Sometimes I smile back and a man throws fruit and small parcels of nuts or olives to me. I wave my thanks. I am thin, and wonder if they see yet that hollowed-out look I met in Alex.

On the day I walk out of Venice, I feel my son with me, a light. I want to be alone with him, and will not try to hitch a ride today.

I walk sometimes with another traveler, but I have turned inward. I am not at all lonely. I choose this way of being in the world. I know I would scare people at home. But I have nothing to say to anyone. I have not been in touch with my family since I left to meet James in Amsterdam, and their voices are finally silent in my head. My backpack is lighter. I hum Bach's *Partita No. 2* and head through Trieste to the next place that waits for me.

Beograd: I am up to my old tricks—thieving food, a bed. I hoard the thirty-six dollars in my pocket. I like this enormous country very much. Tito watches me from posters and framed photos in every building and home. The Danube makes its lazy way past the city and on to mysterious places far away. I get rested, and ease my constant hunger for food. My jeans hang from my hips. My legs are strong. I ask a soldier, "What way is Greece?" and follow his finger.

There are fewer and fewer hitchhiking kids as I move from farm town to farm town. Boys drive oxen with goad sticks, stopping to stare open-mouthed as I walk past. I sneak into barns and sheds at night, pulling my old sleeping bag snug against my neck because of the rats and mice I hear in the hay and chaff. The nights are still cold, and my army surplus bag offers no warmth at all. I curl my legs tight to my chest, trying to get warm enough to slip into a tired sleep. I have learned the arc of the sun; each morning, before the roosters call the day to a start, I slip out into the dewy gray light, orienting myself, continuing on my way.

Athens is beautiful, crisp green and white in the brilliant sun. It is crawling with travelers, and after weeks in the quiet countryside of Yugoslavia, I feel thrown back into a forgotten world. People speak to me in English and French and I understand what they are hoping for from me—momentary connection, shared experiences. I pretend I don't understand and back away without smiling.

I sell my boots to a shoe vendor on a dead-end street, and buy a used pair of sandals from him, giving me an extra $7. I sell my red sweater and all my socks and a yellow jersey. I have $21 left. I sit for long afternoons in the little parks lined with orange trees, considering what will happen when I actually can't raise more money. Going home is not an option I consider.

I live inside my brain now. The walking is an underlying rhythm for my thoughts, like an obbligato, persistent and reassuring. I have accomplished the disconnect, and my wanderings are entirely solitary, free of any voices from the past. Grief is my companion. As the child grows bigger, the hole carved in me grows, too. Silent, solitary, moving—step by step, I measure the distance between me and the woman I thought I was going to grow up to be.

Three times I try to cross the Bosporus and enter Istanbul. Gathering speed in Athens, I sweep up the coast of Greece, through Larissa and Lamia, up through Thessaloniki, through Alexandroupolis, walking, catching rides, and each time I balk at the border, unable to broach Turkey. I am hungry. I have less than $10 left. Each time, at the door to Asia, facing the dark mystery of Turkey, I stumble at the threshold, afraid.

Asia lies behind a curtain, masculine and remote and secretive, having absolutely nothing to do with me. In northern Greece, as Europe gives way to Asia, dark men sit outside their shops smoking hookahs and drinking tea from small glasses. They stare as I walk past. I feel naked, lost. There are no women anywhere. Small dusty-legged boys run in packs beside me, screaming their excitement as they jump to touch my sun-bleached hair. I am all white, a floating apparition; their dark hands and shrill voices chase me in the village streets. Nasal prayers blare from minarets, and the sun sears the land.

I slide back down the coast to Athens, confused, and worried because even here there is not enough room to move; I feel trapped. Remembering the freehand maps we drew in seventh grade, I know the world opens and extends beyond the Bosporus, and I want to be lost in its expanse. Again I roar up the coast. Sometimes rich men in Mercedes pick me up. They feed me at restaurants hidden in the hills and smile at me, baffled and aroused. Again and again I approach the shadowy world that sprawls beyond Europe.

Finally, too tired to turn around, I slip into Istanbul at night and let a kind young student lead me to the cellar where he rents a room with four others. I do not go out for three days, paralyzed with fear. And then one morning, pushing myself to recklessness again, I leave the dark hideaway. Muezzins chant their minor-key call to prayer from the minarets of the mosques. I gather my things and enter the old bazaar. It is dark and dreamy and heavy; wool rugs and pungent spices and dates and plastic dolls tumble from doorways into the alleys. I spend one dollar on a length of dark cloth and a needle, and, sitting in a wavering pool of light within the gloom, I sew a shapeless shift, long and loose. I sell my last blue jeans, and my bra and my sandals, and, finally, my pack. I save my belt, which I pull tight around my rolled sleeping bag.

I have heard I can get three hundred dollars for my passport. I make my way slowly through the labyrinth of shops and paths, watching for men who might return my gaze and invite a deal. I wander in the maze, making eye contact with the dark men who embody danger. Everywhere, men slide next to me, touch my arm insistently, and whisper, "Hashish? Hashish?" "No money," I say, emboldened, and then, "Passport? Passport?" The men move away quickly. I know I have scared them.

I am lost. The bazaar is an ancient city of stone tunnels, roofed in places with great vaulting domes. It is dark and very noisy. Children run past, barefoot and dark-eyed. They pull back against the scarred walls when they see me, so different from the brazen village boys. I walk slowly, watching the men. "Hashish?" "No. Passport?" Finally a man stares back at me and signals for me to follow. A small man with a sharp nose and scuffed-down shoes, he leads me for five minutes through the maze, without glancing back at me once. He stops at a stall selling spices from big wooden barrels; the bright orange and green and yellow and red and brown spices fill the alley with a rich, heavy smell, mysterious and seductive. The man speaks to a younger man sitting high behind the barrels. That man stares at me coolly. I make myself stare back. He nods, then says something to the older man, who turns to me and says in English, "Twenty-five dollars."

"No," I say. I am shocked—I know that what I am doing is a serious crime. It has to be worth it. "No. Three hundred dollars."

Both men return my look of shock. They shake hands with each other, and the younger man motions me away. I hesitate, but he yells something at me and I turn away. I am shaken. My plan seems naïve and unworkable. Later, I spend four dollars on a large, peaty chunk of hashish; I sew it into the hem of my shift to sell when I need money.

I need food. A fat man watching me from his stall with serious eyes calls me to him. He doesn't smile as he puts me in a chair and lays a tin plate in front of me. He hacks the head off the lamb roasting in his brazier and places it on the plate. I spend an hour picking and sucking every sweet bit from the skull. The man shakes his head when I offer him money. I wander through the bazaar, watching at the end of each tunnel for the light outside, the path out. Then I head south with seventeen dollars.

Beyond the city, across the Dardanelles, I am free in that vast far-off space I remember from my childhood maps. This is where I want to be. Nothing here is like home. The disconnect is complete. I sleep alone under the trees at night. It rains some nights, and I am cold and wet. I share dark sheds with small animals, rats, I think, and I sneak out before dawn when men come to do their chores. The land is spare and mimics my stripped life. Voices call across the hills, shepherds as alone as I am. Goat bells answer. Calls to prayer. Wind. Everything has slipped. I am not me anymore.

It is warm in southern Turkey, and very dry. I am always thirsty. My bare feet are strong and calloused. The land is beautiful, rolling and arid and silent. This is an enormous place. I am lost in it.

For several days, I have been following a dusty track winding south. I don't know how far away the coast is and can't remember how it fits on the planet. I think the Middle East comes after Turkey, and I head that way. I have forgotten about India, the hitchhiker's mecca. I am wandering. The track has been getting smaller and smaller, and now I know I am on an animal trail, or maybe a shepherd's path. It winds up and over the dry brown hills. I have not seen a house or shepherd's hut for two days. Sometimes I hear the heavy *tonk* of goat bells on the distant hills. I am not lonely. I hear my steps muffled in the stone dust, and the pulse of blood in my ears. I hum a fragment from Bach, the same bit over and over. I am hungry.

Night comes quickly here. In the near-dark I feel the clinking of pottery under my feet; I am walking on tiny mosaic tiles. Fragments, brilliant blue and yellow even in this erasing light, stretch for hundreds of feet in the sparse grass. I know nothing. I know no history. When did Homer live? The Trojan War—could that have been here? Crete. Minoans. Phoenicians. Did they lay these bits of clay? I have no sense of what belongs where, or when. I am old, an old woman walking across time in the dust. Other women have walked here. Other women, I know, have been alone. I feel a momentary jolt of connection, of steadying order.

A small stone building, round and low, rises in the dark. I feel my way to a door. I have to step down three feet to the floor, where more tiles crackle each time I step. It is damp and smells green inside. I feel for the roof—it is a low dome, and tiles clap to the floor when I touch them. There is a raised platform in the middle, an oblong, covered in tiles. I listen, but hear no rats. Pleased with my find for the night, I spread my sleeping bag on the platform and wrap myself up as well as I can against the coming cold.

I wake abruptly in the night, knowing suddenly that this is an ancient tomb. I am a trespasser. I am in over my head. The old, deep shame creeps back to me. Glued to that altar all night, I stare straight into the pitch-black dome. At dawn I crawl up into the faint light, the air, the patterns of lives etched for millennia in the soil. On my hands and knees, I study the tesserae of the mosaic design, searching for clues, a map for how a life gets lived, how it all can be contained, how the boundaries can hold against the inexpressible and unnamed. How I can hold against the past. People called to God in this place, a god who was, I think, furious and harsh. I am not ready. I may never be ready. I gather my sleeping bag and walk toward the rising sun.

Night is coming. I am somewhere in southern Lebanon, on the coast, in a place I can't name. I need to find somewhere to sleep before it is dark. On a narrow beach I discover a cement-block house still standing, its roof and one wall blasted away. Its whitewash gleams in the dusk, and it is oddly tidy. The shattered glass, the splinters of wood, the furniture and clothes and dishes that must have been left behind when the Israeli mortar shells flew through the night—everything has been scrubbed clean by the winds and shifting sand. Eddies in its corners have left tiny dunes. I push them flat with a sweep of my arm and drop my sleeping bag. It is all I carry now, this bag rolled and bound with my belt; my passport, my pocketknife, and matches are tucked into the foot. I shake out the bag, dirty and musty, and lay it neatly in the corner of the ruins. I slide my passport back inside, and lay the matches on top. I keep the knife in my hand. In the deep dusk, I wander the beach, gathering driftwood. The little fire whooshes up, and I am home.

I have not eaten today, and have no food for tonight. The bats are out, as always, their syncopated bursts felt but not seen. The Mediterranean Sea is not dramatic. It pulses in and out softly, in and out in the dark. Sparks snap and rise. The nights are chilly and I am cold. I am always cold at night, my body too thin now to generate enough heat. My bag is lumpy with wadded cotton batting and only serves to keep the bats from touching my skin. I am almost content. I am free from most things. Recklessness has become a drug, and I am walking stoned. I live in my head, all eyes and ears, a receptor with nothing to return. I have no heart anymore and cannot be afraid.

I hear men shouting suddenly. They come nearer. I can hear their pants legs swishing up the beach, and the clatter of what I instantly know are weapons. I wait in the dark, hoping they will march past me, past my small fire, past this already ruined house. They stop in the gaping hole that was a wall, soldiers in camouflage with automatic weapons drawn. There are six of them. I stay sitting, wrapped in my flimsy bag. They are very young, some with no hair on their cheeks at all. One of them, short and thick, is older, my age, maybe twenty-one or twenty-two; he shouts at me. I cannot tell if they are Israeli or Lebanese. Maybe I have walked out of Lebanon and into Israel along the shore. I don't know where I am, or what the soldiers are protecting, and I know I am in trouble.

"Passport?" the stocky one demands. I know enough not to hand it to them. It will bring them quick cash and I will never see it again. My answer is long, as if there is a logic to my presence on their beach, as if there has been no War of '67, as if I know what I'm doing here. He shouts at me. I don't know if it is Hebrew or Arabic. "Passport!" I hear in English.

Suddenly one of the boys jostles another, points at me with his elbow, and says something. I know what it must be. They all laugh, excited and a little embarrassed. I flare to life after all these months and I am suddenly afraid. I do not dare to stand up. My dress is thin, and I have no underwear.

My fire has died to a glow. They shove each other and giggle and jostle as if they are drunk, but they are not. They are soldiers, a team, and no one knows I am here. They sit in a semicircle around me, their rifles across their laps, their smooth olive hands and cheeks luminescent in the night. They are quiet for minutes at a time, watching me. Then they burst into joking laughter. I sit silent, tense, surprised that I care so much suddenly what happens to me. The bats flick down around our legs and heads and shoulders. The stars are out, the Milky Way stretching across two seas to my other life. I am sitting on my passport, my little knife gripped in my hand. I stare back at these boys, these boys with guns, and I am puffed like a frightened bird to make myself seem brave.

I sit, stiff and cold. Suddenly all the walking away from my past, from my home, from the baby I abandoned in a hospital, alone, just born; from my mother, cold, her love evaporated; from my father, his love withdrawn; from the child I was myself—all the walking has taken me nowhere. Here I am, alone and scared. I remember the days after my baby was born. My young breasts, still a girl's, were large and tight and hard, swollen with milk. My shirt was soaked. I stood over the bathroom sink, crying, pressing the milk from my breasts. My milk flowed, sticky and hot, down the drain of the sink. I could hear my lost baby cry for me from someplace far away, as if my own cry echoed back to me.

I clutch my arms tight to my breasts and face the soldiers who surround me. The night goes on slowly, hour by wary hour. The tides are small here, and the creep of the sea is no measure of time. Occasionally the stocky leader shouts at me, asking for my passport. "American?" he asks. "Yes. American," I say emphatically. "Passport!" he demands again and again. I shrug my shoulders, gesturing no, as if these are my lines in the play we are all rehearsing. Not one of us moves. The constellations reel around the polestar, and we sit through the deep night. In the quiet minutes, one or another lifts his rifle, clacking and clipping metal against metal as he opens and closes the breach. The sound bangs against the bombed-out walls and echoes back to us. They laugh.

At the first seep of light, the leader suddenly rises. The other boys jump to their feet, brushing sand from their laps. They all look frayed with sleeplessness. The leader stands upright and nods to me. They all turn without speaking and move back down the beach in a slow drifting line. I shake my bag out, place my passport and matches and knife in the foot, and strap my belt around it. Images rise: my mother's face turned from me; the white and metal hospital where I left my baby; my swollen breasts, my milk slipping slowly in thick lines down the sink. The sand in the bombed-out house is scuffed in a half-circle around me. Suddenly I don't know if these boys spent this long night threatening me or protecting me.

I don't know where I am. My fear settles again as I walk. I head north, pretty sure I'm in Lebanon.

It is my birthday. I want ritual. This place in Lebanon is called Jbeil, "the beautiful place." I wash slowly in the Mediterranean Sea at dawn, dipping my head back into the cool, still water, an anointment. I wash my dress, and sit for the rest of the day on a long smooth ledge which falls away into the water. I have been feeling the disengagement acutely, the absolute lack of attachment. It frightens me, because I know I have slipped into the deepest current and may not come back. But I like the narcotic of walking and will not stop. I know the roads to Damascus and Latakia and Tyre. The walking claims ground as mine, and I am as much at home here as I have been anywhere since I was sixteen.

Between me and my mother, me and my father, me and my castaway child, beyond this quiet sea, is the dark and raging Atlantic. The sun on the Mediterranean stuns the mind. I am blank. I am here, in this beautiful place. I am alone. I have nothing.

It is hot, dry, brown, peaceful in the hills. I wander from Syria to Jordan to Lebanon to Syria. I am among Palestinian refugees. Soldiers with machine guns lie behind sandbag bunkers on every corner in every country. The low, flat roofs are sandbagged, and soldiers train their rifles on the dusty streets below. I know that Israel invaded Palestine in 1949. I know that Israel occupied Jordan's West Bank and Syria's Golan Heights in the War of '67; armies of American kids joined the kibbutz movement to help the Jews come home. I don't know anything else, except that the Palestinian refugees suffer. They live in vast tent cities along every highway, and in crowded warrens of shacks in every town. Everyone, Arab and Jew, has lost someone; some have lost everyone. They try to tell me their stories, and weep. My own grief feels smaller here.

I walk with no plan, through Ba'albek and Masyaf and Saida and Sabkha and back through Masyaf. In every place, men and women greet me with hands extended. They smile, drawing me in as if I belong to them. I have no idea who they think I am. They share food with me, flatbread and warm tangy yogurt from the bowl on their door stone; it always means they leave their own meal hungry. A woman beating a rug in her yard calls to me as I walk by her house. She looks sad and tired, like all the people here. She holds up her hand: Wait. I sit against the low cement wall surrounding her dusty yard. In ten minutes she comes to me with two eggs, fried warm and runny and life-saving, and flatbread to sop it up. She stands smiling while I eat, her black skirt and thin black shoes powdered with dust, her hens wandering near us, pecking in the dirt.

Several teeth ache. Sometimes in the city I steal packets of aspirin from vendors. When I can't sleep, I lay one against the gum. It burns the tissue, but I sleep.

I sell my blood to the Red Cross whenever I am in a city. Three dollars, enough for a visa to cross back into Syria or Lebanon or Jordan. I try to hide the bruise from last time; sometimes they scold me and send me away. Sometimes they need the blood badly and reach for the less-bruised arm. I feel vestiges of a familiar shame, broad and deep, with these American and European workers. They ask me if my family knows where I am. I always say yes. They ask, What are you doing here? But I have no answer for them and leave quickly with my three dollars.

Abrahim offers me hot bread from the doorway of his shop. He speaks some English, and tells me that he is getting married. He brings me home to his mother in As Sarafand, the refugee camp south of Beirut. She chatters at me in Arabic while she and four other women crowd around the fire to cook for the feast. There is joy here. I have forgotten this kind of happiness, happiness that looks forward. I stay in this tiny plywood and tin house for three days, basking in the large, soft peace of family. I sleep with Abrahim's sisters on mats on the floor; his father snores, and his mother murmurs to him in the night until he stops. I leave on the morning of the wedding. Abrahim's mother wraps a black and white kaffiyeh around my shoulders as I leave. I feel a new stab of dread as I walk away, unsure in which direction to head.

The nights are very cold. I have no jacket, no sweater, no shoes. I squat by my little fire, the kaffiyeh wrapped around my head and neck. I am always hungry. I have slept on this rocky beach in Syria for two weeks. The first few days, just before dusk, a very old man walked the length of the beach with his sheep; he murmured to them as they rustled, grazing, among the debris of seaweed and trash. He didn't look at me.

Then one night, he came across the beach toward me, his sheep following. He was very thin and everything about him was dark—his frayed wool jacket and his old shoes and dirty cap and his lined face. He smiled at me; he had two teeth, both on top. He spoke softly to me in the same vowelly voice he used to herd his animals. Kneeling by my small fire, he took a leather sack from his belt. He used the dented little pot inside to milk out one of the ewes, the milk hissing again and again against the tin. She stood for him without moving. His voice hushed in the falling light, he put the pot on the fire. The milk quickly boiled up. He jerked it off the fire and dumped a brown clump of sugar into the creamy foam, stirring it with a stick. Sitting back on his heels, he waited while the milk cooled and gave it to me.

He watched me drink it down, delicious and sustaining. I came to life. He nodded and smiled and smiled.

Every night now he stops and warms ewe's milk and sugar for me, talking to me softly like a father to a child. His old hands are creased and knobby. I don't want him to leave, and I drink the milk slowly, holding him to me. I am nourished, and feel a father's care. All day I wait for him, feeling how mute I am, how distant I have become from anything I once knew.

One night I try to tell him that I have a child. I hold up six fingers, and show my belly large and round. I point to the west, across the sea. I very much want him to understand. He finally makes a loud, kind noise of understanding, laughing knowingly, smiling and nodding. But I know he cannot imagine what I am talking about. That night I feel very alone under the black sky.

I say good-bye to him after I have drunk the milk he offers. He smiles and nods at me, and turns several times to wave good-bye as he makes his way with his sheep, their bells *tonk*ing their hollow peaceful course along the shore.

It is always almost night, the time when I must find a place to lay down my sleeping bag, a place to attach myself for a few hours. The decision feels enormously important every night. When I am tired, the unspoken thoughts that ride under the rhythms of my walking begin to seep out and over an edge I cannot protect. I feel at this haunting hour like a stray animal, desperate for warmth of any kind. Each night I watch the country go gray, then black. I keep walking. Voices I know—my mother's, my father's, mine, the cry of a child—press at my back.

In a dusty field, twenty women stoop, preparing the rocky soil for planting. Many of them have babies tied with bright cloths to their backs. Small children stand listlessly by their mothers in the sun. I am walking on a track from nowhere that skirts the field. Heads come up and watch me, but they continue their work. The children stare, slowly turning to follow me with their eyes as I pass. The dust rises. The barren hills lift behind us onto the high plain. Suddenly, at a signal I cannot see, the women stand and call their children out of the field for their midday meal, moving together toward me on the path.

I am suddenly struck with shyness. I cannot remember how I got here, what it is I am looking for. I don't know if I have found it, if it can be found. I am outside the world, drifting. I don't think I am lost, but I cannot explain where I am. I want so much all of a sudden, but I cannot name what it is. I am empty and very tired. I don't know where to walk next. I don't want these women, with their babies and their gray dusty feet and hands and careful eyes, to wonder what brought me here. Things gone rise up in a flood. Suddenly I am scared of myself and of how far I have drifted.

The women do not speak to me. They lift the baskets they have left by the road and sit to eat their meals on the little ridge of hard dirt beside the field. I walk along in front of the women and children, feeling exposed. We eye each other; the children lean against their mothers. Goats bleat far off in the hills.

Suddenly a woman smiles up at me and wags her hand— Stop. She is wearing a 1950s short-sleeved sweater, bright red. She swings her dark-eyed baby onto her lap from her back and opens her bag. She lifts her sweater up over her swollen breast, her skin the same soft dusk as the soil around her. Holding a dented tin cup under her breast, she presses milk, creamy white, hissing again and again, into the tin. She smiles against the brilliant sun as she hands it to me. I hesitate, then take the cup, sitting down beside her in the dirt. She lifts her child to the same breast. The other women nod and smile while I sip the milk. It is hot and thick and sweet. For a few minutes, I am bound to this woman, a mother, to her baby, to these women and their children. I remember what it is to belong, to be loved. I imagine my child loved somewhere.

For a few moments, I am suspended within this circle. But I do not belong here, and when the cup is empty, I slowly get up. Nodding again and again, I wave to the woman in the red sweater. A different hunger steals into me. Memories of my old life—when I was a girl in a family, a girl with dreams of the life coming to me—flash white and clear as I start to walk away. I want to go home, home to my adult life, with its losses carved forever in my path, with its possibilities, like unformed clouds, calling me forward. I head back the way I came, against the current, orienting myself north and west, back toward the Atlantic. The sun is warm. Behind me, I can hear the women and children talking and laughing as they eat and rest. Their voices rise in soft floating prayers as I walk.

Chapter Eight

A River of Light

It is late Christmas Day, eight years since I have seen my father, since I have been forbidden to enter my father's house. My new son, Alex, is six weeks old. I am filled to bursting with happiness, with love and completion and gratitude. I hold my baby and nurse my baby and sing to him and sleep with him and walk in the pure clear beauty of winter with him.

There is a lot that should make this holiday complicated and sad. I am twenty-seven. I am with my mother, ailing now, and with my sister and brother and their families. We all walk carefully around my history, never speaking of any of it, especially not of my father's abandonment of me and their decisions to silently comply with this family outcasting. By now I know my role in this holiday routine by heart: Christmas Eve and Christmas Day in my mother's little house. Polite laughter and food and presents. Then, in a chaotic swoosh, Michael and Sandy and their families will pack up food and their presents for my father and drive thirty minutes to Epping, to his and Catherine's house for their other Christmas. I am not welcome. I will stay at my mother's, imagining Christmas with my father. No one speaks of any of this; my troubles are an intrusion on family peace. I am stunned by the grief of loss, by the injustice. By the terrible, aching missing of my father.

But this Christmas, I hold my perfect baby, Alex. I decide during the afternoon of brewing emotions, joy and loss, that my father would like to meet this grandson. I decide that I will go to my father, holding my baby, that I will go with my brother and my sister, and my baby and I will enter my father's magical circle of love again. I decide that what has happened will come to an end. But my sister and my brother risk too much by defying the outcasting, and refuse to ride over with me. I am very tough, and don't flinch. I pack up my baby and my presents for my father and Catherine. I put tiny Alex in his car seat and drive my own car to Epping. Everyone else rides in my brother's car. I follow them over the snowy dark roads, their brake lights and the backs of their heads to me, my son's face a beautiful calm oval in the dashboard light.

My father and Catherine have finished restoring their large old colonial house since I was there, pregnant and hiding, ten years before. The old maple trees stand bare by the driveway. Terraced gardens covered in drifts of snow spill over stone walls from the front door. Candles burn at each window. Cars I don't recognize sit in the yard, my father's and Catherine's. My brother pulls in by the barn and my family climbs out, their arms loaded. They hurry past my car, not pausing. I don't know what to do. The formal side door opens as they approach. My father—my father!—stands by the door, large and gray-haired and handsome. Light pours over him, pours out onto the walkway. Each member of my family—my brother, my sister, his wife and her husband, their children, the family—file past my father. He hugs each one. He smiles. I hear laughter. As she enters the house, my sister turns and nods toward my car. I sit in the dark, looking up the river of light to my father. The door closes, and the river abruptly disappears.

Alex sleeps. I can't move. Shame floods me. I scold myself. "Stupid. You are so stupid. Stupid stupid stupid girl." Figures move across the windows in the warm light inside. I can't find my father. I am suddenly sobbing, trying to find the ignition and turn the key. Just then, the door opens again. The light! My father stands framed in the light. He leaves the door open, walking slowly toward me, toward us. I don't know if I should open the door and get out. He comes to the window. I roll it down and say hello.

"Hi, Meredy," he says, smiling awkwardly.

"Hi, Dad. This is your grandson Alex." I wrestle with the straps of the baby seat and lift Alex toward my father. I feel as if I am making an offering.

He looks at my son and says, "I'm not nuts about babies."

"Well," we both say, as I buckle my son safely back into his seat. My father doesn't hug me or touch me.

"You know how much I love you," he says. "This goddamned situation with Catherine and you. I don't know why you two want to do this to me. Things will change. I promise."

He walks back up the river of light and I drive back over the white snowy roads to my mother's house in Hampton.

Chapter Nine

Double Vision

The movie always starts here and returns here: I am sixteen, and I am pregnant. Today, I have been expelled from school, a shamed girl.

"Meredy!" my mother calls out as she comes in from work, her voice sharp with fury. "Meredy!"

I feel everything—my childhood, my trust in love, my belief in my own goodness, my innate connection to my mother—shake under the tone of her voice.

"You're pregnant, aren't you?" she asks.

"Yes," I say quietly.

"Go call your father and tell him what you have done."

Later, my father asks, "Do you want to marry this boy?"

"No," I say.

"Now what?" my father asks my mother.

"Well," she says vehemently. "She can't live here."

The film ends. The moment of fracture. My mother loved me. My mother exiled me when I was in terrible trouble. There was a qualifier to her love, a condition, which I struggle still to understand. My mother was a good and loving mother. Until I most needed that love. Reckoning: two mothers. I chase one truth, a single truth that transcends the contradictions. She and I are caught forever in a perpetual dance, bound by love and the mystery of its betrayal.

The sound of my mother's typing carries from her room down the short narrow hall to mine. I love this sound: *clack clack clack clack clack*

cluck ding, vrrrrr, clack clack ckack clack clack clack ding, vrrrrr. I am on my bed, reading in the sun. I am eight years old, so I might be reading *Black Beauty* or *The Yearling.* The clean sharp rhythm of my mother's typing is like an old engine chugging again and again, *Safe, safe, safe, safe here, yes, you are safe safe safe safe here.* I know her lean hands work over the keys at lightning speed. She never makes a mistake. It is too costly, the messy rubbed-out place and the smudged carbon beneath. *Clack clack clack clack ding, love love love love always,* my mother at work on some small and careful business, me in my room, the house spotless beyond my door, all the places I cannot see but know by heart tended to by my mother, kept in order, home. *Clack clack clack clack ding, safe safe loved loved here,* steady and fast, my mother's rhythm, capable and a little impatient, while the sun slides slowly and evenly across my blue bed.

My mother's typewriter is an ancient, upright black machine with beautiful gold letters spelling *Royal* in script across the front. Cracked and yellowed glass disks cover the names of each letter. Nothing is in order, the alphabet jumbled inexplicably. My mother isn't thrown off. Her fingers race across the keys in little taps. Pale silver arms stretch at lightning speed from their amphitheater bed and strike the paper, *clack clack clack clack clack clack ding vrrrrr.* When my mother presses the cap button with her little finger, the whole carriage rises and an upper case letter is imprinted on the page. When the little bell rings *ding* my mother's right hand flies to the long bright bar, *vrrrr.* The paper rolls up a notch and my mother's fingers fly again, filling the line left to right with tiny and perfect words.

I like the typewriter and often try to type. I always lay the carbon paper wrong way up and print my letter on the back of itself. *Dear Mummy, I love you. I will be in my room. Do you love me? Love, Meredy.* I fold the paper into a small square, find and address one of her envelopes, and leave it on her pillow or beside her brush in the bathroom.

The typewriter ink is embedded in a ribbon threaded against the paper between two spools. I like to turn the spools with my finger, spinning all the ribbon to one end with a tiny mechanical ratcheting and then back, the smooth hum, retrieving the spool. My mother doesn't like me to touch the ribbon because I confuse the setup, running ahead or sliding behind on the part that still has ink. And my fingers become smudged, then the keys, then the paper, then the desk.

Clack clack clack clack clack clack ding, vrrrr, my mother's rhythm so sure, so safe, so constant.

My mother is a secretary, working for Noel Solomon's insurance office, and later, the magazine. She is good at her work. She graduated from high school in Haverhill, Massachusetts, at sixteen, having skipped two grades along the way. Too poor to pay for college, she took the train into Boston each day for two years and earned a certificate in secretarial work. My mother's penmanship is beautiful, the Palmer Method, with its big looping grace. When she talks with her friends Margie or Marcia on the phone in the kitchen, she covers scraps of paper with long, perfect coils of *O*'s, like tunnels leading nowhere. Roaring with laughter at some shared joke, Mum sweeps her arm over the page, tracing *O*'s without a hitch. She types like a demon, and knows shorthand; she teaches me to write my name and *I love you* in her mysterious code. Years later, I will still have day calendars she kept by her bed in which all her secrets are noted in small, careful shorthand. It is a dead art, I think; I will never meet anyone who can decode them for me, so I will look sometimes at the odd, half-finished symbols and wonder—Did she record my father's comings and goings? His final going? Our fights? Her worries about money? Her dreams? She always wanted to be a writer, a journalist. These bits are her only manuscript, a fragmented testimony to her full and separate life, kept forever from us.

I don't know where or when my mother and father met. I do know that my father was also an only child, and that he, too, skipped two grades of school, graduating from nearby Lawrence High School sometime in the late 1930s. I think they were in love. My sister has a tiny oval photograph that was once in a locket; my parents' faces are pressed together, and they are grinning for the camera. They married on an August day just before the war and moved to a little rented cottage in Granby, Connecticut, where my sister, Sandy, was born. My mother speaks of this house and this baby and this time with so much joy and longing that it becomes entangled for me with fairy tales: Snow White and Rapunzel and Granby. I learn to long for it, too. Then things seemed to become complicated quickly. My mother and sister and the next baby, Michael, lived with my grandmother in her apartment in Haverhill while my father worked somewhere else. They were still dreaming, though. They bought land in Hampton on the coast of New Hampshire, and built their own little box of a house. I was born that spring, and my father left for good ten years later. My mother never got over his going; she would love him until she died. I know that her grief was deep and frightening for her. I grew up in a strange and intimate climate of love, private sadness, private loss, courage, and a mother's duty.

Sometimes, I wake to my mother crying on the couch in the night. I lie in my bed, the lights from the cars on High Street careening across the walls of my room, the light breaking and streaking on at each wallpapered corner. Frightened, I lie in my bed weeping with her, helpless. I sink on those nights inside my mother's dark life, understanding that she cries beyond me, beyond her love for me, beyond anything I can fix.

My mother is a miracle of perpetual motion. On two pots of percolated coffee and a pack of Winstons, my mother goes to work and comes home and cleans and gardens and cooks her way through each day and long into the night, singing George Gershwin and Ella Fitzgerald tunes. She waxes the floors on her hands and knees with Butcher's Wax. When my brother, Michael, and I come home from school, she puts her old wool socks on our feet and tells us to skate

until the floors shine. She changes the wallpaper or makes new curtains on a bored Saturday. Sometimes Sandy and Michael and I come
out of our rooms early in the morning to find the couch reuphol-
stered in red or green or gold. "Do you like it?" She beams at us. She
strips and refinishes chairs and dressers and beds. She sews clothes
for herself and Sandy and me, pleated wool skirts and jumpers and
sundresses from curtains she has taken down a month before. Her
gardens slowly spread around the house, pansies and hollyhocks and
winter creeper and pinks that smell like cloves. Until Michael is old
enough, she mows the lawn and shovels the driveway. She cleans the
fireplace and keeps red paint on the clapboards and replaces wiring
in old lamps and helps Sandy build pens in the garage for her sheep.
We wear her knitted mittens and sweaters when it snows. At Christmas she spray-paints milkweed pods or pinecones or fir boughs with
white and gold paint and decorates every surface of the house with
balsam and candles. In bitter wind sweeping up from the beach a
mile away, she stands on the stepladder and tucks gaudy blue and red
and gold Christmas lights around the yews by the front door.

And she reads. Trash when I am small, then bestsellers, and later
Loren Eiseley and Shakespeare and C. S. Lewis and Homer. An in-
somniac, she reads in the long quiet of the sleeping house. The next
morning, we hear her moving quickly around the house, humming
as she meets the new day head-on.

"Okay, Meredy," she says. "Concentrate. What card do I have this
time?"

My mother is in the bathtub. I am four or five years old, kneeling beside the tub, leaning in, overjoyed to be playing our game. The
room is warm and close with steam, with sunlight luminous in the
hanging mist. Here, she is slowed, the day's chores ignored, and she
is all mine for these minutes.

"Ummm," I say.

"Think," she says softly, smiling at me, the playing card curled
in her hand away from me. "What is in my mind?"

She is thin and strong and naked in the water, my beautiful mother, her knees and small breasts visible above the line of steamy water. I want to look like her. I want to be her.

I stare into her eyes, eager, embraced.

"The four of hearts," I whisper. It is not a question; I know.

"Yes, my love." She leans up and kisses my cheek as she puts the card back in the deck face-down. "It's as if we share one mind, isn't it?" She settles back into the tub, the water sloshing lazily. "Okay. What do I have now?"

I concentrate, flooded with her love, with my belonging to her. I feel the sun on my back as I stare into her eyes. We are one person, my mother extended into me, her youngest child. I know she finds her reflection in me, and I am happy to be absorbed into her.

But somehow my mother is always just out of reach. She appears to be present, loving me, yet she always feels elusive, illusory. Once, when I am ten, I come home from school instead of going to a friend's house. I am astonished to hear someone playing the piano, a jazzy piece rolling surely, powerfully, emotionally through the house and out into the yard. It is my mother. I have never heard her play; I have never seen her touch the piano. I stand quietly in the kitchen, confused and awed. I want to rush to her, to share this miracle with her. But I feel like a trespasser, and hang back, uncertain.

Suddenly she stops. "Meredy? Meredy! Is that you?" I come into the living room, smiling, scared. "That was amazing, Mum. When did you learn to do that?"

My mother jumps off the bench and slams the cover to the keys down hard. The metal strings boom and echo in the hushed room.

"Don't you ever sneak up on me like that again. Shame on you. How dare you sneak up on me?" She walks past me, down the hall, and into her room. I don't see her again until supper. After I go to bed, I listen for her, hoping she will go back down the hall, lift the cover of the piano, and fill the house with her music. But I don't hear a sound all night long.

I find out, somehow—I'm sure she does not tell me—that my

mother has been taking lessons secretly from Miss Mears on Mill Road for six years. She works full-time, so I don't know when she practices. But after that day she never takes another lesson. She never plays the piano again.

My mother lives a separate and intensely private life. She loves me. But she withholds herself, guards herself, and I know the boundaries clearly.

When I am five, we all catch chicken pox at once. My mother must be miserable with the illness, but she tends to us as she always does when we are sick—ginger ale with a curlicue straw, cool baths, smoothed sheets. This time, she also reads to us, maybe because it allows her to lie down. It is the first memory I have of being read to. She has saved the weekly installments of *The Borrowers* by Mary Norton, carefully tearing each chapter out of *Women's Circle* and stapling the final packet at the upper corner. The type is in two columns, broken by small, lively paintings of tiny Pod, the father; Homily, the mother; and their daughter, Arrietty; of Mrs. Lender's wicked cat who hunts like mice the little people I come to love; of the grandfather clock that hides the hole down into their cozy home below the floor; of the things Pod borrows from the people upstairs to get by—empty thread spools, a small potato, a hankie dropped by a chair, a hatpin large enough to serve as their curtain rod. I most love the little paintings of Homily sewing by the coal grate with Arrietty nearby, mother and daughter warm and safe beyond the world.

My mother lies in her bed with us for three days, everyone burning with fever and itching and aching, and carries us into an imagined world. It electrifies me. I learned to read before I started school, but beyond Dick and Jane I have never understood what is there for me, waiting. My mother was never read to, I am sure, and has not read to me. I watch her read paperbacks every evening, but I don't understand that someone, a stranger, has imagined a full and instructive world for me. Sick, squeezed uncomfortably between my brother and sister, I move into my imagination and Arrietty's world.

I feel proud of my mother. She reads in a soft, smooth, low voice, and turns the thin precious pages without crumpling them. She runs her finger over the little paintings, pointing out each detail, drawing me deeper and deeper into the story. But most of all I am proud because my mother is so much like Homily. They each love their daughter and say kind, gentle things to her. They each sew nice clothes and tablecloths and curtains from scraps they manage to secure. They cook good food and serve it to their family, and ask each day about the child's adventures. I understand that Homily is a good mother, exactly what Arrietty wants and needs, and I come to see in that bed that my mother is a good mother. As she carries me into the explosive new world of books, I am grateful. Here is my loving mother, finding another gift for me.

We are a perfect family, my mother tells us again and again. She is an irreproachable mother. But when I am small, I wander around the house at her side, asking many times a day, "Do you love me, Mummy? Do you love me?" She always says, yes, of course I love you. "How much?" I ask. "How much do you love me?" This much, she always says, stretching her arms wide. "That isn't enough," I say, afraid. "How much do you want?" she asks. "More," I say. "I want to feel your love."

I once saw a demonstration of Prince Rupert's drops. They are beautiful—small, perfect, delicate teardrops of clear glass with long, delicate tails. What is remarkable about them is that you can lay them on their sides and slam them with a hammer without breaking them. They are made by dripping molten glass from the end of a rod into ice-cold water. The rapid quenching cools the outside quickly, causing it to contract onto the inner core of the teardrop. The outer skin, then, is in great tension, because of the incompressibility of the core.

A hammer blow can't break a Prince Rupert's drop. But if any pressure at all is exerted against its long, thin tail, a crack races down through the core in a flash, creating an outlet for the hidden tension. Suddenly, from the slightest touch to the tail, the drop explodes, the shattered bits flying across the room.

I am a child. Then I am pregnant. My mother says, *Go away from me*. The fragility of her love, the violent moment of tension let loose. The perfect girl with the perfect mother in the perfect family, exploding in a flash.

Our little town of Hampton is in the direct path of the great and destructive hurricanes of the 1950s and early '60s. My mother loves these storms. Her anticipation rises as the reports come in with stronger and stronger warnings: eighty-five-mile-an-hour winds, tape your windows, check the batteries in your transistor radio, put food and jugs of water and blankets in your cellar, plan your evacuation route. My father is never home for these storms. We live a mile from the shore, close enough to make our new little house shake for hours through the worst of each storm. My mother gets ready. She climbs the ladder and tapes the windows, nails the back door shut, brings in the wheelbarrow and chairs, takes down the clothesline. She tells my sister and brother and me to lay rolled towels on every windowsill to catch the rain that will soak through on the driving wind, to bring in firewood and gather the storm candles and lanterns on the kitchen table.

Her excitement is contagious. These preparations feel like the start of a family party. As the sky darkens and the wind starts to whistle softly around the corner of the garage, we wait. The electricity goes out, cutting us off from the world, leaving us a perfect little island. As the hours pass, my mother rises from our place by the fire and moves from window to window, exclaiming excitedly, "Imagine the sea! Children! Imagine the waves crashing on shore!" The rain comes, and then the wind increases to a deep low howl, and it drives the torrent sideways. My mother's joy fills the house. My childhood fears of the noise, the chaos of the rain striking the windows, the shuddering house, all are muted by my mother's sensuous excitement with the great forces of the storm.

When she gauges that the storm is at its peak, she calls her friend Margie: "We'll be down in five minutes." We pull on our rubber boots and sweaters and raincoats, climb into my mother's green Buick convertible, and back out of the garage into the hurricane. When we stop at Margie's, they are ready. Robin and Judy climb into the back with us, and my mother and Margie lean toward the windshield, trying to see the deserted road and dark neighborhood through the pummeling rain. Minutes later we are at the beach. They have a routine: my mother stops at each barricade the town has placed over the flooded road; Margie jumps out and pulls the barricade aside, replacing it after we drive through. The car wallows in the great ponds of salt water gathering over the road. There isn't another car in sight. Barricade after barricade, warning sign after warning sign—DANGER! DO NOT PASS BEYOND THIS POINT!—we make our way along North Beach Road, my mother threading her way intently through the seaweed, crushed lobster traps, logs, and rotten pieces of boats and docks, the drifts of pebbles and large rocks thrown over the low seawall by the roaring surf.

At our spot, she pulls into the parking place, our shiny car like a boat with its bow facing the oncoming storm. The ocean crashes and roils and surges and booms. The sky is nearly black. The wind rocks the car as the rain hisses and drums on the metal and glass. "Isn't this glorious, children?" my mother says, turning off the car, lighting a cigarette, and settling back into her seat. The windshield wipers click back and forth, back and forth. The sea envelops us in our little boat, each wave rising and surging forward and dropping over us, sucking at the car, retreating, leaving us in a small ocean of seawater to the bottom of the doors. The five of us children sit forward on the wide back seat, shrieking as each surging wave drops seaweed and sand and pebbles and rocks onto the canvas roof over our heads. My mother is alert, alive.

Of course, our hurricanes are dangerous. Once, when we return home, with the car scratched and dented, we find that Hurricane Diane has blown over our neighbor's barn, leaving the apple tree standing, lonely, in the wind. But my mother craves the beauty of these storms. She teaches me to crave beauty—lonely, tumultuous, cleansing beauty. And she finds in these eruptions of natural fury and destruction some corresponding capacity in her own restless and potent heart, expressed one terrible night in my living room when I am pregnant and sixteen.

"That's right, darlin'. Just like that. Watch the fabric ahead of the needle, not right at the needle. You'll keep a straighter line. That looks really good." My mother teaches me to sew. She sews beautifully tailored wool dresses and pique skirts and flannel nighties and curtains and drawn-thread tablecloths of fine lawn. She leans over my shoulder at her old Singer, once in a while touching the whirring wheel or pulling my seam back in line. "Okay. That looks fine. Let's lay out the front." I am working on my first dress. I am eleven years old. I have been making doll clothes since I was five. I know how to make my own nightgowns, and shorts with a matching top. The dress is more complicated: a shirtwaist with a gathered skirt, buttons and buttonholes from the throat to the hem, set-in sleeves, a matching belt. I like the cloth we bought at the Handkerchief Factory in Exeter, a creaky old mill by the tracks; the cloth is striped with flowers and vines and has good drape, necessary, my mother teaches me, for clothes to hang well. I take great pride in my skills, and I love these long afternoons with my mother. None of my friends is taught how to sew, even if their mothers still sew all the family's clothes.

My mother's room fills with afternoon sun. We work quietly, my mother's hands occasionally touching mine to correct the position of my fingers or the lay of the cloth. I have trouble understanding that the cloth is laid inner side to inner side when the pattern is pinned on for cutting. That I can make two sleeves or two sides of the front at once, mirrors of each other, left and right, is hard for me to grasp. "It's simple," my mother says. "You fold the cloth right down the middle, inside to inside, and pin on the pattern. Then you'll get a right and a left at the same time." Laying the cloth heart to heart, my mother and me, so like each other, so known.

"That's a beautiful seam, Meredy. Now the buttonholes will all look even. Okay, turn the bodice inside out and pin the right sleeve in. You'll need to baste the edge to make it fit. Good." My mother sits down on her bed and picks up her hand sewing, her fine small stitches binding cloth to cloth.

"Who needs fudge?" my mother asks suddenly as she jumps up from the couch. My sister and brother and I have finished the supper dishes and we are all in the living room watching television. "No nuts!" I say. "No, nuts!" she calls back over her shoulder. "You can pick yours out." My mother has a legendary sweet tooth. At a hundred and two pounds, she can eat as much as she wants, and these late-night cravings always end in something delicious.

I can hear her working in the kitchen, hear her scraping the pan as she stirs the fudge, hear her humming. An hour later the fudge is set enough to cut. She brings it into the living room in the old beat-up aluminum cake pan and we dig in. When she finally says, "That's enough, kids," I ask if I can brush her hair. "Oh, I'd love that, sweetheart," she answers. "Make me beautiful."

I wash the fudge off my hands at the bathroom sink and come back with her old brush and rattail comb, some elastics, a black velvet hair band, and a mirror. In the gray glow of the television, with Michael and Sandy curled in the corners of the couch, my mother sits on the floor between my knees and I brush her soft, light brown, wavy hair, drawing the brush through over and over. Her head tugs back just a bit at every stroke. I try making stubby braids at the sides, and then little pigtails, showing her my styling in the mirror. Sandy and Michael and I laugh, teasing her that she looks like a bird. "Your turn," she says, and I jump down onto the floor. She sits at my back, drawing her brush through my long thick hair, lifting it into a pile on my head, parting it on the side, and finally deciding to pull it into tight French braids. I can feel her fingers tugging and twisting each strand expertly. "My turn," Sandy says, and we all switch places. A while later, my mother asks, "Who needs a back rub?" Michael is first since he doesn't have any hair to brush. We spend the rest of the evening taking turns stretched out on the floor while one of us sits on the back, rubbing the muscles deeply. I think every family spends their time in front of the television like this, touching and laughing. I remember my mother's quiet contentment in her tidy house, the pan of fudge on the coffee table, a good and present mother with her growing children.

My mother teaches me a lot—how to bake the family's desserts, how to paint the house, how to keep her checkbook and manage money, how to write a business letter, how to weed the gardens and know when to cut the asparagus, how to make a bouquet of wildflowers, how to sprinkle and iron my brother's oxford shirts.

My mother teaches me to love books. To love ideas. That my brain is a gift and I have an obligation to nourish it. When I am young, she teaches me that the rules, all rules, apply. And then, later, she tells me, "Always question anything that anyone ever tells you you must do." She tells me I make lovely hospital corners on the beds. But once, watching me change my brother's bed, she scolds me as I lay the top sheet out, smooth and tight. "Meredy, a man likes to have room for his feet. You always make a pleat for him, like this." She draws the sheet into a ten-inch fold at the foot of the bed, then tucks it in tight. "See? You don't need to bother with this on our beds, but you need to learn how to make a man's bed."

Once, my mother interrupts me while I am telling her some small thing about my day. "Meredy," she says very sternly, "never, ever let anyone call you sweet. Let them call you a bitch, but never sweet." I have never heard her use the word *bitch*. Her angriest curse is a compressed, "Blasted!" Another time she says, "A husband needs to feel like the man in the family. You are too independent. You'll need to pretend to your husband that you need him, that you can't do all these things on your own."

There are other lessons. "It's a woman's job to make a marriage work," she tells me many times. She is divorced, and even at the time I wonder what she must feel about her own failed marriage. "A man and a woman must be compatible in their intimate life," she tells me. "If they are not happy in their private life together, the marriage will be empty." But this contradicts a growing message, one that comes to define my sense of who and what I am becoming: "You have quite a little body on you these days," she says in a new voice, tense with criticism. I am barely twelve, confused and uncomfortable with my breasts and hips.

The rules start to accrue: You are not to spend time with boys. You may not be alone with a boy. I want to look at you when you come in from being away from the house. Never let a boy touch you. One thing will lead to another. Only cheap girls let a boy touch them. You better be careful. I'll be able to tell if you let anyone touch you. What do you and Dan do while you walk home from school?

I understand perfectly: I have changed, I have grown up into a very dirty and dangerous girl, and my mother is disgusted. My sister and brother tell me years later that she helped them grow into their young bodies, that they confided in her and she was tender and sensitive. But, somehow, my mother starts to imagine me—her good and earnest and trusting girl—to be a seductress, a daughter asking for trouble.

When I am a sophomore in high school, in early 1965—as Bob Dylan's "The Times They Are A-Changin'" hits the charts and the Voting Rights Act is passed and my mother checks my dresses and blouses for wrinkles after the high school dance—she insists that I study elocution and modeling with Mrs. Dion. This middle-aged woman has a pile of dyed red hair swirled above her sagging face. She wears rouge and lipstick that clash with her hair. She always wears embroidered scuff slippers, and her feet splay out at the sides. Her house is painted blue. Doilies are laid carefully across the cardboard boxes piled in her hallway. Mrs. Dion was once a local radio celebrity. My mother, my old mother from a time before our world shakes out of place, tells me a young woman needs to know how to speak and move properly. We argue over this decision, but I never win these disputes with my mother. When I ask why, she always resorts to her absolute authority over me: "Because I said so. That's why."

Mrs. Dion tries to teach me to open my mouth and throat when I speak—to "e-nun-ci-ate." "How now brown cow," she demonstrates, stretching her neck and letting the vowels roll from her billowing throat. I try to imitate her. The next week, she says, "My dear girl, when a young woman gets into a car, she must not allow her legs to fall open the slightest bit. Now practice." This is easy. My mother taught my sister and me this sit-and-swivel move years before. "Good. Now. I am going to show you how to model your dress. First, lean back a little, lead with your hips. Now. I want you to bend your arm at the elbow, turn the hand up, and let that wrist go limp. Where are your gloves?" I quit after three weeks, winning the battle with my mother finally by simply refusing to walk downtown. The pulse of the jazz she listens to with her new friends each night quiets her response and she lets me defy her for the first time.

My sister, Sandy, who is six years older than I, tells me this story: When she was twelve, my mother was very angry with her for doing something Sandy can no longer remember. Maybe my sister talked back to her as she was being scolded. What she remembers is my mother facing her and saying quietly, darkly, "Sandra, you get out of my sight this instant before I say something I'll regret the rest of my life. . . ." Of course, my mother didn't need to say whatever it was. My sister will finish that sentence a thousand times over the years, with every terrible thing she can imagine my mother might have said.

The 1950s defined my mother's small world, and she fit inside its confines willingly. But the chaos of the '60s jostles at her, shakes loose the stiff underpinnings, and reveals a woman much better suited to the new decade's promises. When she starts working with

Peter at *New Hampshire Profiles*, she changes almost overnight, a silent upheaval that razes the life we have known at home. I miss her when she goes out each night to be with her new friends at Peter's, listening to jazz and drinking scotch until the sun starts to lighten the sky and calls her back to her old life, to me, to her last child at home still trying to grow up.

In 1965, the same year I get pregnant in the aftershocks of these changes, the same year my mother kicks me out, she meets Dan. He is a poet and painter, addicted to Benzedrine, his bennies. He is a great chemist, writing illegal prescriptions for his uppers and downers, balancing them to make his way just right through the day. He has a goatee, drives an ancient and rickety truck, and lives in Philadelphia. I love him. But I am lost in my mother's transformation and I long for the order and safety of our old life.

Dan is an obsessive, spinning endlessly and exhaustingly around the same idea for days on end. "Eliot gets it right there, huh, dear? Old T. S.? Doesn't he? When he says, 'Where is there an end to the drifting wreckage, / the prayer of the bone on the beach . . . ?' You can feel his fear in those soft little lines, can't you, dear? '. . . the prayer of the bone on the beach,'" he repeats again, and again. Dan quotes all his poetry from memory. "You hear that, don't you, Bobbie? Huh, dear? Don't you hear that fragile fear? Moving, isn't it? Stirs you, don't you think, Bobbie? '. . . the prayer of the bone.' Hear that, dear?" My mother loves Dan. He seems to open a door to herself. Her transformation is complete, and all the old rules count for nothing now.

For ten years, my mother and Dan will live together for months at a time between his trips home to Philadelphia, until my mother finds one day that he has lied to her about something small involving the timing of his return. She tells him it is over, causing, I'm sure, great grief in her own heart. When I try to convince her to soften her response, reminding her that he loves her and has never done anything else to hurt her, that this is a mistake they can work around, she turns to me and says coldly, "He lied to me, Meredy. I can't continue to love him after he lied to me." Her old moral sense has been pricked, and there is only one possible response: evict him. I begrudgingly admire her for her righteousness, but it rubs very close to my own outcasting, and I pity him. I never see her cry over this devastating collapse of love, and she never speaks of it again.

I have a friend who donates blood every time the Red Cross holds a drive. When I tell her that I admire her for her generosity, she says, "I only go because I need the mothering so much. It feels good to be touched. The nurses are kind and make me feel loved." I imagine Karen reading the ad and anticipating the day she will have a moment of mother love: She stands in line watching the nurses, choosing the mother she hopes to get, praying that the ones who are efficient and professional are busy as her turn nears. I imagine that she feels the blood pulse in the veins at her neck and wrist, in her ears as she shuffles forward. She gets the one she hoped for! The mother-nurse has a soothing voice, a tender smile, gentle hands as she lays Karen down on the cot and asks her small questions about herself. Karen says too much, speaking quickly and ingratiatingly. The mother sits beside her and slides Karen's sleeve up her still arm. "I'm sorry to hurt you," she says quietly, slipping the needle with a small prick into the vein. The blood flows. Karen hopes the mother can feel its warmth as it fills the vial. Karen smiles at the mother. "Here now," the gentle woman says, offering her a small cup. "Drink this. You will feel better." "Thank you," my friend says, sipping the juice. The woman stretches a Band-Aid tight over the wound and pulls the sleeve back down. Karen asks if she can lie there for a few more minutes. "Of course," the mother says. "I'm just so glad you came." Karen leaves the Band-Aid on for several days, remembering love.

Once, I offer to introduce my mother to a young man I am dating. We meet at a restaurant near the university where my mother works.

Thomas and I dress for the evening. He is exactly the package I believe my mother will like. He is tall and very handsome; he comes from a wealthy family, and is clearly not "common," my mother's harshest criticism. He must be nervous. But he has polished manners and knows how to conduct himself. I know my mother will like him.

She does. We sit at a round table under the glittering chandeliers as the waiter brings each course. My mother glows. She makes conversation with Thomas, directing the talk to books, politics, philosophy, history, making sure he understands that she is cultured. He smiles and lets her talk. I can see that my mother wants me to know she approves.

As we start on our dessert, my mother suddenly becomes serious. She leans across to Thomas and lowers her voice so he has to lean in to her. She puts her hand on his arm and says confidingly, "Thomas, I feel compelled to warn you away from my daughter. You don't know what you are getting into." She draws her hand back, sits up straight, and turns an expressionless face to me. Thomas is silent. I try to replay her words, disbelieving. Thomas and I scrape our forks on our plates. "Well," she says easily, with a smile, "let's eat. Isn't this delicious food?" Like a puppet, I hug my mother good night at the end of the evening.

Well, she can't live here. So abrupt, the end of having a mother. Within a few years, my mother and I will seem close again. I love her. But she will never again be my mother. Love and its failure.

My sister will say later, "It was just the times." But that is not true. There was something more, a secret, something I was missing, something I should have known, a capacity for this betrayal I should have sensed was coming. I could have prepared myself, kept my feet under me better, not spend a lifetime wondering how this could happen, and, always, wondering at my own lack of worth. I wish I had been able to *see* my mother—my two mothers—more clearly, to predict her capacity to judge so fiercely, to withdraw so abruptly her love and protection of me.

I like to watch the whirligig bugs that skitter on the quiet stream behind my house. They are small, shiny black ovals that scurry wildly in their groups, never bumping into each other. If you can manage to pick them up, they smell like apples; my children call them cider bugs. What I like most about them is the way they see, which is unique among water bugs: their compound eyes are divided, making them look as if they have four eyes. This allows them to see simultaneously both above and below the surface of the water. The whirligig can synthesize these two distinct realms, creating a cohesive picture of the world above and the world below. I have always envied this ability. Imagine being able to see what is before you and at the same time what lies beneath the surface, the obscured, the unannounced, the threatening.

I wish that I had had these eyes, had been able to see both realms: what was at the surface and what might lie below, the warning signs. At sixteen, I'd held only one view: my mother loved me.

I once saw a copy of a page filled with the strange, elegant scratchings of Nüshu, a secret writing system used for centuries by women in the Hunan Province of China and still one of the least known writing systems in the world. Only boys were allowed an education and to participate in the public world of ideas and communication. Girls were kept at home and taught the skills required to run a household. When they were old enough for marriage, they had to leave their mothers and sisters forever and travel to the faraway home of their husband to live under the rule of his family. When a girl left her home for marriage, there was great crying and wailing among the women in her family.

Illiterate, the women developed a secret way of writing in order to communicate with their lost daughters. They borrowed some characters learned over time from the Chinese and made up many more. Like Chinese, Nüshu is written top to bottom, right to left in columns, but the writing looks very different from written Chinese. The characters are not square. They are elegant, feminine, elongated like the legs of cranes, with thin swift strokes connecting the vertical lines, binding women together outside the rules.

Grandmothers and mothers taught their girls the secret writing by making up and singing a verse, then writing it on the hand of the girl. Verse after verse, day after day, slowly the girl came to share in the mother-language of secrecy, of connection, of loyalty and love. Forbidden paper and ink, the mother would give her departing daughter a beautiful book of Nüshu she had sewn, stitch by stitch, to comfort her and bind them together forever, the characters themselves little signs of their eternal connection. For years after the girl went away into marriage, her mother made up long verses of steadfastness, stitching them in Nüshu into her little books and secreting them to her daughter.

I imagine the Nüshu verses my mother might have sewn in a beautiful book for me as we sewed in those long, sunny afternoons in her room: *You are a good daughter*, she says to me in her beautiful hand. *I will love you always. The world waits for you with all its beauty, but also its fright and its pain. I will be beside you every day. I am your loyal mother. Don't be afraid.* My mother sews her love into my secret book, this little book with its spidery, secret letters that I carry inside my shirt to this day. With her stitches in the soft cloth, my mother draws her terrified daughter to her. She holds her daughter close. When the father asks, Now what?, she says to me, *You are my daughter. When you were born I bound myself to you. I will protect you. There are very sad times coming. I hold you, daughter.*

Chapter Ten

Killing Chickens

I tuck her wings tight against her heaving body, crouch over her, and cover her flailing head with my gloved hand. Holding her neck hard against the floor of the coop, I take a breath, set something deep and hard inside my heart, and twist her head. I hear her neck break with a crackle. Still she fights me, struggling to be free of my weight, my gloved hands, my need to kill her. Her shiny black beak opens and closes, opens and closes silently as she gasps for air. I hadn't known this would happen. I am undone by the flapping, the dust rising and choking me, the disbelieving little eye turned up to mine. I hold her beak closed, covering that eye. Still she pushes, her reptile legs bracing against mine, her warmth, her heart beating fast with mine. I turn her head on her floppy neck again, and again, cork screwing her breathing tube, struggling to end the gasping. The eye, turned around and around, blinks and studies me. The early spring sun flows onto us through a silver stream of dust, like a stage light, while we fight each other. I lift my head and see that the other birds are eating still, pecking their way around us for stray bits of corn. This one, this twisted and broken lump of gleaming black feathers, claws hard at the floor, like a big stretch, and then deflates like a pierced ball. I wait, holding her tiny beak and broken neck with all my might.

I am killing chickens. It is my birthday. I was awake through the night, reckoning with a terrible decision. When I woke this morning, the next path was finally, achingly clear. After breakfast I sat with my children, Alex and Benjamin, and struggled to ease the news that their father and I are divorcing. They were stunned into silence.

Now, as I crouch over my quiet hen, my sons are making a birthday surprise for me at the kitchen table. "It's okay, guys," I had said as I gathered my gloves and went outside, trying with my voice to pull them back to safety. "I won't peek."

I carry Bertie's warm, limp body outside and lay her on the grass. Back inside the coop, I stalk my hens and come up with Tippy-Toes. I gather her frantic wings and crouch over her. My husband normally would kill off my beautiful but tired old hens, no longer laying, to make way for the new chicks that are arriving tomorrow. I don't know how to do this. But I am going to do it myself. This is just a little thing in all the things I am going to have to learn to do alone. I have five more to go. Tippy-Toes tries to shriek behind my glove. I clamp my hand over her beak and give her head a hard twist. I feel her body break deep inside my own chest.

Two down. I feel powerful, capable. I can handle whatever comes to me.

But I need a rest. I am tired, exhausted, with a heavy, muffled weight settling inside. "I'm coming in," I call in a false, singsong voice from the kitchen door. "Better hide my surprise." Ten and seven, Alex and Ben know that a terrible thing is happening to them. They are working quietly in the kitchen, not giggling and jostling the way they always do. Their downy blond heads touch as they lean over their projects. I feel a crush of sadness, of defeat. We are exploding into smithereens on this pretty March day and we all know it.

"I have to make a cake!" I sing from the doorway. "When are you guys going to be done in there?"

"Wait! Wait!" they squeal. It is an empty protest, their cheer as hollow as mine.

Our old house smells good, of wood smoke and the pancakes the three of us ate this morning, in that other world of hope and confidence before our conversation. We live on a ridge high over the mouth of the Damariscotta River on the coast of Maine. From our beds, we can see out over Pemaquid Point, over Monhegan Island, over the ocean to the edge of the Old World. The rising sun bursts into our sleep each morning. At night, before bed, we lie on my bed together naming Orion and Leo and the Pleiades in whispers. Monhegan's distant lighthouse beam sweeps the walls of our rooms all night at thirty-six-second intervals. Our little house creaks in the wind during February storms. Now spring has come, and the world has shifted.

"Help me make my cake," I say to the boys. They drag their chairs to the counter.

"Mum, will Dad be home for your birthday tonight?" Alex asks. Both boys are so contained, so taut, so helpless. They lean against me, quiet.

Guilt and fear tug me down like an undertow. I start to cry.

"I don't know, my loves. I think maybe not."

Bertie and Tippy-Toes lie side by side on the brown grass, their eyes open, necks bent. I close the coop door behind me and lunge for the next hen.

"It's all right," I say softly. "It's all right. Everything's going to be all right. *Shhh*, Silly, *shhh*." I crouch over her. Silly is the boys' favorite because she lets them carry her around the yard. I hope they will forget her when the box of peeping balls of fluff arrives tomorrow.

"It's okay, Silly," I say quietly, wrapping my gloved hand around her hard little head. She is panting, her eyes wild, frantic, betrayed. I cover them with my fingers and twist her neck hard. Her black wings, iridescent in the dusty sunlight, beat against my legs. I hold her close to me while she scrabbles against my strong hands. I start to cry again.

When I go back up to the house, Bertie and Tippy-Toes and Silly and Mother Mabel lie on the grass outside the coop.

Benjamin comes into the kitchen and leans against my legs. "What are we going to do?" he asks.

"About what, sweetheart?" I hope he is not asking me about tomorrow. Or the next day.

"Nothing," he says, drifting off to play with Alex upstairs.

We frost the cake blue, Ben's favorite color, and put it on the table next to their presents for me, wrapped in wallpaper. I want to call someone, to call my mother or my sister. Instead, I bring in three loads of wood and put them in the empty wood box.

"Alex, will you lay up a fire for tonight? And Ben, go down cellar and get a bunch of kindling wood."

Like serious little men, my children do what I ask.

"What are we going to make for my birthday supper? Spaghetti?"

"I thought we were going to Uncle Michael's and Aunt Ashley's," Alex says.

"Know what?" I say. "Know what I want to do? Let's just stay here, and have our own private little party. Just us."

I feel marooned with my children. I sit at the table watching while they do their chores, then head back out to finish mine.

Minnie Hen is next. She lets me catch her and kill her without much fight. I lay her next to the others in the cold grass.

Itty-Bit is last. She is my favorite. The others chewed off her toes, one by one, when she was a chick. I made a separate box for her, a separate feeder, separate roost, and smeared antibiotic ointment four times a day on the weeping stubs. She survived, and ate from my hand after that. She has grown to be fierce with the other hens, never letting them too close to her, able to slip in, grab the best morsels, and flee before they can peck her. I have come to admire her very much, my tough little biddy.

She cowers in the corner, alone. I sit next to her, and she lets me pull her up into my lap. I stroke her feathers smooth, stroke after stroke. Her comb is pale and shriveled, a sign of her age. I know she hasn't laid an egg for months. She is shaking. I hold her warmth against me, cooing to her, "It's all right, Itty-Bit. Everything's going to be all right. Don't be scared." My anger and fear center like a tornado on having to kill this hen. I get up, crying again, holding Itty-Bit tight to me. I lay her gently on the floor and crouch over her. The sun fills the coop with thick light.

That night, after eating spaghetti and making a wish and blowing out thirty-eight candles and opening the presents Alex and Benjamin made—a mail holder made from wood slats, a sculpture of two-by-fours and shells—after baths and reading stories in bed and our sweet, in-the-dark whispered good-nights; after saying, "I don't know what is going to happen" to my scared children; after banking the fire and turning off the lights, I sit on the porch in the cold, trying to imagine what has to happen next. I can see the outline of the coop against the dark, milky sky. I touch my fingers, my hands, so familiar to me. Tonight they feel like someone else's. I wrap my arms around myself—thin, tired—and wish it were yesterday.

Tomorrow morning, I think, I have to turn over the garden and go to the dump. Tomorrow morning, I have to call a lawyer. I have to figure out what to say to Alex and Benjamin. I have to put Ben's sculpture on the mantel, and put some mail in Alex's holder on the desk. I have to clean out the coop and spread fresh shavings.

Chapter Eleven
Threshold

An American flag, brilliant red and white and blue against the clear Maine sky, snaps in the crisp September wind. Lions lying on either side of the wide stone steps watch me pass. They know I don't belong here. I am running late for my first class at Bowdoin College. I am a freshman. I am forty years old.

A flag never holds any inspiration for me, but today it fills me with a sense of great purpose, of capacity, of change. The campus is almost empty, the students already in their classrooms. I have been up since five, have fed and watered the sheep and chickens, turning them out for the day. I packed a large lunch for Alex and Ben. I made a hot breakfast, and while we ate at the comfortable old table, we went over the plan for the day: I will be home to meet Ben's bus at three. We will grab a snack and go back to the school for Alex's four-thirty soccer game. Alex has a bag of food for before the game—another sandwich, fruit, trail mix—and his soccer bag. I tell him to run down to the drying rack for his clean shin guards. Ben has his sign-up sheet for sponsors for the free-throw contest on Saturday.

I have no degree and can't support my family. I have been working for a sheetrock company, sanding walls and making dump runs. Sometimes they get the painting contract and I roll out white paint in three coats over the raw sheetrock, a break from the sanding and dust. When there isn't enough work to keep me on the crew, I clean houses for people who leave their dirty underwear on the floor for me and don't wipe last night's grease from the stovetop. I haven't always done such demeaning work. Before the children were both in school, I stayed at home with them on our little homestead. We raised the sheep and chickens and gardens, and wandered the woods and shore and pasture. We read books and made clay towns and stacked firewood. Once the kids were in school, my husband and I rebuilt old houses for resale. But now I am on my own, and I'm scared.

At first, with no degree, I stupidly applied for teaching jobs. Then teaching assistant jobs. Then library helper jobs. Then school secretary jobs. Then lunch lady jobs. There is nothing in our small Maine town between working in the school and working as a laborer. I sand sheetrock and scrub bathrooms for a living. Today, the flag whipping in the wind, so clean and unequivocal, announces that something big has begun. I am a college student. I will graduate and get that job as a high school teacher, and I will be able to support my children. I am stirred by the snapping flag, as if it is an announcement of my new start.

I'm not just a college student. I am the only nontraditional student at Bowdoin College. I wrote a desperate letter asking to be admitted. It wasn't the first letter I had sent to Bowdoin. When Alex and Benjamin first started school, I sent a letter inquiring about going back to college. I received a cool and formal letter back, informing me that Bowdoin is not a community college, and suggesting that I attend the state university's small local campus. But I am desperate this time, and send a passionate letter: *I am turning forty this year*, I say. *All these years of Cambridge and a fishing boat and the Middle East, of a homestead and children. Of learning what it is I need to know.* I do not mention my dark and secret past, the long, strange path that has brought me here finally. *I am hungry*, I say. *I am asking for a chance to learn.* This time, a letter comes from the admissions office. *We have received your (very moving) letter of application. I am delighted to write on behalf of the Admissions Committee that you have been admitted as a student at Bowdoin.* I'm in.

Today, I hurry under the giant trees and cross the near-empty campus, feeling already the complications of also being a mother and the family wage earner. I push to the back of my mind the looming truths: Bowdoin has given me full tuition support. But I will have to cut way back on my work, and we have four years ahead of very precarious finances. In the end, I will remortgage my house to the maximum, and we will slowly eat our way to the bottom of a very deep well of debt. I will live scared for many more years. But I do not know yet just how frightening this is going to be. Today, all I know is that I have leaped onto my next new path.

My first class starts in four minutes. I find Massachusetts Hall, a small and classic brick building from the earliest years of the college. Up a delicate, curving stairwell that has somehow survived nearly two hundred years of student traffic. I hear young voices at the top of the stairs. As I near the doorway, I forget my fears about supporting my children, forget that I am here in order to gain the credentials to make a living. Suddenly, I am a student. I am a college student. I am here to finally become educated. I am starved. Suddenly, I want to cry. I am on a threshold. I understand that my life is about to change, that there will be a past, a time before I came to this place, and an after, a time in which I will make my way knowing how to feed the wild hungers that have haunted my life.

The young students look up as I enter the classroom—a white-plastered garret filled with odd chairs, the leaded windows opened to the fall day. This is a very smart place. I can feel that I am among smart people, an energy that pervades the room. The boys wear baseball caps, some backward. Their faces are open, expectant. I can see in them my own sons not long from now. The girls lounge in their chairs, confident and lively. I don't remember ever feeling like these young people, so at ease in the world. They all stop speaking for a moment, staring at me, an old woman in their classroom, the only one they will see here for the next four years. I am embarrassed, and my feelings of great anticipation deflate instantly. I forgot: I am forty years old, a girl who somehow became a woman and missed this crucial step, a catch-up woman among kids. In that hushed pause at the door, my history of shame and mistakes and decisions that threw me outside the world rushes up in me.

Then a girl smiles, the young students graciously turn back to their conversations, and I find my way to a chair in the old room. I pull out a new notebook and pencil, feeling like a child. Professor Diehl strolls confidently into the room and organizes her papers on the table. She is younger than I. "Welcome back," she says to the group with a smile. Her eyes catch mine and she doesn't hesitate. Has she been warned that I will be in her class? "The Politics of Genre. I'd like to go over the syllabus." I have never heard of a syllabus. I pay absolute attention to every word. I will graduate summa cum laude in four years, buried in debt, filled with hope and urgency, a grown woman ready to move into an unimagined new life.

Chapter Twelve

Propitiation

I close the cabin door for the last time and climb into the truck. It is snowing lightly even though it is early June. For a year, I have lived in Colorado at eight thousand feet, several miles from the nearest people. I look out over the Continental Divide, with twelve-thousand-foot Mt. Thorodin looming in a ghostly purple light against the serrated white and black backdrop of the Colorado Rockies. I am headed down the mountain to the highway, and will drive east. I have troubling work ahead: I have received a letter at General Delivery from my mother, saying that she has been diagnosed with multiple sclerosis. I am twenty-four years old. We have never talked about my pregnancy, the adoption, her expulsion of me. It will take eighteen years for my mother to finally die from this disease, but I don't know that now. I am stunned with the news and am going home to help my mother as she dies.

It is true that the definition of us as mother and daughter shifted forever in that moment in my living room when I was sixteen. I have never again sought mothering and comfort from her. But it is also true that I love my mother very much. I cannot stand to see her suffer, and want to bring the relief that will ease her fear and aloneness.

We have been writing this year. Our letters have been comfortable but carefully ignore our past. They have reminded me of the strange and intimate likenesses we share. My mother writes passionately and humorously of her everyday life, of work and books and dinner with a friend and the squirrels raiding her bird feeders and a mixed metaphor or misplaced modifier she found in the paper and finds hilarious. She cuts out and sends articles about theories of evolution and the beginnings of life and the origin of speech in humans, about constitutional law and the Bill of Rights. She sends her recipe for biscuits. I hand-copy portions of my diary describing the drama of the mountain storms and the humming birds that drink from the feeder in my hand on the door stoop, their wings a mist of figure eights. I send her pressed pasqueflowers. I describe Azara, the Iranian girl who sews at the machine next to mine when I pick up work at the factory down in Boulder; I am the only one who will speak to her, and she shows me how to write my name in Persian script. I do not tell my mother that I will never come home to New England. That she is not my mother. But we are women bound together, women sharing our ordinary days, our complex history held outside our mundane conversations.

Multiple sclerosis is an incurable, progressive disease of the central nervous system. It is an autoimmune disease, in which the body itself attacks the myelin sheath that surrounds and protects the nerves in the brain and spinal cord. My mother's body does not recognize itself, and is destroying itself cell by cell.

MS is not a kind disease. Before she can die, my mother will have to say good-bye to her hands, then her feet, then her arms, her legs; to living her days without pain; to her sight, her bladder, her bowels; to her speech. She is, in the end, blessed, because the nerves in her brain outlast the rest of her and she does not, as she had feared, go crazy.

I marry and buy a tiny decrepit house that needs renovation on the coast of Maine. Pregnant, and then a new mother, I drive the two hours to Hampton twice a week to see my mother. She has had to quit her job at the university after two bad falls down the stairs, breaking ribs and hands and her jaw. She lies on the couch or on her bed through long lonely days, the house silent, dirty. I have never seen my mother lost like this, paralyzed with fear and depression.

She is suddenly vulnerable, and I want to protect her. I feel her fear and grief powerfully. I want to fix her life, to provide some magic that will undo her loneliness and dread and her struggle with this disease. She is grateful, calling me her angel of mercy when I clean her house or bring bags of groceries and make a big pot of soup. But I do not feel like an angel. I felt impotent, helpless; my own life darkens with my mother's suffering. I cannot fix her life now. I cannot fix her past, the losses and unknown sorrows that she carries so silently. I cannot fix our past, make it different, erase it. The terrible truth comes slowly clear to me: with her weakening, I will never be able to hold my mother accountable for her outcasting of me. There is no time for our history to be righted. Our story is carved forever. My mother is sick. My mother will die a slow and terrible death from this sickness. I spend the next eighteen years caring for my mother in a complicated dance of love and forbidden anger, of compassion and unspeakable resentment, of tender respect and the old, silenced betrayal.

My mother leans against the jamb of her closet door, her heavy metal crutches hanging from her forearms. She is looking for her winter coat in the back, among the suits and dresses she never wears anymore. I watch from her bed where I am folding laundry for her. Mum is still tan in November; her hair is shiny, Miss Clairol Honey Brown. She is small and hard-bodied. She pulls out her purple wool dress and bolero vest she sewed when I was young and laughs. "Remember this? God, I sewed a lot. When did I find time to do all that sewing?" I do remember the dress, and my mother in it, clicking down the little hardwood hallway in her black spike heels, efficient, moving fast always, *click click click*, dressed for work and the house clean and lunches made and the bus coming for me and my brother and sister and then off to work, smart and handsome in her tailored dress and fake pearls. I say, "You made me a dress just like it for my Ginny doll. I think I still have it somewhere." She laughs and reaches back into her closet for the coat. Suddenly she stumbles, her crutches clattering, and she falls into her hanging clothes. I jump to her and pull her upright. She often falls, and this is just a little wobble. I expect her to laugh. "Are you okay?" "Yes," she says quietly. "I'm all right." But she is crying. "I just mourn the death of me, Meredy. I'm watching myself die cell by cell." It is the only time I ever see my mother cry during all the years it takes her to die of multiple sclerosis.

My mother's gumption re-emerges slowly. She makes adjustments. Reimagines the life she might live. With too little to do, and no energy or strength to do even everyday chores, my mother lurches around her house trying to create busyness. She organizes thirty years of family photographs and tucks notes inside the odd pieces of family china we use at Thanksgiving, telling us where each piece came from. She draws a chair up and cleans drawers. She sorts through her private papers. After reading that sunflower seeds and soy might slow the progress of the disease, she learns to cook beans and soups and hard little nuggets she calls sunflower muffins. She reads and reads and reads, because already her eyes bother her and time is running out; she goes to the library and hauls home a dozen books at a time, as if she can absorb all the wisdom and beauty of the human soul in a cram course. She feeds the birds and learns to identify every migrant passing through her yard. And she listens to music—Gershwin and Fitzgerald and Duke Ellington and Coltrane, singing along still, but her sure and rich alto voice wavers and cracks as she loses muscle control.

We sell the house in Hampton and move her to my new town on the coast of Maine. Alex is two and I am pregnant again, with Ben. My sister and brother and their families come for visits, her house filling with laughter for the afternoon. But she is quiet, stunned, as she faces the loss of herself one cell at a time. She never speaks of how she feels, either physically or emotionally, holding hard to her life-long stoicism and intense sense of privacy. She is brave. Her legs give out fast, then her hands. She walks like a drunk, and she figures out how to ignore clucking tongues and doors slammed in her face. She learns how to walk with a cane, how to walk with heavy, clanking metal crutches, how to get hand controls on her car, how to drive with her hands, how to sit at the counter in Porter's Drugstore drinking coffee and making new friends, how to give up her car, how to cook sitting down, how to visit her mother as if she is still the child, second in line to die; how to call me when she needs bread or milk or a voice to calm the panic, how to think about her past without crying, how to think about her future without crying, how to hold grandchildren in her lap and read quietly when she is tired and in pain, how to dress without falling over, how to find clothes with no buttons, how to make it to the bathroom on time, how to wash out her panties when she doesn't and hang them out of sight to dry.

Mum never says, "I am in pain." Instead, she develops a clinical language of understatement: "I am in an exacerbation." That means that her muscles one morning turn to pudding, that her eyes are filtered with a gray, shifting lens, that she has soiled her bed, that her perpetual headache is now cracking her skull. It means that the muscle spasms she usually experiences ten times a day—when her body stiffens suddenly, her legs and hips rising straight out, muscles hard as iron, her gasp of pain—come twenty times a day and are so severe they leave her feeling bruised. It means that she can barely walk, cannot read, cannot sleep, cannot bear music inside her screaming head. That her tongue becomes a dead, thick lump that cannot pronounce words. I do not know what any of this feels like for her. All she says is, "I am in an exacerbation," and all I can do is say, "Oh, Mum," and rub her head softly.

Then one morning her head stops screaming; now it is again just a good, steady headache—and maybe she can make it to the bathroom and maybe she can make a soup for supper and maybe she can get to Porter's for a cup of coffee. "I am in remission!" she proclaims, the words clear again. "Remission!" We celebrate—the relief, the release of grief, of fear, of dread. Mostly, maybe, of guilt—for my helplessness, for the absolute promise of my own future life, for my desire to turn away from this hideous thing, this wrecker of bodies and lives. Guilt that I have children to raise in happiness and a living to earn and a house to paint and books to read, that I am stretched too tight and tired and breaking from the sadness of watching my mother suffer. Guilt that I feel sorry for myself. Guilt that I cannot fix any part of her rupturing life, that the casseroles I bring and the overnights at my house and the long days at her house with my children are easings and not a cure. "I am in remission!" means that whatever defines the boundaries of her life, what she can do and how much pain she feels and what parts of her have died, that the circle is closing in. There is never a going-back.

It is called the plateau effect: Along you go on that plateau, figuring out how to live without your hands and your legs and then any peace inside your skull or behind your eyes, you figure it out and find a way to say, "Good-bye forever to that part of me but I can still do *this*"—and then the slide, the abrupt plunge over the edge, giving up more and more of yourself without time to say the good-bye. And suddenly the screeching halt, and a new plateau. There is never a going-back, never a reclaiming, never a surprise against all odds that your eyes or your hands or your bladder will return to you. *Remission* means that you have time to catch your breath before the next slide; if you're lucky, this plateau will be home for months or even years.

Sometimes my mother is lucky, sometimes not. But her joyful relief at the dawning of remission is a window into the extent of her pain and fear. I celebrate with her; the house lightens, laughter again, outings and food and maybe a new book. Mum sets the bar high for all of us; her silent tenacity demands the same of her children. There is no room for crying or pity or railing at God.

And no place for resentment or anger at her. There is no room in this new world for our past, for my deep feelings of bewilderment and pain over her abandonment of me when I was in trouble, for my need to disconnect from her into my own protected life. We circle around it like a lake between us. The fracture will have to be mended silently and on my own. My inability to change the course of her life, to fix this awful flow of events, tangles confusedly with my inability to redress our past.

Worst of all the rapid changes is the wheelchair, emblem of an end, of losing the fight, of complete and irreversible helplessness. Mum starts to have bad dreams: she has fallen beside her wheelchair and is screaming, helpless while the house burns down around her. I carry those dreams with me still, her terrible fear of what is coming, her loneliness.

Michael and Sandy and I buy a commode and a seat for the tub, widen doorways, and build a ramp to the front door. We lift her in and out of her chair and her bed. For a while, she can put some weight on her feet and we can pivot her around and ease her down. But slowly that slight strength disappears and she becomes dead weight. No bigger than she is, I become a mother, lifting her gently, hugging her, body to body, both of us startled, both of us struggling to understand how this all has come to be; I lift her and spin her carefully and lower her into her chair or onto the commode or her bed. Then I lift each leg, heavy, swollen and shiny, oddly hairless, dead, into the footrests, straighten her clothes and her hair, maybe hitch her up again and even again so she is upright and comfortable. She smiles every time and says, "Thank you, my darlin'."

She needs diapers. At first, we put them on just to go in the car, but soon she needs them at night, and then all day. I develop a careful choreography, designed to soften the hard edge of humiliation and transcend the inverted roles we each find ourselves playing. I lay her down on her bed; she lies stiff with muscle spasms from being moved. Looking straight up to the ceiling, she talks about the birds migrating through her yard or the Iran-Contra debates on C-Span.

"I'm sorry my hands are so cold, Mum," I say, sliding her long skirt up to her hips, and ripping the plastic diaper tabs. I always feel awkward and rough, no matter how hard I try to lift her hips gently and slide a flannel pad under her to catch any mess, no matter how tenderly I pull the sticking diaper from her tissue-thin skin, no matter how much I smile and pretend none of this is happening. Her belly and thighs are doughy, white and swollen. I have learned the private landscape of her body, and wash her carefully, slowly, talking with her as if we are sitting at lunch. Her urine always gets on my hands, warm, its smell potent.

"I'm listening to some of Nadine Gordimer's short stories on tape," she says. Her voice is thick. She sucks her breath in in a little gasp. I don't know what I have done to hurt or shock her body; I pause, letting her relax again. "If I could write, it would be like Gordimer."

"Know what I heard this morning on the radio?" I ask, wringing out the warm cloth and rolling her gently onto her side. Her paralyzed body yields to me like that of a sleeping child. "I heard that Mandela may be moved from prison to house arrest." We never look at each other, not until the clean diaper is on, her backless skirt is pulled down, and she is sitting upright again in her wheelchair, a cigarette or cup of coffee in her hand. I learn to do this confusing dance by heart. She learns, somehow, to let me do these things. "Thank you, my darlin'," she says.

Sometimes she slips through my arms to the floor, quietly, a rumpled heap. By the bed, by the commode, beside the car, I feel my own muscles go weak, and am afraid I will never be able to lift her back to her chair. We struggle, my arms around her, leaning over, summoning my love and protectiveness into strength. Sometimes I can't budge her. I sit beside her on the floor, or the snowy driveway, or the wet parking lot, leaning against her shoulder, and we laugh hard. "See how nice it is down here? I've always liked sitting on the ground," she says. I am so grateful for her laugh, for her belief that everything is ridiculous, us too, and for her letting me go weak with the relief of silliness for a minute or two before we face her struggle again. Eventually I will find a way to heave her into her chair, and we go on.

Her reading diminishes with her strength. Philosophy and the classics and poetry give way to mysteries. It is hard for her to hold up a book, and we invent holder after holder, but still she only reads paperback mysteries. Her beautiful penmanship is now almost illegible, the spasms marked by sudden scrawls across the page, and so she stops writing letters. Friends come to see her occasionally, but she is a housebound, wheelchair-bound sixty-five-year-old woman, and it takes more stamina than most people have to sit with her for a few hours as she slurs her words and heaves off the seat of her wheelchair in muscle spasms. More and more often, if she laughs at something, she stops and asks, "This is not the MS euphoria, is it? I'm just laughing, aren't I? You thought that was funny, too, didn't you?" She lives in terror of losing her mind. Part of her sits outside herself, constantly monitoring her dignity as she has all her life.

I know that I cannot empty my anger and hurt to my mother now, that I have missed my chance. But I wait for her to offer regret, to suggest that maybe she made a mistake, to redeem me, to redeem herself with just one comment that she should have held me at home with her when I was in so much trouble, to hint that she recognizes the devastation her daughter experienced in those years. Each time I am with her, I wait. There is not much time left.

I wait for an acknowledgment, a confession. I know she thinks about dying every day. We eat lunch at her old round table. We sit by the door and watch the birds dance and fight at the feeders. We ride in the car, our eyes forward. We talk quietly as I tend her body. But she makes absolutely no move toward an apology. I know there will be no reckoning. And still I wait. I cannot always sustain the tenderness, the empathy, the generosity of my heart. As her health deteriorates, as the quality of each of her days decreases, I struggle against a hardening that works at the edge of my love. She has a second chance now. She refuses to take it. Some days, driving again to her house for the same dreary and heartbreaking routine, I feel the old hurts threatening to surface. Rage flares up inside me, forbidden and hidden. I pray she does not feel my anger simmering when I walk in her door. She is a pathetic sight, and there is no room for challenging our history.

My mother dies on a starry December night, eighteen years after she was told she had MS.

She has been in the hospital, hooked up to machines, all but her brainstem dead. Her body is pitiful, the ravages of the MS absolutely visible. A tube fills her mouth; her tongue is dry and cracked and too swollen for her mouth. We watch this body inflate and deflate with a hiss for five days, when finally we all agree it is time to let her go. We move her to a quiet room at the end of a silent corridor; it takes her twelve terrible hours to die.

Michael and Sandy leave in their grief. I sit with my mother in the twilit room for several hours, holding her hands and kissing her face. I expect to be stunned with grief. I am not. Instead, as my mother's body cools, I watch a great and mysterious transformation. Slowly, slowly, she becomes radiant, white, waxen, smooth as a river stone. The devastation from the illness recedes, as if time is in rapid reverse. Her skin smoothes. Her arms and legs and hands thin, as if muscle again holds flesh to bone. Her paunchy belly flattens. The etchings of courage against such fear, of effort and grit, leave her face. As her body recedes into death, I watch its return to the vital and youthful body, to the life she imagined, to the promise and hope of her young life, slipping back and back, an erasing of all the years of struggle. And then she is gone. On the bed lies a pure and perfect—sublime—casting of a woman's form, my mother's body. Finally, here is peace, for her and for me. God seems to move in the room, incomprehensible, brutal, embracing.

It is still, all of it, a complete mystery—her years of pain and fear, the loss of her chance at a full life, her courage, her transcendent beauty in death; the unbearable weight for her daughter of her mother's suffering, the effect it had of silencing the grievances and angers of a mother and daughter living out their entangled lives. There was no atonement. My mother died with our past laced between us, love and its failures, love and its gravity.

We gather to lay my mother's ashes in the ground in the little cemetery near my brother's house. We have chosen her old wooden jewelry box with its carved lid and broken hinges to hold her ashes.

The grounds crew has dug a small hole, and we carefully lay the box in the soil. The workers wait at the edge of the woods in the December cold so they can refill the hole and go home. Just as we stand and turn to leave, I am struck with a sense of panic, that this is not where I want to leave my mother. I run to Michael's house and find a jar and a large silver spoon. I run back to the cemetery, passing my family one by one as they walk home. I get there just in time to open the lid of my mother's familiar box and scoop some of her ashes into the jar. The rest I leave, and the men move in with their shovels.

For one year my mother stays in my dresser drawer. I am not in a hurry to finish burying her. I often lift the heavy jar—a mustard jar—and hold the weight of my mother. One day, I unscrew the lid, wet my finger, and dip it into my mother's ashes. I touch my finger to my tongue.

The next day, I drive to Hampton and sneak into our old backyard while whoever lives there now is at work. I scrape the soil away from her spirea bush and lay her, finally, back at home. Barbarian acts. My mother and I.

I sometimes dream of my mother. I am at home in Hampton. I hear her clicking, clicking, clicking down the hall, across the kitchen. I listen to her moving easily and busily in our house. She is happy and busy and singing with Ella. I want to stay in the dream, where we have no regrets.

Chapter Thirteen

Chimeras

He drives a little bronze car. He drives slowly along my dirt road. He glances at me quickly as I stand waiting on the steps. I can see blond hair, curls. He turns off the car. He reaches for something, gets out, looks at me, and never takes his eyes off me again. He shoulders a soft old book bag and walks slowly toward me. This is my son, the son I am meeting for the first time, meeting on this warm fall day after twenty-one years of waiting. He is thin, graceful as he walks toward me waiting for him in the sudden sun. He is not a baby. He is not a child. He is a young man, and he walks toward me while I wait. He wears jeans and a sweater striped around his chest. We are in a slow-motion film. Waiting. Receiving. His feet are in old loafers. He comes toward me, his feet crunching on the stone path in the silence that joins us. Our eyes draw us together, lead him to me, a force joining us, a connection fierce and overwhelming as he slowly comes along the path. His teeth are brilliant white; there is a space. My father has a space like that. I step toward him. Every day for all these years I have played this scene in my mind. I have never known what to do. I do not know now. I think I must be smiling. I think I am breaking, breaking with joy, with love, with grief because here he is a grown young man, here I am middle-aged, all the years gone forever and we know it in this moment more than ever before. I reach for him and hold him in to me, a stranger, my son, this beautiful, radiant, terrified son.

It is ten o'clock, October 18, 1987. The leaves in the trees glow red and gold in the sun. We are very shy together and have no idea how to do this. We walk without talking to the railing of the porch and stand, three feet between us, facing the river, looking out over the sheep in the pasture, along the coast of Maine, over the ocean and Monhegan Island, the light dazzling. We do not speak. I cannot find the question that will start our life together. I want to ask, Will you forgive me? Have you felt my love calling to you every day? Are you healthy? Are you happy? Have you been loved? Where have you lived while I loved you? Have you felt this binding cord between us? What did you do each day for twenty-one years? Will you forgive me?

Instead, I ask, "Do you like UNH?"

"Yes," he says, his first word. His voice is soft and deep.

"What year are you?"

"Well, I'm working my way through so I have another year."

"Did you have trouble finding my house?"

"No. No trouble."

His body is taut, as if he is ready to run or to fight something off. But his face is open, his eyes enormous, blue, set wide apart. He has a scar across his chin. His nose has been broken. He is very serious, like a boy who has known a lot of sadness. He turns to me and smiles suddenly. He has deep dimples. My brother. His uncle has these dimples. We turn to the ocean again in overwhelmed silence.

"Do you want to go for a walk?" I ask. Joy and the old sorrow tangle in wild confusion.

We walk down the little dirt road to the river. I feel as if I am walking next to myself, step for step, cell for cell. I want to feel the warm and absolute presence of my son walking down the familiar road with me. I want to tell him I love him.

"This is the owl tree," I say. "Alex and Ben are my sons. Your brothers." I see him tense for just a moment, then slip back into the rhythm of our walking. "They find owl pellets here and we dissect them. We find tiny teeth and fur and bits of bone."

He says, "My mother let me play hooky to go fishing with her."

My mother. I breathe. Of course. Two mothers.

We sit on an old bench above the undulating seaweed. We start slowly, searching for words, for a place to start. Then we speak quickly, saying every thought that comes, our conversation leaping as we try to reconstruct the lost years for each other. I know he will drive away that afternoon, and I don't know if he will ever come again. He must wonder if I will want him to.

"I used to walk along the train tracks that run along the bottom of the pasture, all the way to school," he says. His school, tracks, a pasture: I frantically try to paint the picture of his childhood. "My mother and I grew the best tomato plants in town. People drove all the way out to the farm to buy our plants. We'd heat the old green-house with a kerosene heater."

"Alex wants to be on the baseball team," I say. "I quit college," I say. The sun glints gold on the water, warming us as we fight the cur-rent of sorrow running between us. Sometimes, we find ourselves laughing. The silenced past seeps upward; twice he says and twice I say, "I've never told anyone this before...." The sun shimmers on the water. The tide ebbs quickly, time going.

We climb back up the hill, and I show him the downstairs of my little house.

"This is the living room. This is the kitchen where I like to cook a lot of food for my family. These are the stairs. Do you want to see your brothers' rooms?"

"Yes," he says quietly, as if it is a trial he is ready to face.

He holds back, glancing quickly into their sunny rooms, at their toys and books, at his brothers' lives, their lives here with me where they are loved, safe, not given away. We go back down to the kitchen, the woodstove unlit because it is a warm and beautiful day. We eat tuna sandwiches across from each other and return to our stories. The joy we feel right at this minute lies like a shimmering pond within our grief, the landscape of our lives.

"Would you like me to tell you about your father?"

His hands stop midair, a picture of our first day I will never for-get, the image of his powerful hunger to belong.

"You look like him," I say gently. "He's Italian. He lives in Massachusetts. I was sixteen, and he was a senior at Boston College. We met at Hampton Beach. His name is Anthony."

I watch him struggle to understand what this information means, to integrate it into his twenty-one-year-old identity.

"It doesn't matter anyway" is all he says.

We hug each other silently at his car, trying to prepare for whatever will happen next. He drives back down the road. I can hear his car moving away long after I have lost sight of it. The days of the following week roil tumultuously around every word he has said in those sunny hours, every gesture, his glance, a movement of his hand. I do not sleep. A letter comes on Friday, asking if he can come again, maybe on Sunday.

The call had come in May.

"Hello," she had said. "My name is Janet Larsen. I work with the New Hampshire courts. I want you to sit down. Your son is looking for you."

I had been hoping for this call for twenty-one years, and it came so quietly into an ordinary spring day.

"We will take this very slowly," she said. "This can cause enormous problems for both the child and the birth mother."

"But I'm ready now. I've been waiting for years."

"You will write letters for a while, through me. It is devastating to the child to experience a second abandonment."

"I would never abandon him."

"But you did."

"I could never abandon him again."

"But it happens a lot," she said.

"Where is he?"

"I can't tell you that yet."

"Can you tell me his name?"

I felt myself separate from my voice. Suspended time. A hush, inside me, in the air I breathed.

"His name," she said, "is Paul."

This sound, this soft little sound, was electric. Twenty-one years and my son had a name. A name! Paul. I could hold this tiny word. I could hold Paul. My son had a name. My son was named Paul.

"Your son," Janet told me, "is extraordinary. Paul is a spectacular young man."

I waited every day for Paul's first letter. Finally, after three weeks, a letter came through Janet. There was a picture enclosed, my first sight of my lost child. It was blurred and gray, but here was Paul—serious, a strong jaw, intelligent eyes looking directly at the camera. A young man, the child gone forever.

Dear Meredith, he wrote. *I don't know what to say. I don't know how to do this. Paul.*

His handwriting was big, strong, slanted along the page as if he were in a hurry. I carried his note in my pocket, reading it again and again as I stared at his photograph.

Janet called and said, "Write back to him right away. He is very scared. Ask him some questions."

Dear Paul, My name is Meredith Hall. I live in East Boothbay on the coast of Maine. I have a son, Alex, who is ten, and a son named Ben, who is seven. We keep sheep and chickens and big gardens. Please tell me about yourself. Tell me about your family. Tell me about what you like to do. I want you to know that I have always loved you.

Janet edited our letters for revealing details. They came to us blacked out: *My name is Meredith_____. I live in _____ on the coast of_____.*

My name is Paul _____. I grew up on a farm in _____ in southern _____. My mother and father, _____ and _____, are very loving and supportive. I work sixty hours a week for _____ Construction Company to pay my way through the University of _____. Slowly, piece by piece, our ghost lives took shape.

Our letters went back and forth, back and forth, faster and faster, three a week, four. I was in a dream. I held Alex and Benjamin close to me. Everything was changing for them, a new brother, a mother with a history. My guilt deepened. I did not tell them yet.

Janet called me on October 17, at nine in the morning.

"We have a mess," she said. "Your doctor let a family in your father's town adopt your son. I have never seen anything like this in twenty years. I was hoping it would turn out all right. But yesterday at lunch in the college dining hall, your son was talking to his good friend, a woman your age. She has been like a mentor to him since he was in high school. His friend, he found out, is your stepsister, Molly. He's known your father for years, and doesn't like him much. Now the man is his grandfather. The implications for him are very complex. I think we should change our plan. I think he should meet you immediately. Do you want to meet here in my office tomorrow?"

"No," I said. "We need to be outside."

And so he came to my house on a brilliant and wrenching October day. October 18, 1987.

He does not disappear. He comes again on Sunday. And the next Sunday. Each time, I ask my friends to take Alex and Ben for a few hours. On the third visit, late in the afternoon, we drive in his little car to pick them up at Carrie's. He drives twenty miles an hour. I ask him why and he says he is afraid we might crash. As if I am glass, as if I might disappear again forever.

Carrie smiles at him.

"This is Paul, an old family friend," I tell her and my children.

Carrie is curious. Paul and I look very much alike. He looks like my brother, like Alex and Benjamin. They lean against me, and Paul is pushed into silence. Alex and Benjamin are hesitant with me, as if they know something huge is here with us, as if the world is now spring-loaded. Always I have surrounded them with my fierce armor, my love, my absolute protection. But I am thinned out, tentative, and they start right then, in Carrie's yard, to make the adjustments I am going to ask of them. I feel them draw back, just a little, to watch this thing that is happening, this enlargement, this end of what we have been. Paul stands among us, part of us and terribly alone. None of us knows what is next. I am caught between loves, my two children suddenly three, on an unnavigated course. The confused waters swirl around all of us as we drive home.

Paul tries to ask his brothers questions but has nowhere to begin. "How do you like school?"

"Okay. It's boring."

"I saw your bedrooms..."

"You did?" This surprises them.

"—and your baseball cards. Wow. That's quite a collection."

"Yeah."

"When I was your age, I collected baseball cards, too."

Alex and Benjamin smile and are polite. "Oh," they say.

Paul becomes quiet, driving us slowly back to our house. The boys chatter with me. I think that this time when Paul leaves, I might never see him again, that he will feel too outside, that he will be too lost to fight his way into us. That this life I have made without him can never open enough to hold him.

He lets me hug him good-bye when he leaves. He calls on Wednesday and says he is coming on Sunday.

"Can the boys be there?" he asks.

I am overcome with his courage. It is the beginning of this new family.

It is winter. He comes most Sundays. He spends part of his Christmas break here, still the mysterious family friend visiting. He is very, very funny, with an irreverent view of the world. His intelligence shines. But his sadness deepens, the price he is paying—the given-away child with a separate history, struggling to belong. I think I have time to start again, to forget the years of grief, to love him so fully he will forget the life he has lived, the terrible cost to him of my actions when I was sixteen.

It is time to tell the boys. "My loves," I say to Alex and Benjamin. "I have something huge I need to tell you." I ache with guilt, understanding that I am asking them to take in stride the effects of my own enormous history.

When I tell them they have a big brother, they don't hesitate. They stand in front of Paul and grin. They climb on him, giggling. Like monkeys, they study every inch of his face and hands, studying his ears and his toes and his back, comparing their own hands and feet and hair. They peer inside his mouth. Alex drapes his arm over Paul's shoulder while they sit on the couch; Benjamin gets in under Paul's arm. All of my children are together, here in our little house in Maine. The worst seems to be over; the young children I love so completely will be all right. I am enormously grateful for their capacity to include Paul, to give him part of me.

Paul says to me, "No more sorrow, Meredith. We are done with sorrow."

His first birthday with me is coming. Is it May 30 or 31? I have to ask.

"Are you kidding? You don't know when my birthday is?"

"You don't understand," I try to say. "The labor was so long. It lasted over days. It was a long, long, terrible dream. I was so alone. I didn't want them taking you away from me. I never knew if it was day or night when you were born, how many days we had spent parting from each other."

I want him to understand the longing that comes to its tightest knot every year on his birthday. I want him to understand what happened to me when he disappeared out the delivery room door forever. But I do not know the day he was born, and it devastates him.

The hurt is in his eyes. "Well," he says sharply. "It's Memorial Day. Every year I watched the parade. When I was little, I believed it was all for me. For my birthday. That the whole town was out there celebrating my birthday."

Paul does not call me Mom, or Mum, or Mumma, like Alex and Ben. He has a mother, Ruth. He has a younger sister, Debbie, adopted when she was two. He has a father, Armi. Paul grew up poor. Very, very poor. He grew up on a farm in the poverty of rural New Hampshire, the poverty of previous generations of French Canadian farmers and grain elevator workers and shoe-shop laborers, the poverty of families living in buses in the woods and neighbors shooting a son in the face with a shotgun and rats drowning in the dug well and cardboard being laid in a pad in the soles of shoes and newspaper being stapled on the walls of the house to keep out the wind. When Armi and Ruth adopted Paul and his sister, they had to add two new bedrooms to their tiny shack and bring the plumbing indoors. Armi worked Paul like a hired man, a child who was cold and bloodied and exhausted and frightened by the work and the machines that did it.

As a boy, Paul crept out to the living room in the night to listen to the people on the television; he studied how they spoke, shedding *ain't*s and *don't*s as he whispered back at the television's dreary light, "I am not going," and "He doesn't own a car." He became bilingual, with a language for home and a language for the world. Paul was harassed on the school bus for smelling of cow manure. Eventually he stopped taking the school bus, and eventually he did his own laundry, stashing clean clothes for school in plastic buckets in the woods. He learned to sit with his feet flat on the floor so the soles of his shoes didn't show. He learned how to fight, which he did most days of his life in Epping, how to fight dirty, how to win. But he was small, and Armi carried fury in his strong, tough body.

Armi put the scar on his chin. He put the thin white lines across the backs of his thighs and calves. He shaped his nose this way. He put the knobby bumps on his ribs, front and sides. Armi used his fists, the back of his hand, his boots. He used a shoe, lilac switches, whatever was within reach. He used his mouth: *You fucking little baby. You're no son of mine.* He burned his drawings. He kicked him as he made him burn his books, his notebooks of stories. Paul hid from his father on the top shelf of his closet. He hid in the woods and in the barn. His mother, his other mother, hid under the table and cried.

When he was six, eight, ten, Paul slept in the barn beside the huge warm cows or out under the pines on the hill in the pasture. He hitchhiked to New York State to his uncle Dan's when things were too bad. He was ten, twelve, tough, scared. He protected Ruth from Armi. He did a man's work outside, and cooked and did laundry inside for his little sister. The state tried again and again to take him away. Fuck you, he said to the social workers, his scrawny little arms flailing. I fell down the stairs. No one hits me here. Fuck you.

What is it like to learn that your child has grown up so harmed? Sometimes I condemn out loud the man and woman who raised him. Immediately, ferociously, Paul comes back at me. "Don't you dare criticize my mother and father," he says. "They raised me." I know instantly that he is right. I abandoned my baby. Who am I to condemn the strangers who took him home?

"My mother thinks I am Jesus Christ," he says. "She loves me very, very much."

He is right about that, too. He and Ruth were like besieged children together, and Paul was the heroic older brother. Ruth worked at the shoe shop all day and tended the large market garden every evening and weekend. But she didn't cook, didn't clean, didn't drive, didn't do laundry. Paul was the mother, cleaning, protecting Debbie, writing notes to the school explaining absences when the welts and broken bones threatened to blow open the house. But he was also Ruth's playmate. They looked for kittens in the sweet hay in the barn and shot snakes in the field. Ruth would invite Paul to play hooky from school. Like conspirators, they crawled around the front yard in the dark, collecting a coffee can of night crawlers. Leaping with joy the next morning after Armi left for work, Ruth took the can from the back of the refrigerator and she and Paul headed miles through the woods to one fishing hole or another to catch hornpout. Sometimes they walked together to the dump and threw bottles over the edge into the pit, watching them shatter into sunlit shards. By the time Paul was seven, he was earning his own money by hustling the neighboring farms for work shoveling snow and weeding gardens and stacking firewood. Paul saved his money and walked with his mother to Fecteau's, where he would buy her a steamed hot dog. Often he tells me, "My mother loving me is what saved my life."

When I was sixteen a doctor gave my baby to a very poor woman who cried every time she came to his office. He gave my baby to Ruth and Armi. I was told my baby would live in Virginia. I thought he rode his bike to school, humming. That he held his father's hand when he walked along the river that must flow behind his house, that he made birthday cakes with his mother, standing on the kitchen chair by the counter. I thought he went to sleep warm and safe, curled maybe around the empty place of adoption but safe and loved. Instead, he lived a mile from my father. Armi made him cut lilac switches and bring them to him. Armi had a wide, white leather belt with rows of holes all the way around it. Of course, I have never seen this belt. But I remember it now, always.

When my baby was born, I had never known a pregnant woman. I had never seen a newborn baby. I had never heard the woman-stories of birthing. Terrified, helpless, shamed, the birth was a long, dark nightmare. The labor was induced, a violent high-forceps delivery. I was anesthetized for the last few minutes to prevent me from seeing my child. When I woke up, there was no baby. No one spoke to me as they cleaned me up, a slutty girl who had just dropped an illegitimate baby.

When my baby was born, he must have cried like all babies cry as they greet this life. He was not laid on my exhausted body. He was not held to my familiar heartbeat, my breathing rhythms, the sound of my voice. He would have been washed of my blood by a nurse, maybe tenderly, maybe not. He would have been carried under bright lights to a nursery and placed, unheld and alone, in a metal bed.

I stayed for five days on the maternity ward, among all the cheerful, busy mothers, the fathers and young children and grandparents visiting. The babies were brought for food and comfort throughout the day and night. Of course, no one brought me a baby. A nurse would have picked him up every four hours and given him a bottle. His diapers would have been changed. A hand would have washed him with a wet cloth each day, his head and tiny feet and knees and chest. Back in his hospital bed, he would have stared at the lights overhead, watched the shadows of people moving in the sterile world around him.

Paul has a revised birth certificate, without my name on it. He was born to Ruth and Armi. They picked him up seven days after he left my body, my warmth, the *whoosh*ing pulse of my blood, my voice whispering to him in the long night. For seven days, my baby was motherless, unloved, absolutely alone in the vast circling universe. I have a photograph of Ruth standing next to a farm truck holding a baby. It is the day of their new arrival. She holds this little stranger out in front of her body like a hot casserole being taken to a neighbor. How long does it take to learn to love someone else's child?

Paul says that when he was very young, he clung to Ruth. He remembers leaning against her legs, climbing into her lap. He was teased by his country aunts and cousins for being a mama's boy—the shame of needing love. That I loved him and longed for him was not and is not of help. There is no going back. The mystery is this: by some great power of the heart and will, Paul brought himself up to be kind, and full-hearted, with an immense capacity to love and be loved.

We visit Ruth and Armi in Epping often—driving past my father's house, the house in which I lived until my baby was born, the house I have not been allowed to return to for many years, the house Paul's new grandfather lives in, driving on a mile, past the dump, to Ruth and Armi's house. Ruth and Armi have changed. They want Paul to forgive them.

"Hi, everybody," Ruth says, hugging Alex and Benjamin and me and her son. "Oh," she says, "I'm a mess. I'm so glad you guys could all come down. Look at you, Benjamin. Don't you look just like Paul. Paul, your brothers are getting taller than you! Alex, I heard you made it on the soccer team. Someday we're going to see one of your games." We know that Ruth and Armi never saw one of Paul's games, or school plays, or science projects, or graduation. "Come in. I need to go change. My God. I'm a mess. Armi is going to make us some bologna sandwiches. You like bologna sandwiches?"

Ruth is small with short black hair she cuts herself. She is gentle like an imaginative child, but her voice is strong and husky from cigarettes. Her house is small and cramped. It smells of mold and regret and bafflement. The television is on. The tiny rooms are messy, as if Ruth and Armi did not know we were coming. Paul is embarrassed, and angry with himself for being ashamed. Paul and Ruth stand close together in the kitchen, Paul's arm over the shoulder of his little mother. "Oh, Paul," she says playfully, adoringly.

He roughhouses with his brothers, entertaining his mother and father. Alex and Ben crowd with him into the worn chair, their arms around his neck as if they are protecting him.

"Paul really had to raise himself, you know," Ruth tells me. "I really regret that. From the time he was five or six. It was tough. I'm so glad he found you."

Ruth and I feel something very close to love for each other, woven of our love for our son, warp and weft. We are two mothers, full of guilt and love.

Armi wants to show Paul the new water pump he put in his old truck. Paul leans under the hood, nodding.

"Good, Dad," he says. "That's really good." He is polite, respectful, but the violence of this family's past lies like gunpowder under the calm.

We eat bologna sandwiches, Alex and Ben leaning on Paul at the table. Ruth sits next to me on the couch.

"Oh, my God," she says, "aren't they something, all those boys?

You must be so proud, raising such great kids. Paul's doing pretty good up there in Maine, isn't he?"

"Yes," I say carefully. "He's doing all right." How can I tell her that even this, the coming together of his two families, works relentlessly at Paul's old wounds?

"He's so lucky to have you, Meredith," she says.

I feel like a thief, stealing her son. Paul is right. She loves him so much she will give him this. But every time we sit together at her kitchen table, she tells me stories that circle her own failures. Each time, our son—the son I gave away, the son I left to strangers, the son I abandoned—shuffles his feet and clears his throat and says, "So what about them Red Sox?" Ruth meets the joke smiling like a child, saying, "Oh my God, Paul, what are you talking about? Are you hungry? You want some cake?"

"I used to be Swedish," he jokes with me, the past tense catching me hard. His blond hair and blue eyes were his only evidence.

Sometimes he says, "I am an alien, dropped here on Earth alone and weird, like no one else. I belonged to no one."

"You are Italian. And English and Welsh and Dutch," I say.

"No, I'm not," he says. "I am an alien."

We sometimes stand next to each other at the mirror over the desk, mother and grown son. We search for proof of the powerful tie we feel. The eyes, maybe, or the set of the shoulders. The hands. We are pleased when people tell us we look alike. It feels important that in this elemental way, we are part of each other.

I have read about the mythical chimera, a mix of creatures with the head of a fire-breathing lion, the body of a goat, and a serpent's tail. There are human chimeras, too. It has just been discovered that women carry fetal cells from all the babies they have carried. Crossing the defensive boundaries of our immune system and mixing with our own cells, the fetal cells circulate in the mother's bloodstream for decades after each birth. The body does not tolerate foreign cells, which trigger illness and rejection. But a mother's body incorporates into her own the cells of her children as if they recognize each other, belong to each other. This fantastic melding of two selves, mother and child, is called human microchimerism. My three children are carried in my bloodstream still. Benjamin and Alex and Paul, their cells crossing permeable boundaries and joining mine, float every day through my body, part of me. How did we not know this? How can this be a surprise?

Less incredibly, perhaps, the mother's cells are also carried in the child. During gestation, maternal cells slip through the barriers of defense and join her child's cells as they pulse through his veins. My children carry me in their own bodies, mother and child joined forever, both beings bumping against each other every day.

Of course, the implications are stunning. Mother and child do not fully separate at birth. We do not lose each other at that moment of severance. Every day we spend preparing our young children to live apart from us, independently, we do not have to feel the sharp pain of separation. And incredibly, every day I spent longing for my lost child, he was roaming with me still, part of me, unknown but there. All those years, I moved in his bloodstream, part of him. We belong to each other, cohesive and mysterious. We are joined in an *us*, past, present, and future.

Through this first spring and summer my three sons all play together. Paul has rented a cottage in the next town. They are brothers, noisy and wild. They ride in the car, laughing until they are yelling. They camp and hike and muck around in low-tide coves, bringing home jars of seawater to look at under the microscope. They hunt for frogs' eggs in the old ice pond in the woods and dance to loud music in the kitchen while I cook. They play cabin ball in the yard and read books and collect eggs from the chicken coop. They devise a coded language of brothers that leaves me happily outside.

Somehow, Paul knows how to love us and how to be loved. He is tender, patient, generous, funny. In the kitchen at suppertime, he walks in the door yelling, "Who wants cake for supper?" On the sidelines at Alex's or Ben's soccer games, he calls out, "Way to go, Alex! Smart play! Wow, Ben! Great work!" Afterward with them, he remembers their every move. One day he says, "You guys need a new woodshed. This thing's going to fall on your heads one of these days. Get out some paper and let's design a good building." He buys them carpenter's belts and tools and they spend two weeks building the woodshed, raising walls and setting windows and roofing the steep pitch. He says, "What you guys need is a salamander. Come on. We're all going out to look for a salamander. We can't come back in until we find one."

But these months are also confusing, upheaving. Sometimes, we all rest in our deep love for one another. Then Paul or I suddenly fly apart in despair or hurt or too much remembrance. Some days we want to be loved, we need to be reassured that this is forever. Other days, we fight for our lives, the lives that have worked pretty well before. Sometimes we can't contain everything that has been lost. Once, Paul punches the barn door again and again, sobbing, for the first time in years he tells me, and his hands bleed. Sometimes I cry, pain rising from the place before he came. Now he is here and I finally grieve, crying in the field while Alex and Ben play in the house.

My friends tell me, "This is a miracle. It is a fairy tale with a happy ending."

Paul and I get lost in our histories, each of us a child who has been betrayed and abandoned, each of us carrying mothers, fathers. We lose sight of whose grief is playing out in the circling, churning conversations and outbursts. I carry my own story each day. It is my intimate shadow: when I was very young, when I was in very big trouble, I was abandoned by my mother and then my father. The harm done has become a bony structure surrounding my life, and I carry its weight.

But now I am the mother. Whatever I have learned is put to the test with my children. Do I know how to love, how not to harm, how to protect and defend, how to be sanctuary? I have believed from the moment I gave birth to Alex and Benjamin, my kept children, that I know the obligations of a mother's love. My two young sons are growing up inside their trust in me. I try so hard to be a good mother. I am safety, tenderness, praise. But I am also, always, the child cast out to the world a long time ago. I move between the sorrows of my past and an unrelenting will to love my children well. I am child, and I am mother.

And I am also guilt. I am a mother who gave her baby to strangers. For twenty-one years, my unnamed child held me hard against the mystery of harm. I loved him. I longed for him. But I did not protect him. There is one truth in my son's life: his mother gave him away. Whatever griefs and rage and questions of my worth have haunted me through my life, here is my child, his chin scarred and his eyes flashing the stories of his own great injury.

Whose griefs are these? I never intended harm. I know how to love. And yet I have not loved well. Maybe all of us at some time move from our compass point of true north, that place in which we determine to correct the failures done to us, and we circle, waver, and find our own direction outward in the world to create injury. The rhumb lines of navigation are not straight. The wounded and cast-out child, I hold my abandoned son to me asking forgiveness for casting him to the world.

The silent home movie Ruth gave me is herky-jerky. Paul is smiling, maybe five years old. Someone off-camera speaks to him. He turns away tentatively, then grins back at the camera. He has no shirt on. He is very thin, his pants hanging off his little hips. His hair is buzzed short. His eyes are enormous. He is laughing, but he looks as if he is ready for a strike, that something just out of sight might sweep down at him. He has something, a toy, I think, in his hand. I stop the film. I want to know what it is, what he holds, what is his, but I cannot make it out. Dark wall paneling and a cluttered counter jitter behind him in the shaky film. I want to hold his jersey over his head while he pushes his thin arms into the sleeves, like Alex, like Ben. I want to protect him. I can see knees and pant legs and dress hems around him—aunts and uncles who call him Paulie and know his father beats him—and for that minute he is the center. I watch him smile, his gentleness and powerful intelligence playing across his face even then. Play, stop, rewind. Play, stop, rewind. Crying on my living room floor, I study my child. I want to hold him. To hear his voice. I cannot stop watching, and feel the old undertow of loss taking me.

Paul comes in and sees what I am doing. He grabs the film from the machine. We shout and I struggle for the film, that tiny window into a few small minutes in my lost child's life. He hurls the film out the front door and it breaks against a tree. I gather the flowing tape against me. We cry, holding each other, rocking on the cold, dry grass.

Once, in a class at Bowdoin, I saw a short film of a man crossing the sealed border into South Korea with one hundred other North Koreans for the first time since the Korean War broke out, in 1950. They had been granted a three-day reunion, held in a hotel ballroom, with relatives they had not seen for fifty years. The film showed this man's meeting with his eighty-six-year-old mother. Sixty-nine years old, the man leaned over his old mother in her wheelchair, rubbing his tear-soaked face against her clothing. "Mother! Mother!" he cried. "Your son is here!" The wailing of hundreds of other people filled the room around them. His mother held him fiercely by the neck, crying, "I thought you had died, I thought you had died, I thought you had died."

Another man met his hundred-year-old mother. They clutched each other desperately. "Mother," he said, his tears flowing, "I have missed you every single day." He was seventy-five years old, the child coming home. The buses waited at the curb to take them all back into exile.

Mothers and sons cast apart, reunited. Paul and I clutch each other, every day trying to trust a little more that there will be no more parting. "Mother! Son!" we cry. "I am here! I have missed you every single day."

I wish I had been the one to find Paul. That he would have been the one to receive the call: "Your mother is looking for you." I watched for him every single day for twenty-one years, looking into the faces of every child I passed, hunting for some sign of me, something that would call out to me and say, "I am your child." Blue eyes, brown, green; blond hair, black, brown; skinny boy, boy running, child curled up reading, child crying, child wading in cold water. Teenager hugging his knees to his chest and watching the wind take dried leaves across the lawn. Young man calling over his shoulder to a friend. And always, always, I watched every car: the child, the boy, the young man slipping past, the force of my gaze drawing his eyes to mine. Is it you? I asked as the car sped on away. Every child might be mine. But I did not try to find him.

A girl who had a baby in 1966 was not only shunned, not only cast off to her own lonely orbit. She was shamed. When I sat the first time at Dr. Quinn's desk, a stranger to me, he surveyed me silently and said, "Don't try to tell me who the father of this baby is. I know you have no idea. Girls like you never do." He said, "You need to give this baby up. You don't deserve a baby." He said, the lasting message, "You must never try to find this child. After the birth, you are nothing to him. You will destroy his life if you have contact with him. If you try to find him, it will be the most selfish thing you could do. You are nothing but trouble." I understood. I was a filthy girl, a contaminant in my poor child's life. No matter what, I didn't deserve him. If I interfered, I would hurt him, again. It all seemed correct to me, the irrefutable truth. Shame, crushing shame, silenced me for those nine months, and for the next twenty-one years.

If I had believed that I was an ordinary girl who got pregnant because of irresponsibility, not because I was destined to harm the world, my son would one day have received a call. It would have made an enormous difference. That call, coming at ten years or fifteen or twenty, would have said, I have loved you. I am waiting for you. Please come home.

October 18, one year, a birthday of sorts. Our days have found rhythm again. Laughter erupts between us often, and the upheaving emotions are quieting. We learn to dare happiness, relief. My friends are right: it is a miracle, a fairy tale, although it feels fragile every day, as if it all might disappear again if we turn our backs. Our old lives recede, and our new family holds together. I have my son. He has his mother. Alex and Benjamin have accepted their new brother. That has to be enough.

I give him my small clay owl, something I have had since those devastated years after he was born. "This is to remind you every day that this place in my life is forever," I say.

He gives me an acorn. "My renaissance," he says, his voice soft and hopeful.

There are no patterns for how to do this, how to hold each other safely and fully after a lifetime apart. We cannot plot out the future. We are a family. We love each other. We need each other. That is our only map.

Chapter Fourteen

Reckonings

My son's other mother, Ruth Marie Hobbs, was born in Watertown, New York, in 1935. She married Armand Laurent, a New Hampshire farm boy fresh out of the Eighty-second Airborne, when she was barely eighteen. Seven days after I left my baby on the third floor at Portsmouth Hospital, Ruth and Armi Laurent took him home to the farm in Epping. They named their new baby Paul Armand Laurent. From the day I met my son when he was twenty-one years old, Paul has had two mothers. Ruth and I move in an indefinable circle of love and gratitude and tenderness, asking of Paul and each other forgiveness for the terrible failings of both mothers.

Ruth is less than five feet tall. Her grandmother Hobbs in New York was Seneca Indian, and it shows in Ruth's black and gray tussle of coarse hair, her flashing black eyes and dark skin, the slight downturn of the corners of her mouth, even in her perpetual, playful smile, a smile that seems to be half a step ahead of the silly joke, the wisecrack, the tease that she wants to come her way. It is also a smile of surprised unease, of sadness, of something like fear.

Clinging to Paul's hand, Ruth greets me with that smile the first day I meet my son's parents. "Oh, my God," she says to me, "he looks just like you, don't he, Armi?" And then she says, "I'm just happy to meet the person who gave him to me." That is all. We sit at the table staring at each other, studying our son's genes and his nurturance, eating sandwiches from paper plates, both of us smiling and staring, while Paul—twenty-one and struggling for months to find his new self, son of Meredith, brother of Alex and Benjamin—stands against the counter watching us both, his sensitive face masked.

Ruth and I hug each other when Paul and I leave. "I want you to come here all the time," she says. "You're part of the family. Oh, my God, no wonder he's so smart. He's just like you, you know that?" Smiling at me, whatever panic she is feeling is submerged beneath her love for Paul.

"Well, that was pretty surreal," Paul says as we drive back to Maine, back to the life he now shares with this mother and his two new brothers. "Hello, I'd like you to meet my mother, Ruth. I'd like you to meet my other mother, Meredith. Jesus. Who ever says that in their lives?" He laughs, a tight, tired laugh.

The farm was Armi's great-great-grandfather Macy's, and his great-grandfather's and grandfather's and father's, forty-seven acres of the best soil in town. The big house had burned to the ground when Armi was a boy, around the time his mother abandoned her five kids —four girls and Armi—to their drunk and abusive father. In its place they built a shack, sided with asphalt roof shingles, with two rooms and no plumbing. Armi quit school in eighth grade and worked on both his brother-in-law's farm and his father's. He enrolled in a vocational program in a nearby town, studying carpentry, but he was kicked out for a vicious fight with the instructor. He was in the army by the time he was seventeen. Stationed in upstate New York, he met Ruth when she was seventeen years old, the baby of thirteen Hobbs children.

Ruthie was spoiled, her sisters say, the pet of the family. There wasn't much to spoil her with. She told me once, showing off her collection of dolls she'd found at the dump and dressed in new lacy clothes, that she had never owned a doll. She loved her father, who worked in the grain mills and liked women, was silent, and made Ruth feel protected. Her mother was strong enough to carry the family, cleaning houses and stitching shoes and scavenging junk for resale. She once closed herself in the woodshed with an intruding skunk after no one else would try to get him out. She fought him into submission and held him high when she emerged stinking. Ruth told the story with glee. I have seen pictures of Ruth in some of the many houses they lived in, as unpaid rent chased the whole family town to town. There is never any furniture; the floor is bare wood or worn flowered linoleum. There are no curtains. But there is tiny Ruth, smiling, smirking, laughing with her sisters, a broom handle or pan or hairbrush a prop for whatever gag she was up to. She quit school her junior year, when her father moved them again midyear to a new town.

Armi dreamed of owning and running a gas station in New York with one of Ruth's brother's. But Armi was illiterate. Armi is still barely literate, unable to read the newspaper or instructions on the box of instant potatoes. He didn't dare try to start a business of his own. Then his father got sick and called his son home to the farm, the place of such misery for Armi. Ruth and Armi got married on November 5, 1955, and Armi took his child bride home to the little shack in Epping. She tells me often that she felt duped when she saw the farm, but it was too late. I have also seen photographs of Armi at this time. He is short, with jet-black hair greased into a showy series of waves. He is very muscular, a worker, and always has a cigarette in his hand. He smiles for the camera, as if he believes things are going to be good sometime soon.

I don't know when Armi started roughing up Ruth, when he started drinking hard like his father and threatening her, when the poverty and his own abusive acts finally succeeded in wearing away any dreams he once had. Little Ruthie, far from home and her family, was easy to intimidate into submission. Paul prayed throughout his childhood that she would divorce his father and they would flee to New York. Unlike Armi's own mother, she never cried uncle, never left her husband. By the time Armi's father died, they had carved their life in Epping too deeply to start again somewhere else, and the emotional forces that drew them together had them both in a vise.

In spite of the rich soil and Armi's very hard work, the farm couldn't support them. Armi worked as a mason, and plowed roads for the town, and hired out to help hay other farmers' fields, and then came home and worked his farm nights and weekends. He kept dairy cows and raised beef cattle and pigs. He traded animals at auction, trying to leverage ten or twenty dollars from a steer he bought a month before and fattened. He cut hay and grew a big market garden. He managed to build and keep working the equipment he needed, converting his grandfather's horse-drawn tedders and potato harvesters to clanking machines he towed behind his '33 Massey Harris tractor. Everything was broken all the time. Armi kept the ancient carburetor working by carving floats from poplar. He welded parts from dead trucks in the field to the plow or the baler or the sickle bar mower.

Ruth worked at the shoe shop until the next round of layoffs. She baby-sat neighborhood children. She planted the garden and weeded and picked string beans and beets and corn and tomatoes, selling them at the stand under the huge maple tree by the driveway. There was no play in her new life, I am certain of that. And there were no children. Until her doctor—my doctor—told her he knew of a baby coming. He also knew about Ruth's bruises and crying and medications for depression and hysteria and acute withdrawal, her hospitalizations for "nerves." On June 6, 1966, Ruth and Armi Laurent carried my unnamed baby home. Two years later, they received Debbie, a two-year-old girl from a drug-addicted mother.

Armi worked his son like a man. His aunt told me once, "Everyone in the family knew it wasn't right how hard Armi used Paul. No one stopped him, though." Armi beat Paul with the same force he used on the men he fought downtown at Bea's Bar or the Legion Hall. But here is the hardest part, for Paul and for Ruth, and for me: Ruth hid. She slipped under the kitchen table at the first whiff of trouble, which came daily. She cowered, hiding her face, and cried.

When it was all over, she crept away to her room or the bathtub, locking the door against the mess outside. Worse, she would tell on Paul to Armi, like a sibling managing to foist the inevitable beating onto someone else. I have heard these stories from my son, and from Ruth.

But the connection between Paul and his mother was powerful and intuitive. "I can remember how much I liked being with her," Paul says. They raised tomato and pepper plants together in the makeshift greenhouse behind the barn. Working side by side in the warm enclosure, with February snow still on the ground, Ruth and Paul grew hundreds of plants. They believed that they shared a special magic that made the plants grow huge and healthy. Customers came from far away every spring to buy flats of plants, the best they could find anywhere.

But Armi always came home at the end of the day, filled with his own private rage. Finally, when Paul was fourteen, he stood up to his father. One night after supper, Armi raised a large glass vase over Ruth's head, threatening to kill her. Ruth was backed up against the counter, crying. Paul grabbed a knife and pushed it against Armi's back, screaming, "If you touch her, I'll fucking kill you, I swear to God." I imagine frozen, silent minutes. Armi threw the vase to the floor, left the house, and didn't come back for three days—the first time in Paul's memory he stayed away all night. When he returned, Paul says he looked twenty years older, beaten. After that, Paul shared the house with his father but didn't speak to him for three years. Armi has never had a drink since, and has never again touched anyone in his family. The Armi I know is a weak and broken man who wants desperately to be forgiven, who knows in fleeting flashes what he has done and senses but can't identify the link between his father's rage and his own. He says to people moving around the kitchen making lunch or supper, "I thought I was doing what I was supposed to do." He says to Paul before they hang up the phone each month, as if he is pleading, "Love you."

Paul always knew exactly where on the farm he was going to

build his house someday, on the south-facing pine knoll beyond the first pasture. The farm shaped him. It is inside him, in spite of the terrible demands of work and the grim kind of love he knew there. But when Paul was fifteen, as the town prepared to take the farm for back taxes, Armi abruptly announced that he was selling out and paying off the debts. He believed that if the family left the farm, they would leave behind their history together, that Paul would slide back into being a son and Ruth would love him again. Paul broke his silence and begged him to let him clear three house lots on Old Route 101, on the back side of the farm, beyond the railroad tracks. "Dad!" he argued. "Do you know how much land is selling for? We'll have enough to pay the taxes for the next twenty years."

Armi wouldn't budge. "That's not for people like us," he said. "Don't be getting above your upbringing." He sold the farm for a song to the first people who came along, a middle-aged couple from Massachusetts. Armi sold the animals in four days, and Paul spent two weeks hauling every piece of equipment from the old barn to the dump, generations of work—harnesses and sharpeners and baling wire and grain scoops and ox yokes. The family moved into their new home on the dump road, a tiny box on a half acre in a new subdivision named after the developer's daughters—Bren-Lo. There was barely any insulation and the walls were made of flake board. But Armi was determined to start new, and Ruth was relieved to be done with her lifetime of hard work. Of course, a new and pure love didn't come.

Ruth never makes me feel that I am anything other than a gift to her. She speaks often, always obliquely, about the rage spent by Armi in their old house on the farm. She blames Armi, but says to me in each of these talks, "Paul was like a little grownup, taking care of me. He had to be like a mother to me, and to Debbie. He had to run the farm with Armi. It wasn't good for him. I know that. He raised himself. Not like Ben and Alex. You've done such a good job. Oh my God, you must be so proud of those kids. You're such a good mother. Paul should have had a mother like you. Paul never says anything, but I know he carries it all with him. What Armi did." She never places herself directly in that sentence.

Alex and Benjamin and Paul and I drive often to Epping to visit with Ruth and Armi. Paul is fiercely protective of his mother, and feels guilty for finding me, for moving to Maine, for fitting into his new family. He mothers Ruth, teasing her, grinning back when she giggles with happiness, praising her fully and freely and tenderly. The boys like Ruth, recognizing in her, I think, a child like them, a small person brimming with kindness and simple needs and vulnerabilities. And they know that she feels instantaneous love for them, her son's brothers, the boys she thinks Meredith has done such a miraculous job raising.

The house is cramped, hot and steamy. Everything smells of mildew and fried meat. Each time when we get home we have to wash our clothes and jackets, wash our hair and air the car. Armi talks nonstop from the kitchen table, drinking another cup of coffee, with everyone ignoring him and talking over him. Ruth sits in her sagging blue chair in the living room, sits and then jumps up for a cigarette out on the porch, sits and jumps up to bring from her room the new jewelry box she found at a yard sale, sits and jumps up to ask me what I think of the pretty bluebird stencil she has cut out of an old window shade.

A chaotic mix of love and rage, of regret and guilt and beseeching and a struggle to forgive, of a past too heavy to transcend, fills this little house. Alex and Benjamin are a counterpoint, adored and protected children who feel the shifting balance here of love and hurt, clean and protected children who have never been yelled at, never touched except in love, coming as witnesses to this unimaginable history.

Ruth pulls out pictures of the good times from those years, snapshots of my son, part of a family living in its own intimacy and mystery. The boys climb down to the floor with her.

Paul glances at me and whispers, "You all right?"

"Yes, I want to see them," I whisper back.

But it takes only two—Paul at an age I have to guess at, maybe twelve, holding a fish, bare-chested and grinning; Paul in pajamas, maybe four, smiling, his eyes enormous, riding a plastic tricycle in the kitchen at the farm—for me to stumble. Here is proof of Ruth's love for her son. And here is proof of my absence.

"Oh, I'm so stupid," Ruth says. "You don't want to look at these now. I'm going to send these home with you. You look at them there." I leave later that day with this imperfect record of a family, of my son's life apart from me, my son's life I abandoned him to. Ruth and Armi stand on their doorstep waving cheerfully to us as we drive back to Maine, Paul at the wheel. They call out to us, "Thank you so much for coming, Meredith! Be careful driving home! You do good in your games this week, Alex and Ben! 'Bye, Paul! Love you!"

Back we drive to Paul's new world, in a compressed confusion. We all sit at my table looking at the photos. There is Ruth in shorts and sneakers at the picnic table with Paul under the maple tree. Armi and Paul on the battered snowmobile. Debbie and Paul caught surprised by the camera on Christmas morning. Armi and Ruth with their new baby Paul, wrapped in blankets, on the couch at the farm. They are beaming like all new parents, anticipating the joys to come. I cannot see my son's face.

I write to Ruth the next morning, thanking her for letting me have the photographs, for sharing her son. She and I both understand that love is not enough, has not been enough for either of us to protect our son.

There have been changes in the house over the last few years. The house is kept cleaner. Their clothes are cleaner. Debbie's three children and husband, Tim, come most days for lunch or supper or the night. Ruth and Armi plant gardens all around the little house, with lawn chairs and rickety tables for smoking cigarettes and watching the kids in the wading pool or on the trampoline Paul bought. Ruth paints and wallpapers the rooms, hangs pictures of shy and pretty shepherdesses and milkmaids on the walls. She sometimes makes Paul's favorite raisin cookies for his visits. And the bedrooms and cellar fill with junk.

Ruth loves to pick the dump—the D-U, as she calls it. Armi hates that she does this and scolds her every day for it. He is not ashamed of her; I think he just can't stand to be left alone. I'm sure that is one of the reasons she does it—to be away from Armi. Ruth has become creative, even artistic. She finds a broken high chair at the D-U. Armi grudgingly repairs it for her, then she paints flowers and leaves all over it, and sells it for twenty dollars. She finds a small wooden box. Armi replaces the hinges, and Ruth lines the box with paper she makes from a kit Paul gave her, then stencils a primitive and engaging farm scene on the top. She makes ten dollars on it. She starts to make cards that fold like medieval triptychs, with pictures in crayon on the front and cut-out birds inside. She makes Paul birdhouses from Popsicle sticks, with bushes and flowers and fences and windows and red doors and tall cheerful chimneys.

There is something profoundly touching about her projects— their simplicity and innocence. Each time Paul sees her latest effort, he is crushed to silence; here is his mother, finally, claiming herself in the world. As she claims some release from Armi, spending her time at the dump and in the cellar and at her sewing machine, as she leaves the years at the farm behind her, the years of failed obligation to her children, she expresses pleasure in the world like a child. When Paul visits, she rushes to gather up what she has made and show it off to him, her protector and nurturer. When he shares his genuine surprise at her creative skill and praises her, she says, "Oh, you're just saying that, Paul." She slaps his chest. "It's just silly stuff I like to do. You really like it? You can take it home if you want it."

She also stops leaving the house. She and Armi refuse to come anymore to Maine. They refuse to go to Telly's for pizza or Fecteau's for grinders. They refuse to take a drive to the beach. Ruth won't drive over to the fabric store or the crafts store or Wal-Mart. She drives one-half mile each morning to the dump, where she spends an hour rummaging through the recycling room. Then she drives home, parking her car under the old pine tree. Paul is very disturbed by this closing in of her life, which she cannot explain except to say, "I don't want to go." Armi rambles endlessly about nothing, like a dog circling obsessively without ever lying down. There is no love shared between them. And yet she stays in the little house with him every day.

Ruth has a stroke and is on life support in Boston for three days before she dies. She is completely paralyzed, locked inside her tiny body, able to move only her eyelids. For sixty-seven hours—one hour for each of her years—Paul holds her hand and talks with her quietly, gently. Ruth answers his questions yes and no, eyelids lifting up and down. Paul tells her stories from their past together. He teases her as if she is a child being indulged by her father, trying to let her slide away the fragile and innocent child she has always been.

I imagine this is what happens in that faraway hospital room. I am not there because, in the end, Paul cannot navigate between two mothers. "It's just too confusing," he says. He has very little time to finally reckon with his mother's encompassing love, her adoration, her weaknesses that cost him so much.

Debbie is not there during this nightmare good-bye; the love and the pain are too intertwined in this family. But Armi is in that room. Broken with fear and grief and regret, Armi leans over his dying wife and smothers her in his tears and his kisses. Paralyzed, Ruth turns her lids down hard, as if she is shutting Armi out at last. She makes her final stand, a ferocious closing of her eyes.

I do not know what Paul says during all those awful hours. I know that death preempts any undoing of our lapses, any remaking of the love we offer when there is still life. I know that we suddenly find we wish we had said and done almost everything differently, that wisdom and calm come too late for us to correct the withholdings. I also know that Paul has nothing to regret. He loved his mother fully.

Two days before she had the stroke, Paul happened to drive down from Maine to see her. He came home distressed. She wouldn't leave the house for fried clams or pizza, wouldn't walk down the road to the river, wouldn't ride over to Debbie's to say hello. As he was leaving, she held him in her hug longer than usual and said quietly, "Oh, Paul." All the years were in that sigh, profound and flawed love, gratitude, great regret, and the constant haunting hope for forgiveness.

When the stroke hits, Paul says in anguish, "My mother is not a strong person. She won't work hard enough to save herself." When the MRI shows massive brain damage, as it becomes clear that Ruth will be locked in her dead body for the rest of her life, that she will subsist on feeding tubes and evacuating tubes and a respirator, Paul knows he will be the one in the family who will have to make the decision to remove life support. One more time, he will have to take care of his mother, shouldering the unspeakable decision to let her die. But he decides she deserves to know what is coming. She listens open-eyed. Then Paul asks her, "Do you want to stay on life support?" She closes her eyes, no. He asks her again. She closes her eyes. "Do you know what this means, Mum?" he asks. She pauses for only a minute. Tears slip down her face. Yes, she says, her eyelids lifting high. Yes. At the very last, Ruth takes over. Finally, Paul is allowed to be the child, and, at the last, she becomes his mother.

That night, Ruth is removed from life support and given heavy doses of morphine. She dies the next evening. Paul comes home to Maine stunned with grief. But he also comes home Ruth's son, relieved, at the very end, of being the grownup. There is a mystery here about love and all its failings, love and its final redemptions. After her funeral, Paul brings her ashes to my house. Without saying anything, he walks from room to room, holding the black plastic box close to his chest. He finally places the box on my old piano. "Ruth loved you," he says. "I think she'd like to stay here awhile with you," as if we two mothers do this better together.

Chapter Fifteen

The River of Forgetting

I am sitting with my father in his car in the parking lot at McDonald's, on a busy street in coastal Maine. It is a cold, sunny December afternoon. "I drive a black Acura SUV," he had said on the phone. I have seen my father only a few times in thirty-six years, although I periodically hear news of his health from my sister and brother, who see him often. I waited for more than three decades for my father to come to my defense and overturn the outcasting. He never did. I wrote to him a couple of weeks before this meeting, asking if he would like to meet with me, maybe for lunch. If he agreed to come, I knew it would be the last time I would ever see him.

He is eighty-four years old. I have a startling need to unburden my father of whatever guilt or regret he may carry, to say good-bye to him, to tell him I love him. I am afraid that he will die and I will be left with the unending conversation that has hung in the lost time between us all these years. There are many, many things I wish I could say to him, about hurt and betrayal and injustice, about longing. But he is an old man, and the time for all that has passed.

He lives just an hour from me, but it has been so many years since I last saw my father that I do not know him. My recollections of him are singular images. Once, as he sat in the kitchen, my father happily fed toast to our dog, Sam, placing the pieces on the dog's nose and telling him to wait until he said, "Okay!" Once, my father took us camping at a mountain lake. I cried when I caught a little perch. He cooked it in a heavy black pan over the fire, and we pulled the delicate, pure white skeleton, spine and hair ribs, from the hot flesh. Once, my father hung and skinned a deer he had shot. We children helped scoop the lungs and liver onto newspapers on the garage floor. My father cut out and held up to us the large heart, exclaiming on the beauty and wonder of the living organism. His maroon sweater had holes at the elbows. And once, my father whistled as he held my hand and we crossed a street in a town somewhere. The cars stopped and we walked from curb to curb as if it were a stage. My father placed a steaming plank against the ribs of his boat. My father sang in his cowboy hat. Old snapshots, a tiny album that defines my father, a stranger to me.

I have prepared myself for a meeting with a man I don't know. Yet I sit with him in his car in a parking lot, knowing him. What is this sudden deep recognition of so much I should not be able to remember? Here is my father's voice—tenor, quick with sound. These are my father's hands—large, capable, the long fingers knobbed with arthritis. These are his blue eyes, intelligent, hungry, clouded with an old man's fading vigor. This is his large chest and belly, his jowly neck, these are his long legs crossed at the ankles in his car. His white hair, a white mustache I have never seen. I sit next to my father, known to me, loved against reason in every detail, carried through all these years to this moment.

I have also prepared myself for the worst, coaching myself to stick, no matter what, to my clear intent: I want him to hear me say, "I love you. I have always loved you." That is my good-bye. I cannot find any other words worth saying to him now, at the end of our story. I do not know what he will say to me. I have to be ready for anything. I believe he will not be able to face that this is his last chance to make right whatever might haunt him. Whatever he says, I will not react.

"I will see you, Meredy," he had said on the phone. His voice was cold, aggressive. "But no lunch. And there are ground rules. No talking about the past." That's fine with me, this agreement to forget. I'm not surprised he has chosen not to remember, chosen to face me as if I have sprung from nowhere, historyless, a middle-aged daughter.

I have often stood at the mirror searching for my father in me, for connection, belonging, descent. I cannot find him, except perhaps in my own knobby fingers as I age. Nothing binds me to him but our past, the memories of love and of pain. Always, I want to ask the question, "Why?" But with my father's ground rules, there can be no answers. He chooses to forget, and I churn memory to understand.

I once read that the Greeks believed that souls, on their way through Hades, crossed the River of Lethe and drank of its waters, washing away their memories, and all pain, in preparation for their next incarnation. But freed of their pasts, they became like stone, and their voices became inaudible. The past was lost, and with it, all knowledge of how a life is lived, and why. *Lethe:* forgetfulness, oblivion. In response, cults emerged in which the initiates were trained to withstand great thirst so that when their time came to cross the River of Lethe, they would not be tempted to drink, to lose all memory of the lives they had lived. Instead, they were encouraged to continue their journey and choose the waters of the River of Mnemosyne, the river of memory. This must have taken great courage and discipline in the face of such great potential relief, physical and mental. As they drank the water of the Mnemosyne, they remembered everything that had ever happened to them with absolute clarity, suffering again the sorrows and the joys of a life, and in remembering, attained omniscience. Grief coming to wisdom. Wisdom impossible without reckoning with a past.

I have an old newspaper photograph hanging by my desk of a crypt in the small cemetery in Guanajuato, a city in the mountains of central Mexico. For two hundred years bodies were laid to rest in the ground beside the church, until there was just no more room. A tax was levied on each grave; the families of the dead had five years to pay off the fee. The rich were able to rest forever in their graves, but the poor whose families fell behind on the tax were disinterred.

Their bodies, mummified by the dry climate and minerals in the soil, were draped in coarse robes and hung at the necks on pegs in aboveground crypts. In the photograph, sunlight fills the great stucco halls, illuminating long neat rows of desiccated remains. The heads sit above the sacklike robes, and the feet hang below, still at a ninety-degree angle to the ankles, as if they might stroll home. Men, women, children, a baby. Each is unique, a person, a life. The past—complex lives, love and pain, betrayal and longing—stalks the long hall. The faces stare, hideous, eye sockets empty and mouths gaping as though they are calling out to us, their last words still on their contorted lips.

Did they say what needed to be said before they died? Raymond Carver, dying young of lung cancer, wrote his last, exquisite poem, "Late Fragment," the afternoon before he died. "And did you get what / you wanted from this life, even so? / I did. / And what did you want? / To call myself beloved, to feel myself / beloved on the earth." These men and women strung up in the hot dry vault—did they cry out their love before it was too late? Memory, the joy and lull and pain of the everyday, the storied history; at the end, what do we want to say? And the listeners, waiting for the last whispered truth: isn't what we each wait for this—to hear that after all, love is the great offering, the balm, the healer? To hear these gaping mouths sing a chorus of sudden revelation—*Yes, yes, I loved you, no matter what I said and did, I loved you and now I die.*

But do we say in the end what must be said? Perhaps not. Perhaps these mouths call out one simple last beseeching, *Love me.*

A neighbor once had a terrible car accident as she drove her daughter to Girl Scouts. The twelve-year-old girl died. For years after, small shards of glass worked their way out of the flesh of the mother's face, each glinting piece the same story, told again and again. She could not see or feel the tiny bits as they lay embedded in her flesh, part of her. But once in a while, they made their way out of her body, working slowly under the surface until they pierced the skin of her face and announced themselves. Sharp fragments, they hurt as they left her body.

She would call and ask me to come help her remove the glass splinters. The problem was that she couldn't see them. Running my finger gently over her skin, I could feel the jagged tip of each piece as it emerged. As I scraped and pulled with the tweezers, she cried, each tiny, gleaming fragment calling her to all she had lost.

The ground rules. *Lethe:* we forget. Imagine being able to wipe out the memory of war. Of lost children. Of a lover's betrayal. Of exiling by a father. *Lethe.* Imagine, to drink from the River of Forgetting.

Would I like to forget my father's outcasting? His voice when he explains that I deserve it? Would I like to forget the grief of this loss? These questions ask in the end if I would choose a different life. I am certain that I am memory, events, love and failure of love. The mummified poor hang in their rough sacks, records of experience, of happiness and grief and beauty and fear and joy. I carry the past each day, a life accruing in minute detail. Like the tiny glittering shards embedded in a mother's face, the past lies beneath the surface, intransigent truth. Remembered or not, what we say and do remains, always.

Lethe. The initiates trained themselves to resist forgetting, to choose the River of Remembering, wisdom impossible without reckoning with a past. Would I choose to forget? Would I choose a different life? No.

My father turns to me in his car, the parking lot filling and emptying like a tide around us. I am calm. I am sure this will be our last meeting. After all the waiting, I am here, with my father, at the end. This father I have loved so powerfully, so unreasonably, so inordinately, sits with me, finally. I have certain things to say to him, my final words.

On this cold December day, I know him. He is a scared old man. "I love Catherine with all my heart, more than anything else in the world," he says. Yes, I tell him. Yes, I say to my father, I know this. "When she goes, I want to go the next day." I understand, I say. "You know Bob Ellis," he says. No, Dad, I say. Who is that? "He's one of my best friends. I've known him all my life." He sounds surprised, injured, as if this is a failure on my part to pay attention to his life. No, I don't think I've ever met him, I tell him. What about him? "Well," my old father says, "he's got cancer. You know, the same kind that Ted Hines had. In his stomach." I do not know Ted Hines. My father's life, the everyday, so mysterious, withheld from me.

"I'm an old man now," he says, looking straight ahead. "I don't like it." And then what happens, I ask. "Oh, who the hell knows? I wish I had gone to church. I used to, you know, when I was a kid. Sang in the choir." His voice, singing in the living room. Now I will remember that he sang in church when he was a boy. A fragment.

"I considered being a Muslim once." I am shocked by this. "They stress discipline, you know. I was very drawn to that." He laughs. "I guess I wasn't a very good candidate for it, anyway." He is quiet. "What do you think happens?" My father and I have never had a conversation like this. There is a stillness between us, the river current smooth and calm. I think in the end our intentions are all that count, I say. I do not really believe this. I believe we are accountable, that what we do stays in the world. But he is an old man and I am here to tell him I love him. This is not forgiveness. It is an amnesty, releasing him from remembrance.

"I used to be away from home all the time. Never with you kids and your mother. I regret that. I'd come home from a business trip and change clothes and go right back out the door." Always, when I am in the winter woods where a brook runs under its shelf of ice, I am in the painting my father left in the front hall fifty years ago, a watercolor of a brook running under the winter ice someplace he liked to be, far from home. I say, You were hungry for the world, so smart and so creative and caught in such a small life. He turns to me, a handsome old face, my father I know. "I am so grateful you understand," he says. "You have no idea how grateful I am that you understand everything."

Of course, I don't. Memory glitters, shards pressing outward to the light. The lost past sits here with me in his car. It is bound to a handful of images, obsessive and persistent. Tomorrow, I will remember this black car, the tan sweater stretched over my father's large body. I will remember that his hands shook at first, scared of me. I will remember the great substantial warmth of his hand when he took mine and pressed his lips to my skin. That will be the end of this story.

The loss of my father broke something vital in me, and I have fought against it with all my might for most of my life. I struggle still to tell you about my father. My rage has died away finally. I think a lot about forgiveness, about trespasses. About intentions. The capacity of love to sustain, and to harm. I waited all my life, day after day after day, for my father to come and say, I am back. To say, I am sorry. But he chooses to forget. *Lethe.* I have stopped waiting for him to say to me, *Yes, yes, I loved you, no matter what I said and did, I meant no harm.* Instead, as we sit in the darkening car, I hear him say, "I am so glad you understand everything." His final cry, *Love me.*

Lethe. Oblivion. *Lethe,* a forgetting of the past. I will grant my father this. But our history is not erased. Events and our participation in them are not erased. Memory remains, the obsessive images we circle, struggling to make meaning. The uneasy remembering transforms pain into sorrow, and sorrow into love. There can be no oblivion.

There will not be another chance. I say the things I want him to hear at the end, my last words. *My father,* I say, *I am grateful to you for giving me gifts which make my life rich—my love for wildness, and for beauty. This enormous hunger for the world. Don't be sad. I love you. I know you love me. I am here to say these things to you.* Thank you for understanding, he says, holding my hand. His last words to me, beseeching.

Chapter Sixteen

Sojourn

From his little apartment off my kitchen, I can hear my father tap his spoon on the rim of his morning coffee. I hear the spoon's small clink on the wooden counter. The lever on his toaster zips down and springs back up, zips down and springs back up. "Goddamn it to hell," William mutters. He slams the lever down and it stays.

William is not really my father. I haven't seen my father for many years. And William has his own griefs. An old neighbor, he asked if he could live with me and my children after his wife, Eleanor, died. He was eighty-four. When he asked, I said yes. That was more than ten years ago. I am middle-aged, and we have become family, patching together the holes in each of our lives. It was hard to absorb William into my life, but now I no longer yell back and slam doors against his occasional tirades, his willful and childish outbursts. In fact, he has quieted over the past several months. It scares me.

His dogs' toenails click in small circles near him. He has left the fan on in the bathroom; it hums behind his shuffling between the counter and his table. It is seven o'clock on a brilliant Maine winter day. As I sip my tea at my old round table and turn the page of a book, the clean, bright air catches flicks of white on the chickadees at the feeders behind our house. William scrapes cold butter and then English marmalade across his toast. He places his plate and cup on the table, pulls out his chair, sits. He mumbles something to his dogs, and takes a bite from the toast. These sounds are both comforting and mildly irritating to me, repeated every single morning— these sounds of family routine, of my obligation.

"Good morning, William," I say, carrying my tea to his table.

He smiles an open and happy greeting. He is handsome still, with a high round forehead, blue eyes, and fine mouth. His body is thin, strong, and elegant; he sits with one leg draped over the other at the knee like a young man.

"What the hell is so good about it?" he asks. He means to provoke me, to tease me, but the fact is he is ninety-five years old and he is tired.

"The sun's good," I say. "Why don't you sit in the sun by the window after breakfast."

"I'll get sunburned." He is still teasing, but there is complaint behind his smile. He has brown crepey skin after a lifetime of sailing. He sold his beloved boat in November, his body too weak to press against the heeling-over of the hull. He is renowned along the Maine coast because he sailed all his life with no engine or electronics. Once, a strong southeast wind pushed us furiously through the cut into a tiny, crowded harbor at the mouth of the Damariscotta River. My children were scared into silence. But William quietly told us to drop the jib and the main, calmly easing *Lark* on her mizzen among the moored boats. He took a turn around the cove, chose his spot, and brought his forty-foot boat silently to a mooring. I came out of my worried concentration to the applause of a dozen men and women watching in astonishment from the decks of their boats.

"I ought to shoot myself," he says now, mostly seriously but with the window open in his voice so he doesn't terrify me.

"I hope you don't do that," I say. We sip from our cups. We are both smiling, because we know these lines by heart by now, but I feel a sharp familiar twinge of frustration, and fear.

"Well, I ought to," he repeats, "except I don't know how to do it without leaving you with an awful mess." He puts his toast back on the plate and wipes his mouth with his handkerchief. "It's this goddamned knee," he says, rubbing his bad knee dramatically. "I'm fine except for this bugger."

His knee isn't the big problem, and he knows it. His body has suddenly grown tired. He feels vulnerable, and the losses and griefs of his long life press at him.

"That knee is a stinker, isn't it," I say.

"Yes, that's the thing. I just don't know any way out without leaving you with a hell of a mess."

"Why don't you finish breakfast and go up to your loft, William? How's *Dorade* coming?" He's been working on a watercolor of a coasting schooner running on the wind. But each day, I find him sitting at his drafting table, rummaging through his old work.

"Oh! Did I tell you I'm working on a painting of *Dorade?*"

"Yes, you did, William," I say enthusiastically. "I think this is going to be your best work yet."

"I don't know," he says quietly. "I think I'm getting old." He lays his handkerchief flat on the table, ironing it with his strong hands and folding it again and again, pressing hard along each fold. "An old fool. I just don't want to leave you with any kind of mess."

It is the last day of April. William has broken a hip and is in the hospital. His leg is not attached to his body, and the pain is acute; he has slipped beneath the morphine. It has been three days since I have had to decide that at ninety-five, he will not have the hip replaced. I know he will die. The palliative-care doctors say it will take about two weeks for him to go, from lack of food.

While he could still talk, he had spoken to anyone who came into his room, earnest and focused last conversations. He had shrunk, and a glisten of sweat covered his head, but his voice was strong and he spoke formally, the way he always did with strangers. He was accustomed to holding people's attention, the force of his intelligence and love of attention compelling people to him.

"Yes," he says, "my mother taught me when I was just a boy at the Glades that people lived on Mars. We would sit in the chairs out on the big lawn looking up at that wonderful sky. I don't know if you've ever seen the Milky Way. Back then, you know, people believed there had to be creatures just like us out there somewhere. My mother told me all about the canals that were believed to have been dug by people like us. Of course, we know this isn't so now." His fingers work the edge of the stiff sheet. The room is quiet for a moment. His voice softens. "But they still don't know what any of this means."

Later he says, "You might think you're hearing the phoebe call to you. But if it sounds like *fee-bee*"—he imitates the call—"it's a chickadee. A phoebe calls *phee-BREE, phee-BREE.* You listen for that soft *r.*"

He says to me, holding me close to his bony shoulder, "I love you very, very much." He tells me, "I am proud of you." He says, "I have had a very good life living with you and your boys. We have always seen the world the same way." William holds me to his shoulder and says, "You have been very, very good to me." Like a father, he says at the end, "I love you."

William is not my father. My father turned away from me many years ago. I am not William's daughter. Each of us was, I know, lost and wounded. We were both displaced, floating, not even knowing how much we needed. He came to live with me and my children simply because he had to. I said yes simply because I couldn't say no to such an old and lonely man. But somehow, over these ten years of learning how to live together—the nudging, the dodging, the hard pushing, the laughing—we have become family. We have found refuge in each other. What was missing has slowly been provided by each of us for the other. We are a perfect fit, lost beings needing love, finding each other as if there is a plan, a destiny. Loss of love, of safety, of being wanted; love built, step by careful step, safety, belonging. It has been a coming home for both of us.

We are alone in a quiet corner of the hospital, in a big sunny room looking out into a swaying pine forest. I hold his warm hand. I have asked that every tube and monitor be removed. I stroke his head, the large head holding his hungry mind. I tell him, "You are on your journey now, William. It's time to go." The night comes, and then the soft light of dawn. It is day two of two weeks.

He breathes in a morphine sleep—small, shallow, regular breaths. He will not let go of my hand. The doctor says it is a primal response, but I feel loved. The sun moves across the room. The hospital routine is the only grounding in this floating, surreal dream. I have stopped crying and feel an odd, quiet peace. I have put photographs of William around the room: him sketching in his field; riding his horse, Dandy, in the orchard; receiving honors for his conservation work; carving a half-model. His beloved, tattered book of English poetry—given by his sister to him and Eleanor for their wedding in 1939—lies on the bed table beside the packets of mint mouth swabs. I try to read to him the poem he has quoted to me every day for months, Swinburne's "The Garden of Proserpine": "That no life lives for ever; / That dead men rise up never; / That even the weariest river / Winds somewhere safe to sea." But I cannot get through it and stop reading. I sit, holding his hand, watching the trees sway in the silent wind outside. *Dorade*, finished and framed, hangs beside the bed. Along the way, he changed the perspective; he has swung her bow, and she runs stern-first away from us on a steady wind.

He wills himself away in just three days. It feels like a gift he is giving to me, no mess.

Afterward, on the highway north of Portland, I follow a trailer truck carrying a load of honeybees home to Tennessee from the blueberry fields Downeast. There must be millions of bees in the hundreds of hives, all moving at seventy miles an hour on the flatbed. The air buzzes beyond the highway's roar. I can see bees clinging to the sides and entry platforms of the hives, resisting being blasted away by the force of the wind. I admire their fierce strength and commitment, and what may be pure good luck.

But there are other bees, dots of brown energy, unattached, flying along beside the truck as it charges south. They seem to keep up —seventy miles an hour!—as if they can sustain this frenzied clinging to home all the way to Tennessee, as if their fragile wings can beat a billion times and secure their safe reentry to the place they belong. In fact, they must have to veer off finally, to reckon with losses and impossibilities and limitations. Maybe it feels like some sort of destiny, a plan, as the chaotic wind stream flings them out and they find themselves floating quietly in an unknown place. If they are lucky, a hive somewhere in those woods—maybe also weakened by some force of nature—will accept them, one by one. Everything else will be gone, bound in old patterns beyond reach. They will come to rely on each other. They will each take their place, make the necessary adjustments by a few celestial degrees, and orient themselves again on the planet.

Chapter Seventeen
Outport Shadows

I forget that I am fifty-five years old until I look in the mirror. An average, lumpy, middle-aged woman, I move in the world in another body, my younger body, a body I lived in sometime in the past. I haven't forgotten that home. I know it and love it. It is fluid and agile and smooth. Busy. Graceful, I remember. Strong. It loves work. It loves to heap the wheelbarrow with steaming sheep manure and wheel it down the hill to the garden. To dump the load, which requires all its strength. To grab the spade and spread the manure, load after load, over the soil in the hot sun. This body I know loves to lie stretched on its side, reading, my hand—this hand, if I don't look down—absent-mindedly stroking up and over its tight ribs, its bony hip, its long smooth thigh. This body I live inside loves to burst into a sprint to retrieve the mail from the box. To tease the dog with a romp. To dance when no one is home, the childhood ballet poses—arabesques, pirouettes, fifth position. To make love in the light of winter sun, goose-fleshed and generous. This body catches the eye. Its clothes hang easily, comfortably. Its skin is stretched tight. Its hair swishes heavily in a long blond ponytail. This remembered body I live inside moves large in the world, visible, watched, wanted.

But the mirror reminds me I am a middle-aged woman. I have grown invisible in the world. I am shocked by this shift every single day. I walk table to table at a bookstore, moving around other shoppers, picking up books, reading back covers, author's introductions. A young man with soft black curls and gentle eyes steps in tight beside me and reaches across for a bestseller. I smile, move farther down, and say, "Sorry, I'm in your way." He glances at me, through me, and goes on reading. No one looks up.

I stand in front of my college class, a room packed full of hormones and smooth flesh. We are talking about Tim O'Brien, Vietnam. I tell them that, when I was their age, we marched against the war in the streets of Cambridge, that we were chased by cops in riot gear, that we believed we were changing the world. Meghan, a favorite student I know from other classes, says, "It's just so hard for us to imagine you our age. I mean, that you were young and did all these things. You know, that you were ever like us." Twenty young faces nod.

I resist this invisibility. Sometimes the protest is silly: I resent the confident young clerk at the grocery store, her shine and elasticity, her belief that she is here, like this, forever. Sometimes I pity her, her failure to foresee her own inevitable fading. Sometimes I foolishly compete, counting calories and walking extra miles, pretending I'm regaining a few years. Mostly, I'm careful not to look at my reflection in the store window as I walk back out to my car.

But I understand that what I am resisting is not just the inevitability of becoming no longer seen, no longer watched, a giving up of that physicality the world once noticed. What I fight is this certainty: I am slipping along toward erasure, toward no-body. I will die. Once, I was young and vibrant; now, I am in the middle and eclipsed; soon, I will be old, and then I will be gone. Every time I walk unnoted among people, every time I glance in the mirror, every time I look down and see the ropy veins of my hands, I have to tangle, in a quiet, stunned moment, with this underlying truth: I am far along the path.

My mother was just about this age when she was diagnosed with MS. I remember her two bodies. One is young, thin and strong, tanned. In pictures of her when she was young, about the age of my own re-membered self, my mother is at ease, confident, graceful. She is lean-ing against the kitchen door frame, her gabardine slacks and blouse draping loosely on her strong thin arms and legs. Her eyes flash. She smiles. Her other body is just as vivid: white, her spine collapsed, her hands heavy lumps in her lap, her eyes masked. A long skirt drapes her heavy, useless, shiny legs. This body lies as it is put, a stiff swollen case that holds my mother.

Each glance in the mirror startles me not only because I am suddenly, shockingly, a middle-aged woman, but because I am so much my mother, before the disease started to claim her body. Here is her smile, lines creasing her cheeks. Thick hair going gray. The sloping nose with the little ball at the end. Mostly the eyes, my mother's eyes that stare back out at me from a life lived and ended.

Sometimes when I laugh I hear my mother's soft, ready laugh. When I sit, curling one foot under me on the chair, I am settling my mother's strong legs. I read, my thumb and little finger holding the book open in my lap, and I am my mother reading. My mother's body is remembered in me, like an echo rising from the past and carrying toward the future. In the mirror, her eyes speak to me from before those years of illness. Middle-aged woman, my mother, she is a shadow moving just ahead of me, calling back with the news.

I am memory. Everything I have been is carried here in my body. I am written, the pain and the great love, the surprises, the losses and the findings. The young woman's body I live inside still, that unforgotten home, is a text. It is engraved with memory, my life. Psychologists believe that grief and trauma are taken up by our bodies and held, that we envelop the memory and build it into ourselves, make it part of us, write it into our cells. We think we have mostly forgotten, but our bodies do not.

And we remember love. I have often wished that my children could remember all the tender, floating hours of being nursed, of being held into my heart, stroked and safe. I believe now that they do remember, that their bodies know love and safety. If this is true, then I, also, must carry my mother's love, my father's. Whatever else may have gone wrong, whatever of grief and loss is carried by each of us, so too is love. Nothing is lost.

The wind whips in from the southwest across the icy water of the Strait of Belle Isle. My tent leans and shudders like a sail. Surf crashes on the shore just below. The stars are out, millions of them, silent and calm in their dome, and a quarter moon silvers the wave crests. This is not a storm. It is always windy in Newfoundland.

I am seeking the solitude I love on this wild and haunting coast. My tent is crouched up against one of the old houses where I have tried to find protection from the ceaseless wind. There is no one here but me. There are six houses, all of them abandoned. Clinging to the steep, rocky hill rising from the bay, it is as if they themselves are boulders that are slipping into the sea. The bright and cheerful paints of the old Newfoundland—red, blue, yellow, ocher, turquoise —have been worn away over the years; the narrow clapboards are soft gray, black where water has entered the wood and started the slow process of rotting. The houses are square, two-storied, practical cubes of hard work and determination. Their hip roofs, nearly flat, are designed to take as little wind as possible. They needn't carry a snow load; the wind whips it off as it falls. Three of the houses list heavily downhill, like stooped old women. The doors have popped out of their frames from the pressure. Outhouses stand askew. Below, along the shore, several fish sheds ride just above the high water, tilting seaward on rotting pilings. Meadow grass grows high between the houses, but the old paths show clearly still, purposeful paths winding house to house, house to stream, fish store to cod stage, cod stage to shore. In the luminous glow of the night I can see white lace curtains in the windows, tidy remnants of the lives once lived here.

This is Upward Cove, an outport on Baie Verte on the northern coast. It was abandoned in 1967 when the Canadian government "re-settled" Newfoundland's population, forcibly moving families and clans from their ancestral homes in dozens of remote outports to population centers where the benefits of modern life—schools, electricity, medical care, plowed roads—could be delivered more economically. This is a ghostly place. I am drawn here. I sit awake in the night watching the sea roil, listening to the stones roll in the surf, longing to move into one of these lonely houses. The sadness of the place rides on the wind, heavy and unanswerable. All across Newfoundland, the empty outports cling stoically to their mountainsides, resisting the inevitable.

The beauty is so large and so lonely—the green rocky mountains dropping into the sea, the incessant wind, the hushed village—I am content to sit in the lee and watch, all day, all night. Mostly, I listen for the voices that murmur from so many years ago, asking for borrowed butter, reminding about auntie's bulkhead door, calling the child to her afternoon chores. Someone laughs. Then an answering laugh. Men call up from the fish stage. A boy sings as he stretches a net on the hillside to dry. I remember things I never knew.

The sun rises sharp and clear and warm. The wind dies down, the sea flattens. I sit in the sun in front of one of the old houses, listening to the rich everyday murmur of life, to its thread back in time to other voices that haunt this village. Shadows of its inhabitants slip through the grass, coming and going. The curtains hang white in the morning sun.

In the early afternoon, a woman comes in a rumbling old Ford sedan. I am happy for the company. I smile my greeting as she stops in front of one of the houses that still stands fairly straight. She waves and calls out hello as she stretches. She is about my age, middle-aged. Like most Newfoundland women, she is sturdy, strong-shouldered and short-legged. There is a perfect practicality to her body and her clothing—a cotton skirt and blouse, sneakers.

"Hello, I'm Carolyn," she says easily, barely looking at me. "I'm coming to check on me mother's house." She pulls a dry mop and plastic bucket filled with rags and sponges from the back seat. "Would you like to come in?"

I am always astonished at the matter-of-fact welcome in Newfoundland. "Okay," I say, "if it's all right. I'd like that. My name is Meredith. I'm camping below that lower house. I hope that's okay."

"Oh, yes," she says, "yes." There is a soft, drawn-out patience to her vowels. "No one here to complain anyway, is there now. You're not hurting anything."

Carolyn carries her cleaning supplies to the old door, fishes for a key in her pocket, and pushes the door open. I'm curious but don't want Carolyn to know that. I have tried to peer in the windows of all the houses, but the curtains let me see just shadowy shapes. I have imagined broken furniture and boxes, discarded shoes and worn-down hairbrushes—what was too old or too useless to make the move to the modern world nearly forty years before—lying about on crumbling linoleum, the molding newspaper underlayment showing at the edges. We enter a front hall with steep stairs rising to the bedrooms above. It is surprisingly bright inside, the afternoon sun filtering through the thin curtains in a pleasant glow. The wallpaper, soft pink roses on trellises, is faded but in perfect condition. The banister and newel post are dark wood, polished smooth and bright. The air is musty. That is the only part of this I correctly anticipated. I am stunned by the homeyness of this decrepit old house. It feels as if its family has been away for a few weeks and is here now to air it out and get back to the rhythms of their daily life. Carolyn stops still, her hands hanging at her sides. I understand in a rush that she stops like this every time she comes here, shocked herself at the life that still breathes in her childhood home.

"Yes," she finally says quietly. "Yes, lovey. This is always harder than I think it's going to be." She looks to her right into a front room, to the left, lifts her eyes up the stairs, then walks toward the back. "Want to see the kitchen then? Me mother kept a beautiful kitchen, she did. Seven of us kids, five boys, and me mother kept a beautiful home. I wanted her to come out today from town but she says she can't do it anymore. Me sister doesn't want to come so it's just me."

I follow Carolyn into the square kitchen. The chrome trim on the green cook stove gleams. The table and chairs and sag-bottomed rocking chair and tin-covered kitchen counter are spotless. Glasses and flowered plates lie on the pantry shelves. A young man in uniform gazes softly from a framed photograph hanging over the wood box. The door to the icebox is held open with a wooden spoon. Carolyn bursts into tears. I touch her arm and look away.

The dining room and parlor and four low-ceilinged bedrooms upstairs are time capsules of an old-fashioned life still working in 1967. A sweater hangs on a hook beside a crucifix. The beds are made. Small rugs, braided and hooked, cover the painted floors. "Grammy made these for Mum," Carolyn says. "She made so many rugs we all have them in our houses." Water stains course down the corners of several rooms. Except for those terrible reminders that this house is sinking into the ground, that its roof is rotting, its sills, its window frames, the house seems ready for a homecoming. Carolyn moves slowly room to room, opening windows, fingering curtains and bedspreads. "This was me parents' room," she says. She opens a drawer in a small table and pulls out a sewing kit bound in frayed pink ribbon. She opens it, lays it on the bed, then closes it again and ties the ribbon carefully. She shuts the drawer again slowly. "It took the longest time for us to believe we were never coming back, " she says. "We packed as if we were going for a month. I was seventeen. I thought someday I would live here, just like me mother did. I thought I was going to get married here and dry the cod and have me children here. Some people tried to stay. But the government cut the electric and closed the school. They stopped plowing the road and sending in the nurse once a month, and people got scared. That was it. Everyone's scattered now. It's not like it was. That's all gone forever."

Carolyn sits down on her mother's old bed and stares out the window. She looks older now, as if memory is a weight. As if these sun-filled rooms, waiting for an impossible future, tick along in time, vessels carrying Carolyn toward her own mortality. I think I hear a voice below, and a ghostly answer. The white curtains flutter in the summer breeze. I walk back down the stairs and out the front door. Below me, stretching to the shores of Ireland and Scotland and England and France, the sea sparkles in the dispassionate sun. The houses lean toward their own disappearance. They will become heaps of the past, archaeological relics of lives erased. Carolyn picks up her dust mop and bucket, resisting. Someone laughs next door. Shadows slip along the paths in the overgrown grass. I sit by the shore, tossing rocks into the water. The sun creeps across the afternoon, and my shadow follows it. A shadow arm lifts, throws. Carolyn's mother calls from her kitchen. Carolyn answers, "I'm coming."

As night comes, the wind rises again. I sit in the door of my tent watching the sea slip from blue to purple to black. The shadows fade. The forms of the houses disappear, and I feel a sudden moment of fear, as if I, too, am being erased. I touch my fingers to my face. I am here. I still have time.

Among my mother's old papers, I find a small photograph of a young child. She is wearing a red corduroy jacket with a peaked hood. Her small fingers hold the end of the hood's cord in her mouth. Nearly white hair slips from under the hood. Her head is tilted and she stares straight at the camera with a wide, soft, trusting gaze. Her pupils are so large they make her eyes look black with a thin halo of deep, deep blue. Her eyes catch me: a child so ready, unmasked, unguarded. I am this child. There is my hand, my chin, one ear.

There is another photograph: an eleven-year-old girl in a yellow dress she has sewn herself, with buttons from the hem to the throat, a softly gathered skirt and narrow belt. She is barefoot, leaning against a tree. Her arms and legs are smooth and boneless like a young child's, but small breasts press at the buttoned dress. Her hands are clasped around the tree behind her, leaving her exposed to the camera, but her eyes are shadowed in the bright summer light. I am this girl, these eyes, these legs and arms, this thick hair in the same ponytail I wear now. I remember this day, this time of coming to my new body, of the dawning awareness that I lived in the world, that I had a past, and that a future was coming that I could not envision.

I am this child. Sometimes I glance in the mirror as I brush my hair back in an elastic band, and there I am: still those girls gazing back at the world with the same blue eyes. We all recognize each other, the child and the woman we could not yet imagine.

The human body absorbs minerals from the soil in the area we grow up in. These minerals bind with our teeth and bones, and bind us to the earth itself. Ötzi, the Neolithic Iceman found mummified in the permafrost of Austria's mountains, actually grew up in a valley in northern Italy. We know this because his teeth carry molecules of specific minerals—lead and strontium—in a chemical signature unique to that valley. My teeth and bones must carry isotopes— iron? magnesium? selenium?—from the soils of southern New Hampshire, from my small town on the beautiful rich marshes of the coastal plain. I will die somewhere else. When I die, the minerals that have become me will be released into the soil—in Maine or Newfoundland or maybe even Turkey—and will rebind with indigenous minerals in the soil, microscopic testaments to a life. Another girl, there, will eat her carrots, drink her milk, absorb the minerals of her native soil, and carry me in her teeth and in her bones.

I have lived this life, and no matter what others may decide about it, I must claim each decision as mine. I have caused harm, failed in the expectations and obligations of love. I have loved well. What I do each day is carried within me until I die.

The stream roars its steady rhythms as I paint my cabin. A family of otters, two adults and a baby, fish at the old beaver dam where the stream leaves the little pond. The only sounds I have heard since I arrived three days ago are the eagle screaming from the sentinel pines ringing the pond and a pair of loons who fly over at dawn, calling in their wild, warbling voices. I am in the middle of Maine's northern wilderness, seven miles from the nearest electric pole and three from the closest hunting camp.

My grown sons, Alex and Benjamin and Paul, helped me build the cabin two years ago. It's small, sixteen feet by twenty. It was hard, hard work. Every single piece of lumber had to be carried two hundred yards down a steep hill on a very rough moose path. I lost weight, became muscle again, slept deeply in the old square tent we lived in for the summer.

I got to know the land. Just behind where the cabin was going, I found the remnants of an old logging camp where a few men had worked the forest with horses and waited for the spring melt to run their winter's work down the stream to the lakes. The bunkhouse, small barn, and cook camp are just piles of rotten logs; mature trees are rooted in the rich humus of the decay. The old cook stove, rusted, its parts strewn over ten feet, lies hidden under a stand of moose maple. Orange and red and brilliant yellow mushrooms erupt each summer in the camp remains. When the four or five feet of standing snow melts in the late spring, I find more bottles—whiskey, liniment, vinegar—thrust up through the moss by the frost.

We cleared just enough of the white cedar and hemlock trees to tuck the little building into the woods at the edge of the pond. We laid the ribbons and joists, insulated the box, and stapled hardware cloth and screening to keep mice and burrowing insects out of the insulation. Then we raised the first-floor walls, the upper and lower plates and studs, framing out the rough openings looking out on the pond. We decked the second floor and raised the bedroom walls. Then hair-raising days of setting the ridge and rafters, and sheathing and shingling the steep roof. Windows next, a lot of them because I love the light. Then the doors. Outside trim and clapboards. Insulation. We nailed pine boards horizontally on the inside walls, laid the floors, and built a little kitchen with an old slate sink and gas stove. My sons managed to bring an old iron bathtub and a new woodstove down the path, and winter came. In the end, to put together this little cabin took seventeen trailer-loads of tools, lumber, shingles, nails, insulation, windows, and doors, all brought from home four hours away and then carried down the moose path on our shoulders. We built it to last. My sons and their children will come to this wild place, listen to the haunting call of the loons on the pond in the night, and eat good food at the table we built.

Today I am staining the clapboards a second coat. The late-summer day is cool and breezy. The pond shimmers with sunlight. A kingfisher sits in her favorite cedar snag at the edge of the pond and cackles. Below me, a wild garden of ferns and bunchberry and bead lily spreads in the moss. One sprig of brilliant red maple leaves, the herald of winter coming, catches the light like a gem. I climb down the ladder and move it over four feet, climb back up, and work under the eaves with my brush. The wind soughs in the pines and spruces over my head.

The world outside feels chaotic to me. Here, in short respites, I find myself. I remember a slow-motion calm. There is a perfect system here of evolution, the universe silently revolving, expanding. Rhythms of light and dark, warmth and cold, abundance and need, growth and decay. I enter and feel the reassurance that I am part of that perfect order. Here I participate in the fecundity and bene-ficence of earth and water. I come back to myself. I am beautiful, strong, bursting with life.

I catch my reflection in the window as I paint: the middle-aged face. Mine, stretching back to that gazing child. My mother's—fading blue eyes, squint lines, jowls forming. My sons', the carry-ing forward. My hands as I paint are my father's, the extra skin and thickened knuckles. Signs of arthritis, I'm sure, an old woman's con-dition. But here, my small life is measured against such an immen-sity of time I don't panic. I will die. Mystery and no mystery. The pond will reflect sunlight and ice over and melt and rush the two hundred miles to sea. The moss will crumble in drought summers and glow like jewels in wet seasons. The bear who leaves muddy paw prints on my outhouse will be another bear. Venus will continue to dominate the evening and predawn skies. No need to panic.

This is a sturdy cabin. It will hold. Carolyn's house in New-foundland, the ancient tomb in Turkey, the remains of the bunkhouse rotting back to soil behind my cabin keep me from the conceit that it is forever. But as I stain the clapboards and sashes, laid up by these hands in lovely square and true, I am at ease. This is an ordinary story, the story of a search for a steady course. Love, its sustenance and its costs. My mother. My father. My children. Me, the child and the mother.

The day is still long. I have a lot of work to do. Then ripe tomatoes for my supper. Later, I will sit by the shore as the light seeps slowly from the pond. My shadow will float among those lengthening on the water. I will rise and make my way back into the cabin's soft glow, and then return home, part of the world.

Acknowledgments

This book would not be if it were not for the Gift of Freedom Award I received from A Room of Her Own Foundation. I am profoundly grateful for AROHO's extraordinary financial support, encouragement, and friendship.

Thank you to the Maine Arts Commission, the MacDowell Colony, and Jentel Arts for their support.

Thank you, also, to my hard-working and enthusiastic agent, Andrew Blauner; and to Helene Atwan for her compassionate, insightful, and attentive editorial help.

I owe everything to the friends who have believed in this book, and to my family for accepting its necessity.